GROWING UP
QUEER
IN AUSTRALIA

GROWING UP QUEER IN AUSTRALIA

EDITED BY BENJAMIN LAW

Published by Black Inc.,
an imprint of Schwartz Books Pty Ltd
Level 1, 221 Drummond Street
Carlton VIC 3053, Australia
enquiries@blackincbooks.com
www.blackincbooks.com

9781760640866 (paperback)
9781743821084 (ebook)

A catalogue record for this
book is available from the
National Library of Australia

Cover by Grace Lee
Text design and typesetting by Tristan Main

Printed in Australia by McPherson's Printing Group.

Contents

Introduction

Benjamin Law

Some things I wish I'd had, growing up queer in Australia:
- clothes that fit
- less acne
- wavy hair like the local hot white surfer boys
- queer role models
- stories that spoke to me
- gay porn.

Eventually I'd figure out how to access the first three things by shopping in Asian clothing outlets, getting a prescription for Roaccutane, and paying good money for a bad Korean man-perm I don't particularly want to discuss right now, please respect my privacy. But those last three things – queer people, stories and depictions of queer sex – proved much harder to find, and I craved them with a desperation that bordered on hunger. Growing up in pre-dial-up-internet Queensland, the last mainland Australian state to decriminalise homosexuality, any scrap of queer connection or recognition was a hard thing to come by.

So what did I have? Well, there was the 'H' volume of our family's set of *Encyclopædia Britannica*. As a kid, when I was sure no one was around, I'd fervently flip to the entry on 'homosexuality', feeling sick, my heart thumping. Though it couldn't have been more than one or two paragraphs long, the entry represented the entirety of all knowledge available to me at the time about being gay, beyond snickering schoolyard jokes about AIDS and anal sex, which I weakly laughed along with.

As a teenager, there was our household copy of *Everything a Teenage Boy Should Know* – the popular coming-of-age sex-education tome every parent seemed to give Australian kids born in the 1970s and 1980s, written by Sydney doctor John F. Knight. In Chapter 14, titled 'Unnatural Sex', Knight wrote of gay sex:

> The method most commonly attributed to males indulging in this form of sexual gratification is *intercourse* (if such a word can be used in this context) via the back passage. Most normal people would regard this form of indulgence as less than attractive, and indeed downright repulsive.

Lovely thing for a twelve-year-old to read. Truly. But by then, puberty was hitting hard, and not even Dr Knight calling gay sex 'repulsive' could stop me from scouring *TV Week* every Monday for art-house movies on SBS that were rated MA, featuring S (sex scenes), N (nudity) and A (adult themes), and setting the VHS timer accordingly. The A was especially important: 'adult themes' combined with 'sex' and 'nudity' usually meant queer stuff. Without A it was mostly just heterosexual sex, and who wanted that? While SBS movies rated MA (A, S, N) weren't exactly the piping-hot gay porn that I craved, watching them throughout the late 1990s meant I was thoroughly familiar with the collected works of Pedro Almodóvar, Todd Haynes and Gregg Araki by the age of fifteen. One benefit of being a repressed gay teen in the suburbs: you come out literate in art-house cinema auteurs.

The internet was a slow revolution. It was only in my final years of high school that my parents – riddled with divorce guilt – caved and bought us a Hewlett-Packard desktop computer. It was state-of-the-art, with a whopping sixteen-gigabyte (!) hard drive, a base roughly the size of a small microwave and a modem built *inside* the computer. We were living in the future. Needless to say, the first thing I did when I got online in private was to look up gay porn on AltaVista. As one single explicit gay jpeg of two white meatheads going at it in jockstraps loaded – frame by painful frame – I watched with horror as the monitor was infested with pop-up porn advertisements from hell. As footsteps approached, it was a mad sweaty scramble to simultaneously hide the plague-like pop-ups and my popped-up boner, the whole exercise feeling like I was being punished before I'd got any reward.

*

On reflection, it's odd that I grew up without meeting any other openly queer people, and with so little exposure to stories with which I could identify. As Oliver Reeson writes in their essay about being non-binary:

> When I look back on my own life, I feel the weight of not realising earlier who I was, of being scared to tell the whole story. And yet, how could I realise I was a non-binary person when I did not even know of the concept until I was already an adult? How could I have grown up as a non-binary person when it was not a story I had ever heard?

As a reader, I look for two things in other people's stories. The first is the kind of self-recognition Reeson talks about. For queer people it's especially important, because while other forms of prejudice – like racism – can make you feel just as alone and isolated, ethnic minorities like me go home to families and communities who share our backgrounds and experiences, and affirm who we are. Queer kids growing up typically don't have that. I didn't. That feeling of belonging – of understanding you are not alone and not insane – is a core human need. If we can't get that from the people around us, we need stories.

The second thing I look for in stories is the opposite of self-recognition: experiences completely outside my own personal framework. As much as queer people share experiences of marginalisation, fear and facing baseless assumptions about who we are, lesbian, gay, bisexual, transgender, intersex and/or non-binary people also have their own discrete experiences and histories. Our capacity to stay curious and listen to each other's stories is paramount. Embracing difference – rather than relying on simplistic platitudes like 'we're all the same' – is how we learn to forge respect. In any case, sameness is boring. Sameness is the opposite of diversity. And sameness has never been a prerequisite for queer equality.

Yes: we've chosen to go with 'queer' in the title of this anthology. We could've called it *Growing Up LGBTIQA+*. Personally, I don't mind the unwieldiness of that acronym – I like how it makes us vigilant about who might be left out – but it would've made life slightly hellish for booksellers trying to search for it. That said, I acknowledge that there is a sting associated with the word 'queer' – especially for those from older generations, against whom 'queer' was used as a slur and a weapon. Balanced against that, though, there is also a proud and rich history of defiantly reclaiming the word 'queer' for ourselves. LGBTIQA+ people from racial minorities began to identify as 'queer' in response to parts of the gay and lesbian community becoming more conservative, assimilationist and palatable. 'Queer' is not just an identity, but a lens through which the world can be viewed differently. It's a noun, an adjective and – perhaps most importantly – a verb. To 'queer' something is to subvert, interrogate and flip – which all these stories do in their own way.

Here, then, are stories about the ways religion forms and deforms us; how our queerness can transform ourselves and the people around us; discoveries of heady romance; fumbly terrible sex and revelatory joyous sex; the vulnerability and physical danger that often comes with being queer in a bigoted world; how friendship can become love; coming out later in life; finding and making families; how queerness intersects with race, language, size, cultural background and ability; the hurt we can inflict on each other; the ecstasies and shocks of finding our community for the first time; about how so little has changed and simultaneously how far we've come; and why we need to keep going. Holly Throsby notes in the first story that she remains optimistic. So do I.

So here you have it: the book I wish I'd had when I was growing up queer in Australia. It's also the book I want – and invite you – to read now.

Freedom of Heart

Holly Throsby

At the age of eleven I was sitting in my room contemplating whatever it is that young people contemplate. Perhaps the guitar chords to 'Bad Moon Rising'. I was midway through Year 6, and I don't know if it's the same for other kids, but for me it was as if the local pool of people my age had stagnated, basically since kindergarten. I knew the kids at school and the kids from surrounding streets, but I don't recall making any other friends until I was eleven and a new girl moved to Balmain. Not only was she new, she was very beautiful and spoke with a foreign accent. Sitting in my room that day, having recently met her, I found myself diverted by discomfiting thoughts.

What were these thoughts? Well, they were really so innocent: I pictured her, thought how pretty she was, and felt a little stirring inside.

What did this mean? I didn't really know. I have no idea who first told me what a 'lesbian' was, but I guess I must have known what they were, and I'd certainly gathered that being a lesbian was very undesirable, because I distinctly recall wondering with some alarm: *Does this mean I'm a lesbian?*

Surely not. Please, no.

I quickly consoled myself: *Silly me! Of course I'm not.* Besides, I had been in love with Andrew McDonald since Year 3, and I had kissed Mike Daly behind the toilet block! No, I was perfectly normal and fine. And, mercifully, I did not think of another girl in such a way, nor experience such stirrings, for many years to come.

Looking back on my childhood, and how Australia was at the time, I'm not surprised that I felt such anxiety. I was born in 1978 and grew up in the Sydney peninsular suburb of Balmain. When I was young, Balmain was home to a politically progressive and somewhat artistic community. The adults I knew were relatively well educated and proudly left-wing. The year I was born, Labor won 84.2 per cent of the two-party-preferred vote in the Balmain electorate.

And, yet. Even in Balmain. Or maybe because of Balmain?

Neville Wran did say that 'Balmain boys don't cry' and, sure enough, the men and boys of the peninsula seemed stoic and manly. I assume the most terrifying thing one of those young lads could have possibly been was gay. Everyone in Balmain appeared thoroughly heterosexual. To my young eyes, queer people were invisible. And although my mum worked at the ABC (or the 'GayBC' as some have called it) and had dear friends and colleagues who were gay men (so I had heard about those), the true *rara avis* of my childhood was a queer woman. In fact, throughout primary school I didn't knowingly meet one. Where were they? I am sure they must have existed, at least over in Leichhardt, but to me they may as well have been the Easter Bunny or a unicorn: not real.

So on I went to high school, forgetting that uncomfortable thought I'd once had in my bedroom. I began to write songs obsessively, and I had a nice boyfriend for a year and a half – a lifetime when you're fourteen. I was a tomboy in Doc Martens and corduroy pants. Kids took drugs and smoked cigarettes and had sex. But what about the queer culture? Well, it was this: if a boy at school appeared somehow effeminate, the punishment of taunts and social isolation from other boys was brutal.

Perhaps as a teenager I was so determined, on a subconscious level, to be 'normal' that I suppressed any feelings about girls so deeply as to render them non-existent. This is possible. But the fact was, I didn't have any queer feelings for almost all of high school. I didn't have to try not to; I just didn't. I was entirely focused on boys – until Year 12, when a new girl arrived. Or rather, new girls: several of them, from a nearby school that had closed down. These girls were cool and smart and clearly came from a different planet, because some of them identified as 'bi' – a little term that meant so much.

How intriguing this was for the rest of us in Year 12! Or was it just me? One of the new girls must have sensed my interest and began what I recall as a somewhat ruthless pursuit of my attention/ embarrassment. She was so audacious with her flirting! She was so confident and blunt. In fact, one day she yelled at me from across the playground, in front of everyone, a direct sexual proposition. I absolutely died/loved it. I blushed, went home, and sang along to Joni Mitchell: 'I'm frightened by the devil, and I'm drawn to those ones that ain't afraid.'

Now, at this point, anyone who has read my novel *Goodwood* may be raising an eyebrow. For in the book, the protagonist – Jean Brown – becomes infatuated with a new girl at school who shows her that there is more to this beautiful and sad world than she had previously imagined, and that maybe it's okay to be who you are. Perhaps those readers are now wondering if Jean's story is my story, since they do sound rather similar. But: not exactly. When I was writing *Goodwood*, I wanted to give Jean the kind of confidence I had not possessed at the age of seventeen. I allowed her to be fearless. And even though she hides her feelings from the people in her life, she is able to act freely.

So, while I did kiss the girl in high school, I would not say I was free in my heart. It was 1996 then. I had no queer role models to speak of. I had no queer friends or family. There was no *The L Word*. Ellen hadn't even come out yet. And although I was beginning to sense that it was slowly becoming more socially acceptable to be a lesbian, it still wasn't *really*. There were caveats. As in, it was better if you didn't actually *look* like a lesbian; better still if you were merely bisexual; better still again if you were actually straight and only with other women for the entertainment of onlooking men.

Perhaps this is why, when I met my first girlfriend in the year after high school, I struggled to varying degrees, depending on my surroundings. I loved her, and in our private universe it was wonderful. But back then I was certainly cautious about who I told. I didn't want to dress in ways that announced queerness, and for that I suffered the judgement of some prouder queers. I was considered, in those circles, 'not gay enough', which was confusing. Yet the simplest public display of affection would often incur honks and yells from men in passing cars, and I hated that. So I tried to blend in. I was neither closeted nor courageous. And yet I felt safe and open with close friends; I felt free and alive with other queer people who cared for me and had no expectations about the type of queer that I should be.

I have known queer people who came out to their parents and were completely excommunicated – literally thrown out of home, as teenagers. I've known others who never came out to their parents at all. I've known people who left their small hometowns and never returned, for fear of the consequences of their sexuality. I've known people who denied their queerness to themselves for most of their lives; or gay people who felt they 'couldn't be gay' because their sister was already gay, and they 'couldn't do it to their parents'. I know trans people whose parents still use their deadnames. I know a man whose mother announced to him, moments after he came out to her, that she therefore wanted to commit suicide. I know another man whose mother said nothing to him at all in that moment. He came out to her and she merely turned her head to the front window and said, to no one, 'Oh look, a little corgi just ran across the lawn.'

I have not suffered like this. I have been far more fortunate and enjoyed a large degree of privilege. But I have certainly struggled against the sheer force of societal expectations and judgement. As queer people, we feel this. Navigating our lives can seem like a constant task of 'reading the room'. *Will I be judged? Will I be safe?* It is like this – to varying degrees, at various times – for all of us.

So the way I see it now, my life as a queer person has been a slow process of feeling more and more at ease. I had some nice affairs with men, but always fleetingly. By the time I met my second long-term girlfriend, when I was about twenty-six, I had come to accept that being in a relationship with a woman was natural for me. The circle of people I shared my queerness with became larger over time – until finally it included anyone who was listening. Some people may be surprised to hear that I ever lacked fortitude, for I have acted with such brazen confidence! Walt Whitman taught me that we all contain multitudes. I realised I didn't need to be confused about my sometime-attraction to men, but that it could merely exist as a part of who I am. I came to prefer the term 'queer' because for me it means anything that's not straight, and I am certainly not straight. I have slowly found, over a long period of time, freedom of heart. And I have come to believe that the simple act of being validated by other human beings is perhaps the most important and helpful gift there is.

I have a partner now, of seven years, and we have a young daughter and a geriatric Labrador. We have a gay donor, and he and his partner are such a positive force in our lives. We have a lovely community of LBGTIQA+ friends, rainbow families, and so many dear allies, and we make an effort to find our daughter books that show different types of families, so she sees herself represented, and hopefully feels as normal as any other kid. As much as some straight people would like to believe it, marriage equality did not change Australia overnight. There is still a long way to go, especially for our young ones. But I have seen so much change in my short life – in others, in society, in myself. I feel quietly optimistic.

Shame and Forgiveness

David Marr

I was fourteen, standing on the deck of the ferry wearing a snazzy pair of white pants as it chugged across Port Hacking towards Camp Howard. What I couldn't admit to myself then is what I most vividly remember now: the erotic charge in the air. It was frightening and compelling. That week of messing about in the bush, swimming in deserted bays, sleeping out and listening to the Word was suffused with the promise of sex. Nothing happened but a lot happened. Some of it was ludicrous. One night in the dining hall we were given a sex education lecture. The slides weren't of men and women, but chooks. I remember still a cross-section of tubes and eggs and awkward talk of reproduction as that hen glowed on the screen. Afterwards over cocoa – here's the point – a serious, handsome young man spoke intimately to a dozen or so of us about committing ourselves to Christ. I was deeply drawn to the idea of a man who could love me knowing all my faults, indeed who could love me for my faults, even for the worst of them. One day I would need to be saved, but Judgement Day seemed a long way off in 1961. On that night and at that moment I needed to fall in love, and here was this counsellor – a radio sports commentator in later life – telling me there was a man available: Christ. By a miracle that seemed obvious then, Christ would satisfy me and cure me and protect me from the worst fears I held for myself. I didn't have the courage to come forward over cocoa. Two did. I piked. But as I walked back to the tent I shared with half a dozen other boys on the edge of the bush, it struck me that I had committed myself at that moment to Christ. The future would be different now: pure, thrilling and safe.

The school chaplain had already been pursuing my soul for years, hammering on about sin and salvation. Three times a week we assembled in the chapel to be taught the only lesson Anglican schools in Sydney teach thoroughly: the need for all us awful human beings to be Forgiven. I wasn't convinced. There didn't seem anything worth forgiving, until sex came along. Uneasiness at thirteen was turning to shame at fourteen. This was the raw material I took across the water to Camp Howard. I couldn't have been the only one. We were there to be recruited and the counsellors knew what they were doing, setting us free in that stretch of bush and talking sin at the same time. They challenged us to take Christ into our hearts, but that first required deep acknowledgement of shame. First shame and then forgiveness. That's their business.

You don't have to be a young queer for this to work. There's a trace of self-disgust in most of us that can be worked up into shame, especially in those most difficult, precious years when we are on the threshold of sex. But a young homosexual is particularly easy pickings, fearful of himself, his family and the disapproval of his world. Christ offers a gay kid consummation of a kind, strength to resist sin, the minor heroics of teenage self-sacrifice, and a chance – important for children living day-to-day with an undertow of shame – to do good. That was the Christ I took into my life at the age of fourteen. It was a kind of falling in love, tepid compared with the real thing when that came along, but it was love nevertheless. What followed were a dozen wasted and painful years. I wasn't very brave. My circumstances weren't desperate and I got out the other side with most of myself intact. But it's left me unable to forgive those Christians who are still at work, inflicting misery on kids.

Where does shame come from? I look back to my childhood and can't remember anything being said. My parents had no idea what was happening. Children like me were bred in other suburbs to other families. Homosexuality was a vice too dark for the Anglican Church to condemn. All I heard from the pulpit were grim hints. I vaguely knew the Crimes Act promised a decade or so in the slammer and once in a while the afternoon papers had appalling stories of citizens caught in lavatories. The only instruction my school ever gave me came when I was seventeen and the senior year was in the assembly hall for a talk by the school doctor. It wasn't much of an advance on cross-sections of chooks. 'You can tell a homosexual,' Dr Day said, and by my calculation about a dozen boys must, like me, have frozen with curiosity and terror. 'You can tell them by the decor of their flats.'

Though this advice has not been entirely useless ... Silence was the most potent source of shame in my childhood. Preachers like Fred Nile claim Christians have the right to keep their children 'wrapped in cotton wool', and they campaign for the state to collaborate in that. For years I used to scoff at the pointlessness of trying to keep the young innocent in this way. My answer to the Fred Niles was that, try as they might, our subversive bodies will always tell us the truth. But I was missing the point. What censorship is really designed to achieve is the sort of silence that turns what our bodies tell us into shame. This calls for more than censorship of books and films. It also needs the censorship of learning. Those many Christians who still oppose sex education use the rhetoric of intimacy, innocence and faith. What they're fundamentally about is cultivating shame.

If the clergy I met while I was a keen young Christian had been a more inspiring lot, I might have joined them. I was a shame-driven kid hungry for a spiritual life but all I heard were Sydney Anglicans hammering out their formula for salvation. Even so, I thought a lot about joining the church in the year or so after Camp Howard. My reasons were muddled, but strong in the confusion was a sense that the church might be somewhere to shelter while I set myself right. It would be a respected response to my troubles. A cover and cure. But I knew so little of what service to a church might mean; all I saw was a prospect of Anglican boredom for the rest of my life. My vocation was stillborn.

Talking to priests and ex-priests, trying to puzzle out why men commit their lives to religion, I heard over and again the familiar note of gay shame. Often it was deeply hidden or entirely disguised at the time it was doing its work. At first glance it seems an incongruous way of dealing with vilification, to join the church of the vilifiers. But that's the beauty of shame. It drives you inwards towards the pain because somewhere in there is also the promise of relief. The churches offer pain and shame, but provide the mechanism of forgiveness and relief. Catholicism differs from other churches only in offering guilty young men the supreme reassurance of celibacy. For those who fear their sexuality, that vow of abstinence for life looms like a bulwark against temptation.

At some point after Camp Howard I made a solemn pact that by the time I left school for university I would stop feeling this way. I devised a number of spiritual exercises to make certain. These included prayer, daily Bible reading, eating, staying clear of the beach and not letting thoughts of men come into my mind when I wanked. Keeping a blank mind while masturbating seemed a significant moral achievement. There was one image I had trouble keeping out: Johnny M. diving into a creek at cadet camp. His body hung in the air for a moment, naked and beautiful, before it hit the water. That split-second has lasted forever, of course, but back then I thought I could lock it away with all my other troubles and contradictions, each in their separate cell. I suppose the idea was to turn myself into a prison, a sort of Pentridge for inappropriate emotions, then throw away the key and walk into university a free man.

I invested a decade of my life in the pursuit of a profound, sincere, determined and hopeless ambition not to be homosexual. It's an ordinary story with an ordinary ending. Christ failed me. So did alcohol. So did marriage. Whatever damage I did to myself along the way, I did worse to others I loved. Eventually the price of heaven proved too high and in my late twenties, with all these wasted years on my conscience, I set about doing what I might have done in my teens but for that problematic encounter with Christ over hot cocoa – I began to try to live as myself.

From *The High Price of Heaven*, 1999

How to be Both

Giselle Au-Nhien Nguyen

Cô Linh and Cô Trang had been together ever since I could remember. They were friends of my parents, and I'd see them at gatherings where we sat in backyards at long white plastic tables – at least one for the adults and one for the kids – eating *bánh cuốn* and *chả giò*. They weren't any different to the other grown-ups, not really – they'd all known each other forever, and they'd sit at the adult table talking about things we found dreadfully boring as we chased one another on the grass and collapsed into laughing heaps, out of breath.

But of course they were different, because they were together and they were both women. They had delineated roles, though: Cô Trang was soft and feminine, with colourful scarves, bright pink blush, perfectly pouted lips and permed hair that looked like she'd styled it on a cloud. Cô Linh, on the other hand, had short hair like mine. She always wore pants, button-up shirts and an unimpressed expression. There was no doubt about who was the man and who was the woman in this two-woman couple.

Behind closed doors, we called Cô Linh 'Chú Linh', *chú* being the Vietnamese word for uncle. We all did it – my parents, my sisters and me. We'd laugh but we weren't being mean; we didn't hate them. We still hung out with them, didn't we? It was just a joke between family members. It was alright.

*

When I was growing up in the sleepy suburbs, bisexuality was a foreign concept. Either you liked girls or you liked boys – and if you were a girl, you shouldn't like girls. When my sisters and I played The Game of Life and reached the stage where our little movers would get married, inevitably someone would put a pink mover next to another pink mover, and we would laugh and laugh. Such a silly thing to even think about – a girl marrying a girl. Such a good joke.

If we heard about a man who had left his family to be with another man, we would gasp theatrically: imagine finding out your husband had been *gay* the whole time! What if you were the one who turned him? The shame! He was always pretending. He never wanted to be with you. He only wanted to be with another man.

When I was six, I heard the word 'lesbian' for the first time, when my older sister spat it venomously at me as we brushed our teeth. I didn't know what it meant, but by the hatred in her voice, and the way our father's face darkened as he yelled at her to never say that to me again, I knew she'd used a bad word.

When I was nine or ten, we were watching SBS when a beautiful man appeared onscreen, draped in red, make-up accentuating his delicate features. I was transfixed, but my reverie was broken by my father's snarling voice: *poofter*. I should have known better; it was unnatural. I didn't think about the beautiful man again.

When I was sixteen, I told my mother that I was a lesbian (I wasn't) just to see how she'd react. She burst into tears at the kitchen sink. I remember thinking that even if I did discover in the future that I was a lesbian, I could never tell her.

We spoke in hushed tones about my cousin in America and his husband, my other cousin who lived just a few suburbs away and his new boyfriend. I had seen Cô Linh and Cô Trang all my life, so I knew that kind of relationship existed, but we didn't talk about the truth of it. They were just friends who were always together and lived in the same house and slept in the same bed. Roommates. Definitely not two consenting adults in a loving relationship that had stood the test of time for almost as long as my parents' had.

You were one or you were the other. You could not be both.

*

When I was ten, I got a scholarship to an Anglican private girls' school – my family was Buddhist, but we lived in Sydney's bible belt and all the 'good' schools around there were religious. Off I went to this strange new world where we got detentions if we wore ribbons that weren't the regulation blue, or dared to step out into the world wearing anything but our school blazer.

Here was a place where we were told outright that it was a sin to be gay (ironically by a female staff member who, despite informing me I was going to hell for not being Christian, would hand me gifts after class with a little knowing wink, giving me preferential treatment that I only recognised as inappropriate later on). There was an unspoken rule forbidding teachers who were gay from discussing their personal relationships. Whispers shot across the schoolyard about the girls rumoured to be lesbians – how disgusting and creepy. When the time came to get changed for PE, we didn't want those girls around in case they checked us out. We were told that no one was to take a girl to the school formal.

It was during my time in this peculiar place that I met her. I was in the orchestra for a school production of *South Pacific*, and Jessica, a new exchange student a few years older than me, was one of the leads. Her wild, Hermione Granger–esque hair swept over her soulful brown eyes, and she had the most intoxicating smile. I don't remember the first time we met, or how she got to know my name, but every time I saw her my heart would jump into my throat and I wasn't sure why.

'Hi Giselle!' she'd say brightly, and I'd stammer a hello back before running away. We never said more than that, but somehow it meant everything.

I moved through that year like I was in a daze. I had my first boyfriend, if you could call him that – someone I exchanged timid confessions of love with over the phone and on MSN, and met in person just once before he dumped me and I felt the crush of heartbreak for the first time. But Jessica was a physical presence. I'd walk the corridors hoping I'd run into her, although I couldn't quite say why. I thought she was so cool, this older, confident girl – I wanted to be like her, just like I wanted to be like Sarah Michelle Gellar, who I had a poster of on my wall that I loved to look at, staring into her paper eyes, drunk on the feeling of it. I told myself it was because I liked *Buffy the Vampire Slayer*. I'd never watched the show.

Jessica left at the end of the year, moving back to the island she called home. One day she was there, and the next day she wasn't. I never got to say goodbye or tell her how I felt – not that I'd recognise it myself for years.

Life went on without her, as it tends to do. I wonder where she is now – if she's with someone, if that someone is a woman, or if I'm just projecting. I wonder what I'd say to her if I saw her again. *Thank you*, maybe.

Could my love for Jessica coexist with my love for that first boy who broke my heart? Was there a part of me that I had buried somewhere so deep, so secret, that I couldn't find it?

One or the other. Never both.

*

Switching my Tinder to both men and women was an experiment, that's all. I was in my late twenties, a couple of years out of a five-year relationship, and had well and truly played the field with men, but now – especially living in Melbourne with more diverse friends than I'd ever had before – it seemed like anything was possible. I still didn't consider myself to be anything but straight, even though new friends I'd meet would invite me to queer events, always surprised when I adamantly corrected them.

I chatted for months with the first girl I went out with before we ever met up. Something was holding me back, but as I scrolled through her photos I wondered what it would be like to wake up next to her.

Our first date was pizza in the park with her dog; our second was a movie night at my apartment where I cooked vegan mac 'n' cheese and we watched *The Swan Princess*, which both of us had loved during childhood. I felt comfortable with her in a way I never had with men, but it also felt strongly platonic. Although with men I always knew who I was attracted to, with women the lines seemed more blurred because I wanted to be besties with all of them. We became extremely close friends, but sexually, romantically, not so much as a kiss ever transpired between us.

But I fantasised, still: what would it be like to touch a body more like mine, curves and dimples rather than strong, hard lines? The moans, the sighs, the softness. I wanted to be soft. I wanted to play a new part.

Somehow, though, whenever I pictured my future, it was the same as it ever was. I could see myself in bed with women, learning to make each other's bodies sing, but when it came to romantic relationships, I still only ever saw myself with a man. Only after a lot of soul-searching did I come to recognise this as a symptom of internalised homophobia. As I talked to more women on Tinder, dated and slept with non-binary people, I realised that I wasn't straight at all, and yet I still felt pressured to force my romantic life into a binary, to conform to what I'd always been told was acceptable. I could be soft behind closed doors, perform a role I'd never known before, but in public, in a relationship, I still had to seem like I was straight. No matter how hard I tried to fight, I couldn't shake it.

*

It crept up on me so subtly that I didn't even notice until it had burrowed into my bones. At first there I was, a certified Man Lover Who Would Never Ever Look at a Girl Are You Kidding, and then I was questioning, and then I was standing before myself, fully formed, bi as fuck.

It felt exciting, like being born again, or at least like being a snake bursting out of its old skin, revealing something that was always there. I wanted to shout it to the world, but before that, I had to shout it to my parents – at the time I was writing a column for a national newspaper and I knew it would come up in my work eventually, and I wanted them to hear it from the horse's bisexual mouth.

I dialled the ten digits of my parents' landline, hands clammy, throat closed. When my mother picked up, it all spilled out at once: 'Ihavesomethingreallyimportanttotellyou.'

'Did you have an abortion?' she asked, panic in her voice.

'What? No,' I said, bemused. Apparently that's the line – who knew?

'Well, whatever it is is fine, then,' she said.

I can't even remember how the rest of the conversation went, because it was that unremarkable, which is remarkable in itself. My mother once told me that raising children in a new country had been a constant lesson for her – that she became more open-minded and compassionate as she watched us go through adolescence. Somehow, through all of the fear, we had arrived at a place of understanding, and I realised I probably could have told her, told *myself*, about my sexuality years earlier.

My parents are still a little mystified by the concept of bisexuality, and I still have to correct them any time they ask me if I have a boyfriend yet (no, but I also don't have a girlfriend, or a non-binary-friend – please, I am very lonely, stop asking). But they're getting there.

When my cousin married the love of his life and we watched them sing 'Love Me Tender' together with an acoustic guitar (extremely cute), my once unapologetically homophobic father muttered gruffly, 'This is surprisingly nice.' Years later, when the marriage equality postal survey was underway, he urged all of the patients who came into his medical practice to vote 'Yes'. We are getting there together (even though my dad still bristles when he walks past my sister watching *RuPaul's Drag Race* – it's a work in progress).

*

Sometimes I feel like I don't know how to be bisexual, as if there's a proper way. As if someone would doubt a person's heterosexuality if they were a virgin; as if there's any milestone I have to reach before I'm allowed to carry the card. Even though my family is accepting, it still scares me. I'm still censoring myself, wondering how much I should allow.

But I am unlearning.

I am unlearning the self-loathing, the doubt, the pressure, the terror, the worry of being at once too much and not enough.

I have figured out that, just like me, the path to knowing myself is not straight (sorry). I am thirty years old and I am only just figuring it out – how to let go of the fear of the unknown, and dive headfirst into a world that I've always dreamt of fully inhabiting. To be more like Cô Linh and Cô Trang – the role models I didn't even know I had, who defied their conservative culture to be themselves, proud and unafraid, with a love that continues to pulse decades on.

To Jessica. To Buffy. To all the girls who've made my heart flip before I brushed the feeling away.

I can be both.

Rob, and Queer Family

Nayuka Gorrie

I was reticent about my sexuality until I was about twelve or thirteen. I didn't really start living an out queer life until a few years ago. And I still feel like I'm growing up – or at least growing into – queerness. There was no Young M.A, Janelle Monáe, IAMDDB, Kehlani or Amandla Stenberg when I was a kid. All I had was t.A.T.u., and they turned out to be gammin. But there were signs I was going to grow up queer: my crushes on the two youngest Hanson brothers, and liking softball. I didn't know it at the time though; I just existed.

I might not have understood exactly who I was yet, but I knew being queer was bad. Ankle socks were for poofters according to my grandfather. AFL was 'GAYFL' according to the Queensland boys I grew up with. Rugby League was for poofs according to my Victorian uncles. It was Adam and Eve not Adam and Steve. If you annoyed a sibling, you'd be called a fag. You heard about a cousin who was 'a bit thing'. About an aunty who had a 'good friend' and a motorbike. There was a black person who everyone made jokes about because they were visibly queer. These jokes travelled up and down Queensland's coast and apparently black kids are still telling them today.

There were queers in my family, of course, but typically they removed themselves. There was never outright rejection, just whispers and insinuations. I don't blame them for separating themselves from the extended family – us queers have to protect ourselves. But for black people (and maybe I'm projecting here) this is a kind of death, a part of the soul cauterised to protect the rest.

Aside from the whispers and taunts, the other thing that shaped my understanding of deviance was how *straight* everything was. All the things deemed 'normal' and all the 'done things' were straight. Straightness was a given. Every girl I knew grew up, found a man, got pregnant, and stayed with him even if he was violent or they were unhappy, bored or hated each other. Pink was for girls, blue for boys. My mum always worked, but for most other women their place was in the house. Toxic masculinity, heteronormativity and rigid gender roles were enforced and performed under the cloaks of culture, the-way-things-are and religion. This wasn't done in a self-reflective way; there were just no examples of other ways things could be.

There were glimmers of hope though. Dad loved Queen, and he said it didn't matter that Freddie Mercury was gay, because he made good music. When Mum joined the police, she suddenly had a lot of dyke mates. And the sexual rigidity we grew up with eased when Dad left Mum.

I wasn't aware of it as a child, but Dad was Catholic and quite strict about what we were exposed to. We were instructed to cover our eyes during 'naughty' scenes while Dad fast-forwarded.

When he left, Mum started dating, and eventually she met Rob. Rob was the brother of a man she was sleeping with. Rob was my first encounter of the queer kind.

There are so many ways to be gay or queer, but with Rob there were a lot of obvious signs and most of them revolved around Beyoncé. We spent many a summer day and night watching DVDs of Destiny's Child and solo Beyoncé shows, and the film *Fighting Temptations*, starring Beyoncé. He even used 'Beyoncé' as his middle name on his Facebook profile. Despite all this, I didn't realise that Rob was gay. I thought he was just a very lovely man with excellent taste.

I missed these sorts of clues when I was young. But now that I'm older, I realise that queerness was there: it was just coded. Sure, there was no Jayden declaring Tyler his boyfriend, but Tupac and Missy Elliott had an extremely queer aesthetic. Despite being drawn to that, and to Rob – to all this queer coding – I didn't clock it at the time.

The first time I identified what my sexuality was, I landed on labelling myself 'bisexual'. For years, I was closeted about being bi.

A friend lent me a porn magazine, which I kept under my bed. I was out to friends, I pashed at parties and fucked during sleep-overs, but my romances were always with boys and men. These relationships were serious; pashes with girls and gays at parties were not. But once I was in a relationship, it felt unfulfilling. After the freshness wore off, I would get bored. It wasn't the fault of the men I was with: there was nothing wrong with them.

I spent my early twenties with a man, and for most of that time I had to stave off queerness. It was all closeted: gay porn, what I read and who I followed, and who I had crushes on. While I was with this man, I came out to Mum and other family members who didn't yet know. Mum couldn't understand why I bothered to tell her I was bi – I was in a relationship with a man, so why did it matter? She didn't understand that I wanted to be seen and to live truthfully. At various points in the relationship, I alternated between thinking I was a lesbian and thinking I was asexual. The two obviously aren't mutually exclusive, but I thought *something* had to account for the way I felt. I regularly wondered if I wasn't a woman. I often didn't feel like a woman.

Eventually I realised I could no longer be with this man. After the relationship ended, I was really able to be queer. I fucked often and soon realised I was not asexual, I just wasn't into men, or wasn't interested in being a woman with a man. I hated the dynamic and found it distressing. Heterosexual men are conditioned to think they are tops, and because heteronormative society is conditioned with binary thinking, heterosexual woman are expected to be bottoms, which starts to become rather boring if you aren't truly either.

Towards the end of this relationship I started to dress how I wanted to dress and began going to parties to be around people who it made sense to be around. After I left the relationship, I realised these people were all super queer. The cousins I felt most drawn to were gay, the parties I was going to were all queer – everything finally made sense. Unknowingly, I had gravitated towards the life I wanted.

Queer dating for the first time was difficult for a few reasons. Women who are into everyone but have not unpacked their shit can tend to situate men at the top of the hierarchy. There can be a tendency to generally take (colonial white) masculinity more seriously. This isn't clear-cut, obviously. As Allison Gallagher has pointed out, cis people expect trans women to express a kind of femininity they can feel comfortable with – feminine but not too feminine. In the LGBTIQA+ hierarchy, women and femininity, particularly trans women, are at the bottom. I'm probably theorising here to make the waters of my own behaviour murky. Desire and who we prioritise is political, and regretfully I have treated a few women like shit. To be fair, I treated men like shit too. Something we don't necessarily talk about is that it can be much easier to treat men like they are disposable. Or, at least, I did, because I just stopped caring about them. The problem with respecting people who aren't men a lot more than you respect men, and not learning how to respectfully engage with hook-up culture is that it can be hard to just fuck people who aren't cis men. It also doesn't help that even if you do just want to fuck, some queers can be really coy. White queers can be really fucking weird. I was utterly turned off random hook-ups with people who weren't men when one white person I hooked up with at a party randomly rocked up to my house drunk at 3 am on a Friday night over a month after we'd hooked up. At least with men there seemed to be a mutual disrespect – no one expected to see each other again. It was easy to get just sex from men, even if it was uneventful, even if they never made me cum (they never did).

Eventually I realised I was an all-or-nothing person. I either just wanted sex, or I wanted a life (and sex!) with someone. There was no in between.

Eventually I met Witt, who is now my boyfriend, and realised all the things I wanted were possible. I could be passionate about someone and it could stay passionate. It was possible to cum a lot. It was possible to wake up happy and excited. Things just made sense.

I am fortunate to come from a family that has not only produced a lot of queers but also respects my relationship and my choices. Mum doesn't see my queerness or gender as some kind of personal or moral failure – mine or her own. She uses the right pronouns. I have a brother who often gets mistaken for being queer because all his friends and siblings are queer and he's always at our parties. I have a queer lesbian sister.

I am lucky to be in my late twenties in the late 2010s: I did not face ostracisation. But many queer people still do. I see many an Instagram story about loneliness, rejection, homophobia and transphobia. Despite it being '20bi-teen' or '20dyke-teen', depending on who you ask, it is still not always safe to be whoever you are. I'm one of the lucky ones.

Those of us who are lucky – who have never known cold rejection, police brutality or violence from bigoted strangers – should remember that this time in history didn't arise spontaneously. Without women like Marsha P. Johnson and Sylvia Rivera, we would not have our movements. The queer black position in Melbourne, where I live, would not be as strong as it is is if not for Lisa Bellear and organisations such as OutBlack. I'm lucky to live in a city where it feels like black queers are everywhere.

I often wonder if baby Nayuka would be stoked with older Nayuka. I think I'm living the kind of life I would have loved to have seen, even just from a distance. Although I probably wouldn't have clocked what it really was.

*

Until I started writing this essay, I had never reflected on how important queer people are to keeping families functioning. Our family was crumbling when Rob found us. Dad had taken off and Mum was trying to navigate her emotions, single parenthood and reclaiming her youth. Rob, our beautiful fairy godmother, stepped in.

At the tail end of 2004, my sister Likarri, brother Paul and I all contracted chickenpox at the same time. Mum wasn't able to take time off work, so Rob did. While I found my own body revolting, he tenderly applied calamine lotion to my skin and Likarri's. When he decided that we were well enough to leave the house, he drove us to Rebel Sports in Mt Gravatt. Unable to control themselves, people unabashedly stared at pock-marked Likarri and me. Rob, offended on our behalf, asked anyone who dared to stare, 'What the fuck are you lookin' at?'

A year later, Rob took Paul, Likarri and I to Dreamworld. He was so much fun. If he liked a ride, we'd do it three more times. I'll remember his scream and laugh going around the Claw forever.

One teacher–parent interview night, Mum got hammered on passionfruit UDLs. I was upset because I'd started to make an effort at school and wanted Mum to know how well I was going. She called Rob and he made the twenty-minute drive from Oxley to Indooroopilly State High School to make sure I could have this moment and to save Mum and I an argument.

The following year, unsatisfied with the dress I'd bought myself for my Year 12 formal, Rob insisted I buy a different dress. I didn't have the money for it, so Rob asked his boyfriend at the time to help me out. I got special permission from the school to have Rob as my formal partner. We laughed all night.

The day I started writing this piece I messaged Rob and asked him if I could talk about him for this anthology. He said, 'Of course, make me famous!'

Around two weeks later, he was stabbed to death in his Kelvin Grove house.

At his funeral they played 'I Was Here' and 'All the Single Ladies', and when his casket was lowered a substantial piece of my heart was buried with him. He probably has several hundred chunks of heart down there with him.

Words can't capture Rob's smile, laugh, smell or humour, but I hope in some way that as this book gathers dust his memory is kept alive and that I have in some way fulfilled the last request Rob ever made of me: make me famous.

I would not be the queer I am without Rob and I will miss him forever.

Caritas

Jack Kirne

His name was Stephen. Nobody called him that, of course. He went by his surname, Tan. We attended St Paul's together. A Catholic boys' school in the suburbs, it was a dangerous place to be gay. Had I been the type to make a fuss, I would not have allowed myself to be enrolled there.

Tan was thin, with a long neck; dirty black hair flicked over the collar of his blazer, in blatant defiance of the school's dress code. When he smiled, which he did often, crooked teeth jutted out in strange directions; with his mouth closed, his lips were full and slightly feminine. When tasked with reading the daily prayer, he would deliberately fuck it up. For instance, if the prayer read, 'Lord, give us victory over sin and temptation', he said, 'Lord, give us victory, sin, and temptation'. If it read, 'Lead me to the towering rock of your safety', he said, 'Lead me to the towering cock of your safety.' Not very clever jokes, but when the slightest infraction tempted detention, these risks commanded roaring waves of laughter. He wanted people to pay attention to him. My cock swelled if he spoke to me, which he did rarely, thank God. Sometimes, it became too much and I would retreat to the toilets, where I'd knock one out.

Of course, nothing would come of it. I read space opera and spent my weekends building landscapes for my model trains. I dreamt of being a jazz pianist, and hung out with the music kids, an eclectic bunch of misfits who talked exclusively about Coltrane, Led Zeppelin and *The Legend of Zelda*. Tan was different. At lunch, he hung with a crew of boys who lingered at the top of the grassy hill that overlooked the school's soccer oval and the old gym. They slipped down to Merri Creek to smoke, and if they were bored, they'd find a Year 7, and, like cats playing with a half-dead bird, shove him around until it got old. Those boys were sometimes close, pulling each other into rough side hugs, or ruffling another's hair. In class, they would play gay chicken beneath their desks, where an adventurous hand sliding up a thigh was a test – swerve too soon and you were a pussy, but let the hand climb too far and you were something much worse: a *homosexual*.

*

Once a month, our year level was dragged into the school's chapel and exposed to Father Peter's sermons. He was an ancient man, with excretions that leaked constantly from the folds of his eyes. He wanted to make us 'gentle men', and spoke at length on the value of Christian *caritas*, and loving one's brother. These ideas provided ample fuel for the simmering gay panic. Tan called Father Peter a super-pedo for his speech at the school's fortieth anniversary assembly, in which he fondly recalled watching the 'fine boys' shower together. The thought depressed me. Tan and I were in PE together, and in the changerooms, he and the other boys would clutch their towels around their tight waists to hide their peckers. How I longed for the freer days. But I never said any of this; I barely said anything at all. When I spoke, my voice moved with lovely accordion motion; unchecked, my slight hands would nurse my face in an effeminate way. In Year 7, I had been called *homo* a few times, and had since mastered the art of not being seen. In silence was a rough kind of safety.

This silence made me more aware of my surroundings, more so than my peers. Years later, over beers with an old bandmate, I casually remarked on the school's wire Jesus.

'Wire Jesus?' he replied, wiping the beer's head from his lip. Surely I couldn't be the only one who'd noticed. I was captivated by that sculpture of Jesus. Not in the spiritual, believe-he-died-for-my-sins kind of way; it was the oddness of the crucifix, or lack thereof, that got me. Unlike in most churches, where the Son-of-God was well-and-truly nailed to the cross, this Jesus was liberated, a minimalist wire sculpture suspended above, his hand stretched out before him. Waiting in line for the Eucharist, my eyes would fix on where Jesus' eyes should have been but weren't, and I'd feel a piercing pain in my lungs, like the sort I sometimes got from running. I did not believe in God – or His wrath on Sodom – but beneath that chicken-wire Jesus, I felt seen in all my queerness and I was afraid.

St Paul's had a strict uniform policy that extended well beyond its gates; after school, teachers drove in their dusty Volvos to distant train stations to find students wearing their uniform improperly all across the eastern suburbs. After my forty-minute bus ride and twenty-minute train ride, it was easy to believe that I was far away from the institution's reach. But on a thirty-six-degree day, after I loosened my tie just enough to let in air at my clammy neck, Father Michael stepped out ominously from behind the bus stop. He took my name and wrote me a detention slip.

The following lunchtime, I walked to the edge of campus. The detention rooms were famously stuffy, the air too hot and close. I arrived on time, and sat in the back row to avoid the light, split by the venetians. Mr Lee, a dumpy man known as 'Dogfuck', supervised. The nickname originated in the aftermath of an infamous religious education class in which Lee said that masturbation was a greater sin than bestiality.

'I'm surprised to see you here,' Mr Lee said.

I might have explained myself, if not for Tan. He came through the door yelling to an out-of-sight friend, but silenced when he saw Lee. The men acknowledged each other with the wordless nod you might grant an old enemy. Tan shuffled to the back of the room and settled beside me. My fingers started to tremble. I met his gaze with trepidation, and raised my eyebrows, as if to say, *Hey*. He pulled out his laptop. My stomach plunged. We were supposed to tackle our homework in silence, and I thought we might do just that, until I saw him opening MSN and circling his username with his mouse. I don't know why he wanted to talk to me; he had barely shown me any attention at all. To pay this mind would break my rule of silent protection. But I was intrigued by the gesture.

His username was t@nXXX. Mine was Basil Lurhman. In his profile picture, he stood in green shorts at the beach, rivulets of seawater tracing his abdominals. Mine was of model trains.

t@nXXX said: *look at Dogfuck go.*

Mr Lee picked at his teeth with his finger, digging furiously in an attempt to dislodge an indeterminate green speck.

What do you suppose he's digging for? I wrote.

Tan sniggered. *Treasure.*

Mr Lee's excavation expanded into a two-handed operation. His left hand prised his lip over his gums, exposing a raw fleshy mound into which his finger furrowed. Tan sent another message. *You got any games?*

I admitted that I did not.

Nerd.

Mr Lee rose with an exasperated huff. The dig had failed to dislodge the gunk.

'You gentlemen stay here,' he said. 'Keep working, and don't talk.'

With Lee gone, Tan let loose his crooked smile.

'I have a game,' he said. 'Want to see?'

The game's name was *Beer Goggles*. The player shifted a six-pack from left to right, trying to catch bottles that fell from the top of the screen. On the right, a buxom blonde flashed a flirty smile. I didn't understand. Tan collected ten bottles and the game lurched, as if glitching. The bottles sped up. The woman on the right was now sans shirt, firm nipples visible through a white bra. Another ten bottles, and her pants flashed off. She lost her shoes, her panties. Finally, her breasts were free.

Nailed it! the game declared.

'You think she's hot?' Tan asked.

'Yeah,' I replied, though I didn't really think so. Something about the game had left a sour sensation in my mouth.

'The next chick's hotter.' Tan clicked 'Play Again'.

The 'next chick' had red hair. Larger breasts, curvier. I felt nauseated. Then I realised that for him this was porn, and he was probably hard. I eased myself up an inch in my seat, vying for a glance. I saw it stir beneath the fabric of his shorts. My cock lurched in reply. I could tell he had a pornstar dick. I bit my lip, and held my breath.

'You like that, huh?' Tan asked.

I glanced back at the screen. The ginger woman's pants blipped into non-existence, revealing a trimmed strip of pubic hair.

'Oh yeah,' I said, swallowing. 'Hot.'

A bang on the window behind us. Tan slammed his computer shut as we turned around together. Mr Lee's round face was pressed up against the glass – bright red and furious. He too had seen the ginger pubes.

'Fuck.' Tan said.

*

Sex education at St Paul's was folded into a class called 'Personal Development', in which we mostly talked about 'Goals' and how to say no to drugs. What I recall most vividly was a video about 'the change', which featured infrared footage of a hard penis. The boys in my class had screamed 'Sick!' and 'Turn it off!' while Mr Platt, our teacher, yelled, 'Be mature'. I was oddly captivated, and I knew in that moment what others had deduced from my girlish laugh.

So I felt ridiculous, and sick with dread, to be dragged to the vice-principal's office for the porn I had no interest in. Being caught with porn was about the worst thing that could happen to a boy at St Paul's. When Father Peter had caught Bradley Howett gifting his stash to a Year 8, a meeting was organised with the vice-principal, who played the offending material back to Bradley and his stone-faced parents. Bradley told the story through fits of laughter, but terror hung behind the façade. Excuses presented themselves to me as Dogfuck walked us across campus: I could tell the vice-principal that I was forced to watch it. I could say, 'I was as shocked as anyone, I was only looking so I could be sure of what it was, once I knew it was too late.' I could pose a question: 'If someone tapes a knife to your hand while you're unconscious and uses it to kill someone, does that make you a killer?' I had a good record, would probably get away with it. But I couldn't do that to Tan. It felt right that we should both suffer. I thought that, like Simon of Cyrene, the shared burden of our cross would draw us together somehow – that it would become the story we would laugh about and tell strangers at parties when they asked how we became friends.

I was lucky: the school only called my mother, who responded with faint, inarticulate huffs. When I got home, she had burnt dinner, and then she disappeared to her night-shift at the Alfred Hospital without looking at me. I was not surprised. We were strangers in those days, and weathered the disappointments we inflicted on each other as old friends do – we did not believe that the other person was capable of change. The shame I had felt quickly gave way to excitement. Tan had shown me porn; we got hard together. In Pastoral Care the following day, I asked him for the game. I needed him to know: *I was hard too.*

Our detention was escalated to a Saturday. In the days leading up to it, the bulge of Tan's cock crowded my thoughts. I found a photo of him online wearing a lime-green mankini at last year's swimming carnival – the swimwear came with the special DVD edition of his favourite film, *Borat*. I heaved over this photo: it was what I turned to when horny at night and hard in the morning. I could not, did not, believe the fantasy would become real. Still, usually in the heat of it, I opened MSN with the intent of starting a conversation, only to be stopped by the terror and exhilaration that pounded through my body. Besides, I had been unable to think of anything to say except 'Hi.'

Saturday came. In the shower, I nervously scrubbed my arse-hole, just in case. I didn't have any concrete plans, and when I tried to rehearse a conversation it failed. I was unable to imagine what we might talk about – he did not seem the sort to get lost in a discussion about Thelonious Monk. Still, when I saw Tan standing outside Father Peter's office joking with Tommo and Luis, my crotch tightened with anticipation. Tan was leaning against the lockers in the hall, and nodded a hello. I watched him, not really listening to what he was saying. I wanted to touch his body; I kept my hands in my pockets and pinched my thigh when I felt myself getting hard. Then, Kristof rocked up and gave Tan a one-armed hug. He was one of Tan's best mates, a quiet man who was built like a refrigerator. Watching them embrace, the tightness in me evaporated – I wouldn't be able to get between their antics.

We spent the morning picking up litter from the footy oval under the watch of Father Peter. Above, stony clouds hung close like a ceiling. I scooped discarded Smith's chip packets and the lids of LeSnaks and Yoplaits from the dewy earth, while Tan and Kristof trailed behind, taking the piss. They shoved each other and laughed in thick stumbling bursts. When Father Peter asked what was so funny, Tan pointed to a used condom.

'That's too big to be yours, mate,' Kristof said.

'You're right,' Tan said. 'Must be your mum's.'

*

Waiting for the 904 bus, I felt ridiculous. I smelt mouldy from the trash and was hot with disappointment. But what had I missed out on, really? Him fucking me at detention? I mourned him all the same. I tried to escape into my book but couldn't absorb myself in it. What had seemed exciting a week before was now unfathomably far away.

'Hey, nerd.'

Tan settled on the seat beside me and gave the finger to a passing black Mercedes.

'Kristof,' he explained. 'If he isn't the richest cunt we know, I don't know who is.'

His use of the collective 'we' punctured my misery. Perking up, I asked, 'How rich is he? Does he have a tennis court?' *Idiot*.

'Ask him yourself,' Tan said. 'His folks hate me. Won't let me round. Want to smoke?'

He led me into thick bushland and down to a shadowed clearing. Under dappled glow, Tan stared at me with his arms folded as I struggled with the lighter. If he were testing me I was failing. I tried the spark wheel six or so times before the flame leapt up, and when I dragged on the firm tube nicotine seized the back of my throat. I managed to stifle the cough. Tan easily lit his own cigarette and blew smoke into the sky.

'Where d'you live?' Tan asked.

'Close-ish. Montmorency.'

'That's the fucking *sticks*,' he said. 'What do you do out there?'

'A lot of reading, I guess.'

He sucked to the butt and flicked the cigarette into the underbrush. I waited for a fire to erupt in the scrub, and when nothing happened I followed his lead. He lit two more smokes and passed one to me.

'What did your folks think of the tits?' he said. 'Good boy like you, I bet they flipped their fucking shit.'

I didn't like that he called me a *good boy*. I exhaled some smoke.

'They were chill,' I said. 'Disappointed, but too ashamed to say anything. What did yours think?'

Tan pulled up his shirt and pointed to a vermilion bruise below his right nipple. 'Dad.' He made a half smile.

'Shit,' I said. 'I'm sorry.'

Tan laughed. 'Not your fault,' he said. He shuffled across the dirt and rearranged himself beside me. 'Last one,' he explained, producing another cigarette. We shared it close, his leg against mine. He smelt like chlorine. My head spun from fear and nicotine. I wanted nothing more than for this moment to go on forever. I took another drag, and stared at the autumn leaves shivering overhead. Then, his hand settled on my lower thigh.

My heart rattled but I didn't let myself look. With delicate, testing movements, the hand shuffled north. The advance ceased, then continued. My gaze strayed to Tan's face. He grinned manically. His hand moved on to the inside of my thigh, and he was close, so close he brushed up against the firm presence and – 'Fuck!' He leapt to his feet.

'You were going to let me,' he said. 'Weren't you.'

I said nothing. He grabbed his bag and set back up the hill. I realised too late he was playing chicken; hard and horny and bewildered, I had failed to swerve.

I spent the rest of the weekend in a terrified fugue. My insides squealed and roared. What was I going to do? If I asked Tan not to tell anyone, it would be like admitting that something did happen, and I wasn't ready to admit that to myself or anyone else. Should I deny everything, pretend it never happened? Should I fake sick? Move schools? I knew I couldn't come out. My mother had once said, 'The gays live lonely lives.'

I stayed up till four on the Saturday, taking bites out of the block of tasty cheese in the fridge. My skin felt irritable, and poorly fit; like a wetsuit a size too small. Near delirium on Sunday, I logged on to MSN, praying he'd be online. I would pretend my enthusiasm was a joke – and if that failed, beg. He sent a message to me the moment I came online.

t@nXXX: *ive been thinking of u*

Alone, words are dangerous, terrible things.

Basil Lurhman: *Is that so?*

youre gay ... aren't you? its kwl if u r.

He would be laughing at the other end, getting ready to take a screenshot if I confessed.

He said: *I hope u r.*

I wanted to vomit. I wrote: *I think I might be bi.*

I want you to blow me, he said. *I would ... like ... put my dick ... down your throat.*

I unzipped my pants, released my already firm cock, typed: *I wouldn't object.* My most explicit flirt.

t@nXXX: *coz like ... once I start ... im not gonna wanna stop ... for at least a couple of days.*

I came, violently. Shame bloomed in my gut, and I wanted him more than ever.

So, I wrote. *When do you want to do this?*

No reply. I waited a minute, another few.

t@nXXX: *Duuuudeee.* Another pause. *My sister was using my computer.*

I slapped my laptop shut and whispered, '*Shit!*' I opened the screen again, studied the flashing cursor.

I'm not gay, I typed.

I was fucked.

But Tan told no one. And when he messaged me late one Tuesday evening, I understood. We had started to play a game: we sexted and absolved ourselves of perversion post-orgasm, only to return later, filthier and more desperate.

At school, we remained distant. I learnt that he was slightly allergic to Vaseline; that he had to take cold showers to keep his skin from erupting into hives. Mostly, we talked about sex. Then we stopped absolving ourselves. He would steal his older sister's g-strings and send me photos of him barely contained in the underwear. I replied in kind.

When Tan started going around with Mary, a girl from our sister school, I despaired, but the lewd messages continued. We bought webcams. I discovered that his pornstar penis delivered pornstar loads. He loved to watch me swallow.

One night he wrote: *I can promise u ... I want my dick to be aching ... if I fuck you.*

When I took the exam for my learner's permit, he told me not to fail: *take me cruising*, he wrote.

It was my idea to book the room at the Box Hill Motor Inn. I suppose we might have driven to a car park, or secretly fucked in one of our bedrooms, but I wanted romance, the texture of his skin against mine as we fell into sleep together.

I checked in a little after six. I was frightened and excited, my voicing wobbling as I passed my ID over to the disinterested concierge. While she scanned my documents, I wondered if she knew what my night was going to entail and felt suddenly hot, my temples pricking with embarrassment. This was ridiculous, I knew – even if she guessed, why would she care. And even if she did, what Tan and I had planned was legal. Though it didn't feel that way to me then – it felt filthy and illicit.

Safe in the room, I stripped to my briefs and sent Tan a selfie. He said he'd meet me at seven, which gave me forty minutes to kill. I took a beer from my bag and sipped in the shower, where I washed my hair with the complimentary shampoo. I emerged bright pink from the water and checked my phone. *Nothing*. It was twenty past seven. *You nearby?* I typed out. Another hour passed, without reply. I drank another beer, attempted to call – straight to voicemail. I felt furious, and desperately sad. I wanted to scream and throw things around the room, but also crawl under the bed and stay there. Then, the shaking started. I ran a bath, but even submerged, I shook. I drank deeper and deeper into the evening, into the still depth of the night, shaking in the neon light of the motel's entrance.

He never came, of course. He never messaged, not on the night, nor in the days or weeks or months that followed. I tried to contact him. I asked, *What happened?* Drunk one evening, I wrote: *Fuck you*. And then, the lonely messages, months apart. *Hey. Hey. Hey. You there? I'm here for you. Call me?* He didn't call.

*

Years have passed since then. I have dated some good men, more bad men, and one terrific man. Coming out was not easy, but it never is. My partner, Chris, says anybody who tells you otherwise is either a liar or too well adjusted. I don't talk to people from high

31

school, but Facebook keeps me in the loop. Tan has partied, cycled through women, and become a carpenter.

I still dream of him sometimes. He is his best self, muscular and lovely. And smoking. Always smoking.

Three months ago, he sent me a photo. In it he wore tight red briefs and had shaved his body hair. The way the light lingered on his biceps suggested he took time to compose the image, his patient, firm penis an extended olive branch. When Tan messaged, *hey mister*, I didn't hit 'block'.

I didn't want Tan to love me, but I let his slick body and porn-star penis flood my messages. I encouraged him. I replied with a wink sticker, or with *Wow* and *Nice*. It was intoxicating to hold such power over him, to behold his nakedness, arranged and presented just to please me. But Tan and the memory of my original desire – that coming-into-queerness where everything felt wrong, and exciting – rose like a leviathan and swallowed me. When Chris pushed my legs over my head, I closed my eyes and let Tan pound me. When I descended on Chris, his penis petered in comparison. Sex between my real and phantom lover was desperate – a failed negotiation across time and bodies. Chris noticed. One night, naked and sticky with cum, he asked, 'You home?' I tickled him until he begged me to stop.

Not long ago, as I teetered on the edge of sleep, I received Tan's final message.

I'm outside your house.

I rose from my bed and snuck through the dark house, not daring to turn on any lights in case he really was outside. With heavy breaths, I pressed myself against the crisp glass of my living room window. There, on the street, was a car with the headlights on, purring with anticipation. At the time, I couldn't fathom how he'd found me – I'd never told him my address. Later, I learnt that Messenger had been attaching an address to each message I'd sent, courtesy of location services.

In the quiet evening, the muted hum of his car's engine was astonishing. I wondered if he could see me; if he would get out to cross the distance between us. I don't know how long I stood there, the warmth of my breath fogging the living-room window. It was a while.

St Louis

Oliver Reeson

When I was twenty-one and had just discovered the possibilities of writing as art, I heard a Harold Brodkey short story called 'The State of Grace' on *The New Yorker* fiction podcast. In it, the narrator recounts his teenage years in St Louis, particularly times spent babysitting a young boy named Edward. The protagonist prides himself on being able to invent games that were 'wonderful to [Edward] – like his daydreams, in fact'. Yet always, despite Edward's ferocious, trembling love for him, the narrator holds the boy at a cool distance. It is only later, from the vantage point of adulthood, that he experiences regret. 'Really, that's all there is to this story,' the narrator concludes. 'The boy I was, the child Edward was. That, and the terrible desire to suddenly turn and run shouting back through the corridors of time, screaming at the boy I was, searching him out and pounding on his chest: Love him, you damn fool, love him.'

On the podcast, American novelist Richard Ford reads the story and says that Brodkey 'became a kind of perfectionist, which is a bad thing to be if you're a novelist, [but] it's not such a bad thing if you're a short story writer'. Brodkey's novel *Party of Animals* was famously delayed (it took nearly thirty years to be published), and though he was once the talk of New York for his perfect short stories – the great potential, the wunderkind of the city – that wait

33

came to be considered a great sadness. How dare this writer make New Yorkers believe in something and then make them wait for it? His critics spoke of him like he was a grifter, and their impatience with him transferred onto his characters. 'Brodkey is so fixated upon the tragic memories of his childhood and youth that he has virtually no sense of proportion about them. In one story after another, he offers up pages of gratuitous detail, straining, it seems, to squeeze every last drop of significance out of every last inane particular,' wrote Bruce Bawer, reviewing the 1988 collection *Stories in an Almost Classical Mode*.

Harold Brodkey did not grow up queer in Australia and, depending on your view of queerness and its relation to time and self, one might not even be able to say that he grew up queer in America. He died of AIDS in 1996, and although he contracted the virus from a homosexual relationship he never considered himself a gay man – nor, presumably, a queer man. The narrative Brodkey told of himself was that he was a married heterosexual man whose romantic life was separate to his sexual one. That is – or was – his story to tell.

I don't consider myself to have grown up queer in central New South Wales or central Queensland as a child, or Brisbane as a teenager, though these are the places I lived, grew older, fucked in. I began to grow up as a queer person in a doctor's office in East Brunswick when I was twenty-five, when I cried asking for a referral to a gender therapist. In this moment I admitted for the first time that my disconnect from my body was not – as I had often posited lamely to confused romantic partners – so much to do with the surgery I'd had for breast cancer, or with being asexual, but more with that fuzziness that had persisted since my teenager years. Since I'd stepped out of the seemingly genderless space of childhood and into the heavily gendered body of a teenager going through puberty. I had never spoken about it before, but as I entered adolescence I checked out of my body indefinitely. I told myself that this was what puberty was like for everyone, but over the years it became increasingly obvious that this was not the universal experience I had imagined it was.

In high school I had no concept that I might be transgender. I thought, for a time, that I might be gay. In Year 8 English we were taken on an excursion to the Roma Street Parkland in Brisbane to see Shakespeare's *Twelfth Night*. When Olivia tried to seduce Viola (disguised as her brother Sebastian), I felt the melodramatic and engulfing narrowing of my world. I sat in the sunlit amphitheatre in my Catholic school uniform (tartan and large, totally unfit for Queensland weather) and the pubescent voice in my head couldn't utter anything more than *That's really cool*. This feeling never culminated in any real-life crushes, but I still knew that it was the start of something significant, and I remember one night praying to God that I not be gay. *I can't do it*, I said. *I don't know how*.

At times since then I have considered myself a dyke, asexual or pansexual. 'I never really came out,' I used to tell people proudly. 'I just started kissing people and never called it anything. My family didn't care. I'm really lucky.'

More honestly, I never came out because I didn't have any words, no story yet, for why what was happening in me didn't match exactly what was happening in almost everybody else. I would only understand it later in life, as I shuffled through old memories of adolescence. In all of these I have no consciousness of my body. Memories of my youth are of my mind and of a vague feeling of discomfort, like when you don't get enough sleep and your body feels like something you are merely wearing, like clothing.

Like Brodkey's protagonist, having lost my childhood, my most comfortable moments were when I didn't feel looked at. 'It was comfortable for me in the back room, alone in the apartment with Edward, because at last I was chief; and not only that, I was not being seen. There was no one there who could see through me, or think of what I should be or how I should behave; and I have always been terrified of what people thought of me, as if what they thought was a hulking creature that would confront me if I should turn a wrong corner.'

In my early twenties I was unexpectedly diagnosed with breast cancer, and thus was forced to confront the idea of my body: that I had one, that I needed it to live, that it was malleable, and that I belonged to it and it to me. It is only now, as I move into the later part of my twenties, that I am growing up. I have started testosterone therapy and I feel, suddenly, like the teenager I never was. It is as if my

35

physical self is coming into focus, and not just when I look in the mirror. It's as though my mind is one image and my body another, and they are circling ever closer to one another, closer to something unified and clear.

I have a crush on someone, in the dizzying, disorienting sense, for probably the second time in my life, and I have no idea what to do with it. The other night she asked me about the ways in which I feel like I'm going through puberty. I told her I had always found people beautiful but now I find them hot. I find myself wanting to touch their skin or kiss their shoulders. When we talk, my voice breaks when I laugh too loudly or talk too fast, and she laughs at me and asks me why I hate it happening. I say I don't know. I do like the way it signals my growing up, but I feel residual discomfort with the notion of being noticeable.

Mostly, I feel lucky and grateful to be alive in a time when I get to claim who I am, when I can realise something was missing from my life that I deserved to experience and can correct it. Although I *am* correcting it, I think often of the missed opportunities. The incorrect explanations for myself I held for some time. Were they lies, even though I had no concept of the truth? Should I have realised earlier? What if I had had top surgery as a teenager? Would I have developed breast cancer in the residual breast tissue? Or would I have escaped something I never should have had in the first place? Sometimes I want to run back through those corridors of time and pound on someone's chest – but whose? Not the child version of me, who felt genderless and therefore comfortable; not me as a distant and confused teen. No one is at fault, yet the urge to turn and run back towards myself remains.

I have come to view all identity as a sort of constant growing up, a perpetual becoming, a continued reinvention. Our concepts of identity, the categories we use to understand it, are after all simply stories: powerful and important, but not above questioning. To approach them with an expectation of perfection is to stall us, stop the motion of becoming and therefore halt the identity and let it evaporate completely.

I wonder if Brodkey's perfectionism was connected to his choice not to identify as queer. There are countless other factors, of course – he lived in a different time. But the feeling of being adrift, isolated, because you don't have the language to articulate your life perfectly, pervades so much of his work that it gives me pause. It is both heartbreaking and deeply familiar to me.

I want to tell people all the time: there is no deadline for growing up, no submission date for your life's narrative. You can work it out now or later. You can reveal yourself in parts, or as a whole, and make revisions. For better or worse, sooner or later, life conspires to reveal you to yourself, and this is growing up.

Harold Brodkey was a writer with a highly American, masculine intellect. His success, the pressure for him to deliver, the notion that he was gifted – I recognise these as stressful at the same time as I criticise the effortlessness with which they were afforded to him. There were other geniuses at the time, non-male, who could not keep people waiting so long, not piss off their audience so deeply, and still be allowed to publish. As someone who is critical of masculinity and its easy topple into toxicity, I am self-conscious about relating to his work. I relate to it not because I understand the experience of being a man or a teenage boy in America, or because I wish to have been one, but because I recognise someone who couldn't allow themselves to be seen and didn't know why until later in life.

When I look back on my own life, I feel the weight of not realising earlier who I was, of being scared to tell the whole story. And yet, how could I realise I was a non-binary person when I did not even know of the concept until I was already an adult? How could I have grown up as a non-binary person when it was not a story I had ever heard?

Ahead of the release of Brodkey's second novel, *Profane Friendship*, a gay love story released three years after his first novel and two years before his death, Ian Parker wrote: 'Some people publish a novel, are saddened or pleased by its reception, then go on holiday, then write another, have children, write another. Life goes on. But imagine a writer who did not do that. Imagine just one novel; imagine its publication and reception expanding to fill a lifetime; imagine a vast, ridiculous, exhausting palaver going on for twenty-five years – great advances, sneak previews, mistaken newspaper reports of this novel's arrival. Think what this does to your understanding of a normal relationship between writer and reader, between writer and writer, your idea of reputation.'

You can't choose to opt out. If you don't tell the story, others will fill in the gaps for you. Brodkey's story is sad because of its undercurrent of persistent repression. It speaks to me of a heteronormative world that understood and validated his talents but would never allow him the narrative devices his own life needed. Of course, I am projecting – our lives barely overlapped; I can't claim true insight.

'There is a certain shade of red brick – a dark, almost melodious red, sombre and riddled with blue – that is my childhood in St Louis. Not the real childhood, but the false one that extends from the dawning of consciousness until the day that one leaves home for college. That one shade of red brick and green foliage is St Louis in the summer (the winter is just a gray sky and a crowded school bus and the wet footprints on the brown linoleum floor at school), and that brick and a pale sky is spring. It's also loneliness and the queer, self-pitying wonder that children whose families are having catastrophes feel.'

In the opening of 'State of Grace', Brodkey talks of the red brick of St Louis as his childhood and I think of the red brick of the first home I remember living in, in Muswellbrook, New South Wales, where I was born. I wonder if it is the same shade. Instead of being laced with blue, I remember it as being highlighted by the pale orange of the cumquat trees either side of our front door. I recall my childhood in that home not as sombre, but as sharp and free, as running naked in the yard and playing with my brothers and learning to hold their guinea pigs and rabbits and wrestling with their friends. I remember the Christmas when I asked my family to call me Peter because Chloe had gone on holiday with her real family (Some mix-up! Can't remember the details) and my family went along with it, or at least indulged me for as long as I needed this. Perhaps my memories of those bricks are gentler because my childhood there did not stretch, as it did for the narrator of Brodkey's story, until I left for college but, instead, until my dad's job moved us on, as it did every few years. In high school, there are brick buildings once again, a dark red, definitely tinged with blue this time. I went to a Catholic high school, and it's here where Brodkey's sombreness really hits me. My memories of this time are fuzzy with blue, smeared with it.

I don't believe, necessarily, that people are born queer, or that I was born trans. That is not my experience or story. I think I was born free from anything and then stories accumulated on me and some of them turned out to be incorrect. I made my own attempts to write convincing stories too: asking to be called Peter; mistaking the queerness of Shakespeare as relevant to my sexuality rather than my gender (the story I could use to understand my response at the time versus the story I can use to understand it now). None of these stories was objectively true, then or now, but the more I learnt the more I had at my disposal to understand myself. All identities, queer or not, are fictional stories. The importance of queer storytellers is not in how they prove their truth, but in how they prove it is necessary to tell our stories in a way that makes us comfortable.

For queer people, adolescence often stretches beyond the teenage years. I think of familiar queer aesthetics – delicate-featured trans men, butch dykes in patterned bow ties, hairless twinks. Most of my queer friends, in their twenties, live life with the fervent excitement of delayed adolescence, of ascending to yourself long after puberty has passed; of needing to regress to progress, to go back to your adolescence in order to grow up, telling the story correctly this time.

I have two older brothers and although my mum longed for a daughter, she was so certain that I would be a boy that when I emerged into the world and was handed to her, she looked up at my father and said, 'Robbie, what's wrong with his penis?' He looked down at her and replied, quietly, 'Kim, it's a girl.'

In queerness, growing up isn't confined to childhood. The gift of being queer is in the close contact it gives you with the nature of identity, the great many possibilities for becoming and for telling stories. Queerness is the red brick – that heavy, strong thing that reflects the light we see around it.

Boobs, Rags and Judy Blume

Phoebe Hart

'When will I get my boobs?'

I was eleven years old, and ever since I'd finished Judy Blume's seminal work, *Are You There God? It's Me, Margaret*, I was in our kitchen moaning to Mum on a daily basis about my glaring lack of mammary glands (Ms Blume has a lot to answer for).

Mum made no comment, just shifted her weight slightly on her feet and continued standing at the sink with her back to me. I sighed and resolved to return to my bedroom to do some more breast-enhancing exercises. 'I must, I must, I must increase my bust ...'

I'm not sure how this technique was supposed to work, but I hoped it would – and soon! My gaggle of girls (I had dubbed us 'The Gang' so we sounded tougher than we actually were) was due to arrive in a few hours for a weekend get-together at my place and I was still as disappointingly flat as the proverbial surfboard. There were seven of us, and I'd worked hard to make these friends after swapping schools a year earlier, in Grade 6. I watched with envy as they all got their 'marbles', which gradually developed into well-formed little breasts. I only had fleabites where two nice little mounds should be.

I would try to fool my mates by popping down the front of my top some dried up balls of 'Slime in a Bucket', horrid kids' gunk sourced from a showbag I got at the local agricultural show in Townsville in Far North Queensland. That got old when my snot-green goo boobs slipped out of place, or worse, fell out and onto the floor.

'Phoebe's got fakies!' screeched the other girls, as I burned with shame.

Cute as my struggles seem in retrospect, my overdue puberty eventually became beyond a joke.

One by one, members of The Gang came to school with a certain look in their eyes – an unholy mixture of pride and horror – and announced they had got their 'rags'. Each time I felt a choking jealousy that made my head fuzzy. It was like the sensation of sand being sucked out from under your feet as waves break on the beach. My ears blocked up. I barely heard my friends as they gushed through the gory details of the arrival of their monthlies.

'It's raining down south!' one would say.

'Nosebleed in Tasmania,' another would reply.

'Clean up in aisle one,' piped in a third.

Resounding giggles. I moved so I could sit on my hands.

'How about that new Madonna video clip?' I would offer weakly, desperate to appear somewhat mature and cool. 'What do you think she's on about when she says, "Papa don't preach"?'

The girls would stop to eye me before going back to listing their top ten euphemisms for menstruation. For my part, I would resist the urge to flick their trainer bra straps until their backs bled in tandem with their vaginas.

But now was not the time for revenge. Rather, I was making a blue-chip investment in my popularity stock, which would soar to an all-time high when I held a rockin' pre-teen sleepover. This would be our chance to gossip about hot boys and choreograph some new routines to the synth-styles of '80s pop music like 'Girls Just Want to Have Fun' by Cyndi Lauper or, if we were feeling a tad more artistic, something like 'One Night in Bangkok' by Murray Head. It was going to be a bonding time for us all, and I sure as heck didn't want to be on the outer for that.

I spent a lot of time making sure it would all go perfectly. My bedroom was looking just right: plastered with teen idol posters of the boys from Pseudo Echo and Wa Wa Nee and the permanent paint murals Mum had allowed us to splatter the walls with as she was 'going to wallpaper over them as soon as we moved out when we turned seventeen' anyway. The fridge was cram-packed with drinks and snacks – mini pizzas, party pies and fizzy drinks – and my little sister Bonnie had been banished to one of her own friends' houses for the afternoon. Everything was set to go.

Only Mum seemed out of sorts.

I'm not sure of the precise moment when my mother's attitude began to change. It might have been when I refused to wear white t-shirts out of the house unless I had a singlet on underneath. Or it might have been the hours I had begun to spend gazing at my own reflection at all angles in the full-length mirror. Maybe it was when I started bringing up awkward subjects such as pregnancy, abortion and birth control. Mum became a little jumpy around me. I couldn't quite diagnose it, but I could sense her unsettled energy and decided the best course of action would be to steer clear.

Finally, the first cars arrived to drop off my friends. Parents waved farewell to their youngsters behind a plume of Winfield Blue smoke and ash as they sped away down the street, leaving my friends to trudge up our steep driveway. Before long, my bedroom had reached a fever pitch of squeals, shrieking laughter and the other assorted sounds of pubescent lounging and lolligagging.

When one gal pal chucked an unused tampon in another's lap, resulting in an extra shrill scream, Mum poked her head in long enough for me to see her disapproving expression. I pretended not to notice, and she stalked off in a huff.

'Oh my god, Phoebe, I think your mum doesn't like us!' one friend whispered theatrically.

'Don't worry about her,' I said. 'She's probably about to get a visit from Aunty Flo.'

Wild hilarity. Pitch and timing perfect. Put them off the hot topic of my own deficit with some on-topic humour. Excellent decoy.

'So …' ventured another friend, 'has George come to visit *you* yet, Phoebe?'

Damn!

'Er, no, not yet.'

Loaded pause. The girls looked at one another. One broke the silence.

'You're nearly twelve, Phoebe. Maybe something's … wrong?'

'Yeah, maybe you should ask your mother about it?' someone added.

A general mumble of agreement.

'You think?' I said, looking up from my lap at all six faces through my fringe. I'd been avoiding the subject with my mother.

'Sure. That's what we'd do.'

All nodded earnestly, wide doe-eyes. I straightened my back and injected some bravado into my voice.

'Alright then, I'll ask her *right now*.'

A sudden burst of energy and everyone got up as a chattering whole to leave the room together.

'Maybe you guys should stay here.'

My suggestion was met with poutiness and smirks. I turned away from the tittering tits and went searching for Mum. I discovered her in the backyard, watering the plants.

She saw me sidling towards her and angled slightly away, aiming her nozzle at a despondent soursop sapling.

'Um, Mum,' I said sheepishly. 'Can I ask you a question?'

Mum flicked her eyes at me. Muffled laughter came from the back window and I turned to see The Gang all peering through to eavesdrop on the exchange. Mum looked up and saw them too. She rolled her eyes and pivoted, yanking the hose towards a remote corner of the yard.

I shooed the girls and waited until they'd reluctantly moved away. Hearing them retreat back to the bedroom, I approached Mum again with trepidation. A few metres from where she was standing, facing the garden, I stopped and waited for her to acknowledge me.

'What is it, Phoebe?' she said exasperatedly. I swallowed and went for it.

'Umm. Everyone's been asking me, and I was wondering ... when will I get my periods?'

Mum stiffened and half-turned towards me.

I'm not sure why I phrased my question in this particular way. I expected her perhaps to simply say 'Soon' or 'Be patient, it will happen in time', and that would be the end of the conversation. Funny things, expectations.

Mum sighed. 'Phoebe, you'll never get your periods.'

I stood blinking in the afternoon light, stunned. My lips formed a basic monosyllabic response.

'Why?'

Mum's mouth tightened. 'Because ... you don't have a uterus.

So you can't have periods, and you can't have a baby.'

My head began eddying with thick, dark thoughts. The inner part of me was screaming *Whaaaaatt!?!* but the outer part was completely blank, speechless.

'You can adopt, though, if you like,' Mum added.

A beat.

'Really? Are you ... sure?' I said eventually. 'No periods?'

Mum nodded.

'Okay then ... at least I've got something I can tell the others. They've all been asking why I haven't got my period yet—'

For the first time, Mum whipped around and faced me, eye to eye.

'Don't you tell them anything!'

My eyes must have popped out of my head. Mum calmed herself a little before proceeding.

'It's not a good idea to tell anyone about this. Your father and I haven't told anyone else, not even Grandma and Granddad. So let's keep this a secret. Our secret. Okay?'

Her words snapped me out of fogginess into a clear, tangible focus and I sensed blood pounding in my temples. I had a secret. A really, *REALLY* big secret. I couldn't believe even my beloved grandma wasn't allowed to know.

'Is that everything?' Mum was looking at me. I got the feeling she didn't want me to ask another question.

I stood there for a moment longer, before turning around quietly and re-entering the house. My memory of what happened next or what I said is murky. I suspect that, in a trance-like state, I nodded, left Mum to her garden and stumbled back to the bedroom with its air of breathless anticipation. I imagine that The Gang was dying to know what had happened – something, anything! – but I can't remember what I told them. Most likely, 'It's nothing.' But it was *something*.

In the end, my breasts did start to emerge, little by little. But by then I had assigned myself apart from the girls and their feminine ways. There was nothing in any Judy Blume book that could explain this to me, and no one to ask 'why'? It would be ages before I understood the reason – many years before I learnt that I am intersex and that my sex chromosomes and organs are male.

All I knew was I was different. Very, very different. It was a profound feeling that shaped my adolescence and my life for a long time to come.

Looking back, I have mixed emotions about this time. It was the start of my journey towards understanding my body and myself more, although it was rough and things didn't get much better any time soon. I still struggle sometimes to accept I'll never be normal, whatever the hell 'normal' means. In these times, I feel confused and lonely, much like the eleven-year-old me. But as my knowledge of human experience has expanded, I've come to realise I'm not alone in feeling this complicated mélange of shame, loss, discovery and, finally, pride. And now I know I am accepted for exactly who I am.

From Dreams to Living

Nadine Smit

I have a great life. I love my work as a nurse. I have wonderful family and friends. I am addicted to shopping (I guess that could be a problem). I get so much pleasure trying on, purchasing and wearing pretty dresses, skirts and blouses. I think I have good taste when it comes to styles that suit me. I've never had a dazzling white wedding dress, but, hey, there's still time to meet the man of my dreams. I'm fit and healthy. I enjoy the outdoors. I often go to dance classes; I walk, run and cycle most days. And when I look in the mirror, it gives me great satisfaction to see a reflection of the person I truly am. The outside matches how I feel on the inside.

But it hasn't always been that way.

In 1959, when I was born, a doctor proclaimed, 'It's a boy!' All he knew was that I had a penis. No one knew my brain thought I was a girl.

In my pre-teens I had regular dreams about being a girl. I wished a fairy godmother would wave her magic wand and when I woke up I would no longer be a boy. During the day when no one was around, I would go into my parents' room and put on Mum's lingerie. Of course it was too big and I looked ridiculous, but I did this at every opportunity. I even pretended to be sick so I could stay home and play dress-ups. I was unable to stop thinking about being a girl. By my late teens it became more difficult to dress up, and I was certain I had been found out, although my mother later insisted she had no knowledge of what I'd been doing.

These thoughts and desires became a source of torment. I could not understand what was wrong with me. I believed I had to compensate by taking on masculine roles. Maybe they would stop the feelings? I finished high school and went into the banking industry. I met my first wife. Of course I was obliged to get married – that's what was expected of me as a man. Neither of us were truly in love, but my wife had her own reasons for marrying. We had three children, some fairly happy years as a family, and divorced after thirteen years as we simply grew further apart.

During this marriage I began to get a grasp of my feelings. I saw an article about Carlotta, a Les Girls performer who was born in a man's body and was now living as a woman. I was intrigued by what she had achieved. After stumbling on her story, I tried to learn as much as I could about others who had transitioned from male to female. I wasn't yet familiar with the word 'transgender', but I had come a long way towards understanding who I was.

I did have some suicidal thoughts growing up. I felt trapped and confused. It would have been quite easy to end the agony, but I cared so much for my loved ones. I continued to bring up my youngest child, my son, who lived with me after his mother and I separated. He was in his mid-teens when I met my second wife. We were introduced by a mutual friend, got on, and though it was apparent to both of us that we were not in love, it was mutually beneficial at the time. Our communication gradually broke down after a few years, by which time I was deeply engulfed in thoughts of transitioning.

In 2009 I started a nursing degree. It is obvious to me now that this was what I was meant to do in life, and I had never been happier than in my role. The first years were still difficult, though; I had panic attacks from the strain of not yet being able to express the person trapped within. Late in 2013, when my marriage deteriorated beyond reconciliation, I saw that it was time for me to be myself, to begin my new life as a woman. What a huge task lay ahead for me.

I purchased premarin, a feminising hormone, from an overseas website that did not demand a prescription. Pretty dumb, especially for a nurse, but I was desperate to make a start on my transition. I soon realised the risks, made an appointment with my GP, and for the first time I said the words 'I'm transgender' out loud. What a sense of relief. She was supportive but admitted she was inexperienced with transgender patients. I'd done some more research and knew I needed to take oestrogen and a testosterone blocker. My GP rang a colleague who was well known to the transgender community and we adjusted the hormones accordingly. I was now properly on the way to feminising my body. Just the act of taking those hormones had an immediate effect: I felt so much happier and surprisingly calm; I became less anxious, better equipped for the task ahead. Within weeks I noticed an increase in breast tissue. After a few months my breasts were big enough that I thought people might start to notice. I couldn't stop smiling.

It was time to come out to my family and friends. This was the scariest moment of my life. How should I go about this? Would they still love me? I was closest to my eldest daughter, so she was the first person I told, over lunch in the city where she worked. Before we ate, I sat her down and said I had something to tell her. I had felt she would be genuinely happy for me, and she was. We shed tears and had a wonderful lunch together.

It was time to tell my best mate. This was going to be hard. We had known each other for seven years and enjoyed common interests. Though he was accepting, it was more difficult for him to digest my news and he said he would need time to process it. His reaction made me more aware of how my revelation would affect the people I told. He later said it was like his friend had died and he had to pass through a mourning process. I understood, even though I felt I would remain the same person and it was just the outside that would change.

Telling my parents was especially challenging. Coincidently, and fortunately, they had seen a program on the ABC on the lives of transfolk in transition. This meant they knew what I was talking about, at least. But they did wonder how this could be happening to them. As Mum said, she had given birth to a boy, raised a boy and now I was telling her I always felt like a girl. Despite their disorientation, they both pledged to love me as they always had, which made me so happy. Dad has been unable to call me Nadine, but after struggling for the first year or so Mum has made a real effort. She nearly always uses my correct name these days.

I have not spoken to my brother since I told him. But my sister has been a strong supporter.

I was getting ready to begin living as a woman.

A psychologist told me I had 'gender dysphoria', which I knew. I like to think that, rather than having an illness, my brain has always been female but I developed male genitalia. It was good to talk about my transition and hear about some of the ups and downs I may experience. At the end of one visit, the psychologist asked me what my name was going to be. I had given it some thought but had been uncertain. She considered me and said simply, 'You look like Nadine to me.' She was right and now I can't imagine being anyone else.

In preparation for the day I would start living as a woman, I assembled a new wardrobe. Buying my first dress was an exciting yet daunting experience, in a shop that sold larger sizes and vintage styles. I found some dresses that seemed to suit me as well as a pair of black high-heals that I was able to take a few steps in; however, they soon found a home at the back of my wardrobe. I realised I was fortunate to have relatively small feet. I also discovered I have small hands and a non-prominent Adam's apple. It all helps.

The first time I left the house in a dress was quite exhilarating. I waited till it was dark, put on one of my recent purchases and drove to my daughter's house. Would anyone see me? Would I need to get out of the car before I got to the end of my journey? Would I be stopped for an RBT? All these things went through my mind, but of course the drive was entirely uneventful and my daughter was happy to see me. I became more adventurous going out in daylight. It was not long until I was living full-time as Nadine.

Not every transgender person has surgery. Some don't want or need it, and some can't afford it. Having surgery to change my genitalia was always something I believed would have to happen for my transition to feel complete, and I was in the fortunate position of having the required funds.

Years of research had brought me to a leading surgeon in this field in Phuket, Thailand. I arranged a holiday for my sister and me, and booked a consultation with the man who would perform my life-changing (life-saving) surgery. I felt immediately comfortable with him, and then came the real shock: I was a good candidate, so he could do the operation in less than three weeks' time.

I arrived back at Phuket International Hospital late in the evening of 8 December 2014, completed my admission and was shown to my room. My surgery was scheduled for the morning of the 10th. The day prior to my surgery went very quickly with visits from my surgeon and the hospital psychiatrist, and performing various tests. It was surreal; I felt completely at ease.

The surgery took place without a hitch. When my new genitalia was revealed a few days later, I was speechless. Never in my wildest dreams could I have imagined this day. There was swelling and some pain, but it was truly amazing.

I was nervous about my first day of work as Nadine, but I didn't need to be. I was returning to a ward where some former colleagues, including my manager, had been transferred to. The support I received was wonderful and I rapidly settled back in. In fact, work seemed easier now that I had less distraction in my life.

I'd never been certain I would have further surgery. I made the decision to wait for three years – the approximate time for maximum breast growth – before considering breast augmentation. With hormone therapy I had achieved a B cup, which appeared small on my large frame. So, in May 2017 I had 500cc implants and now I am a full D cup. To attain what I hoped would be a totally new body shape, I had a tummy tuck in October 2017. Hormones can sometimes change the distribution of body fat to a curvier figure, but I needed a little assistance. Diet and exercise helped to reshape my body. My waist slimmed and my hips and buttocks increased. Looking in the mirror, I could see a much more feminine silhouette. I had achieved what I believed might be impossible.

I'm often asked: do I have any regrets? Of course not. I have two beautiful children and three gorgeous grandchildren. I've travelled and I've had a fantastic life. I will still have ups and downs as a woman, but I'm far better equipped to deal with the challenges. I can enjoy the future, being true to myself.

All my life I have wanted to dance, but for so long it remained only a dream. How could I explain that I wanted the woman's part in partner dances? Now I learn West Coast Swing. I'm led around the floor by an experienced male partner – and I love it.

The Most Natural of Things

Justine Hyde

In the mid-'80s, we move to a new housing estate in the outer western suburbs of Sydney. I live there with my single mother. It is treeless. All the birds are gone. Everything organic has been bulldozed to make way for dead-end cul-de-sacs, brick veneer houses and concrete driveways. The wasted earth offers up broken remnants of construction in place of the green shoots of life. It looks like a post-war battlefield where mines lie buried beneath the surface.

In summer, the heat bakes down, magnifying the absence of green and making me wilt. In winter, the morning fog hangs heavy for hours. The cold slaps me as I open the front door. Frost creeps a silver veil across the ruins. When it rains, the razed ground turns to clay mud that sticks to my shoes in thick red drifts. I scrape it off against the gutter.

Year on year, the suburb spreads its tentacles, until it crowds out the horizon and I can no longer see past it.

I lift the metal drain cover and drop my bike down into the dark. I ride through the smooth, subterranean concrete tunnels and emerge in a distant street. The houses here are still half-built. I pick through heaped building refuse and fill my pockets with splintered wood and sharp metal. I slip abandoned fluorescent light tubes from their cardboard covers and hurl them against the ground, watching them smash apart. I rescue an abandoned litter of feral kittens. They mew with open, pink mouths and shred my arms with needle-sharp claws.

There is one bus to school in the morning and one home in the afternoon. There is a boy who likes to sit behind me on the bus and bang my forehead against the metal seat frame. The mission kids sit at the back and smoke. You hand over your lunch money when they ask for it. If I miss the bus, I walk the five kilometres home through semi-rural backstreets. The thick smell of shit from the pig farm. Roads eerily empty of cars and people. A few vacant-looking malevolent houses, their yards littered with burnt-out car chassis and rusted whitegoods. One day I stop to inspect a bulging garbage bag by the side of the road. The skewed hind legs of a dog stick out through the plastic.

At school, I hang around in the library to dodge Maths and Sport. The two-level utilitarian building is a place of air conditioning and possibility. I discover Steinbeck, Wilde, Camus, Poe, Shelley and McCullers. I write stories on a typewriter. I fail Maths. I help to care for the indoor pot plants. I stare at the ghostly white axolotl that sits lonely at the bottom of the library's fish tank and wonder what it is thinking.

*

One lunchtime in the schoolyard, I accidently grab a handful of my friend D's breast. Her eyes flash wide and we stand looking at each other, stunned. We both laugh nervously.

'Sorry,' I say, but I'm not.

Something shifts in my brain. I think about girls' breasts often after that. I wonder if this is normal.

*

My English teacher has perfect skin and an Edinburgh accent that makes my nerve endings spark. It is her first year of teaching. She stares me down in class if I misbehave. I start smoking in the toilets at lunchtime when she is on yard duty, hoping she will catch me.

'Justine!' she says, her voice a hard edge.

I want her to push me into the cubicle, lock the door and fuck me up against the wall. She gives me detention instead.

*

I have never heard the word 'queer'. I have heard these words: 'gay', 'poofta', 'faggot', 'homo', 'lezzo', 'dyke'. They are used to cut people: words shouted from car windows, words scrawled in spray paint. No one I know is queer. They must all live in the city, gathered by the coastline like shorebirds; winged creatures.

*

I rattle through the bathroom medicine cabinet and search through my mother's drawers. I line up all the pills I can find. There are blue tablets, white tablets, big tablets, small tablets, capsules filled with white powder and others filled with tiny orange beads. I swallow them in handfuls, choking them down with water. I hear the background rise and fall of voices on the television in the living room. I lie down on my bed, close my eyes and summon a never-ending sleep.

I am gutted to wake up.

'You're too young to feel depressed,' my mother says.

My friend S tries to swallow bleach by putting a funnel down her throat. When that fails, we drink vodka mixed with orange juice and spew all over her granny flat. We set fire to the backyard with a pile of newspapers. We go into Kings Cross and score acid from her cousin at a club called Ziggurat. S has her P-plates. She drives us around and it is raining, a Sydney summer deluge. Neither of us remembers about windscreen wipers or petrol. Her dad, a tough Italian bloke who doesn't say much, rescues us. Years later, I run into S in a dyke pub with her girlfriend. We drink beer and play pool and reminisce.

There is another girl in my grade, A. She has hollowed out eyes, is too thin. And there is a camp boy, C. He has long eyelashes and is only friends with the girls. I find out about them through the grapevine years later. There must have been others too.

It is New Year's Eve and I'm at a house party. I am sixteen. I want to lose my virginity, just to get it over with. I search out a good-looking guy who is in the grade below mine. His girlfriend is away for the summer holidays. We fuck in his backyard, sharp blades of grass pressing into my bare arse, until we realise the neighbour is watching. Then we move inside to his parents' waterbed.

'I can't be your boyfriend,' he says.

'That's fine,' I say.

When we finish, I notice something brown and liquid smeared on my arm.

53

'Did you do that?' I ask.

'No,' he says.

I see a small, white terrier on the end of the bed, looking at me with sad eyes.

'Dog vomit,' I say, wiping my arm clean on the bedsheets. I get dressed, find my friends and leave.

*

On the weekends, I catch the train into the city with my friends, A and M. We wander the markets of Paddington and Glebe, and buy vintage clothes, incense and cheap silver jewellery from women with dreadlocks, piercings and tattoos. We see arthouse movies at the Valhalla. Eat at cafes on Oxford Street. In these suburbs, men hold hands with men and women hold hands with women, unselfconsciously. I watch them for clues on how to be.

On Saturday nights we go to a Goth club in Kings Cross that plays dark tunes and goes heavy on the smoke machine. The boys are dolled up with eyeliner, nail polish and velvet jackets. The girls push up their cleavage with corsets; their tangled hair drapes their shoulders in pre-Raphaelite drama. Everyone is loved up on E; pupils and bodies yawn wide open. When the sun comes up, I sleep on a stained mattress on the floor of a sharehouse, curled up next to one of the pretty boys. His eyes are black-smudged and a puddle of saliva rings his pillow.

*

I answer an ad in the classifieds. I meet X. She is older than me, works in finance and drives a sports car. She picks me up from the train station in the city, takes me out for dinner and drops me off in time for the last train home. I don't call her back.

Next I meet E. We see movies and trawl bookshops. I sleep over at her parent's place and we stay awake to watch the sun rise over the beach. We work up the courage to go to our first lesbian bar. At first, the male bouncer will not let E in because she has long hair and looks too straight. We plead with him.

'Okay, in you go, girls,' he says, winking.

The bar is full of women. Lots of short hair and leather. Thumping techno and sweaty bodies pressed against each other on the dancefloor. It feels like finally being let in on a secret. The air is charged; I feel electric. I am too scared to kiss E.

*

There are many times when I inch towards a confession to my mother. Somehow she always has a sense of what is coming.

'Lesbians are disgusting. I can't even imagine what they do in bed,' she says.

I can imagine. I can imagine touching the delicate skin between a woman's thighs and sliding my tongue across her swollen clit and pushing my fingers deep inside her, wetter and tighter as I make her come and ... and ...

Another time, my mother hangs up from a phone call and says, 'Aunty P's best friend J – who is married with children – has just found out that she is a lesbian!'

'Did she get a letter from the government?' I ask.

The continual effort of hiding myself in plain sight is an incremental act of erasure.

*

I move into a sharehouse in the city. I get a job in a law firm photocopying contracts and making sure the lawyers have enough pens and staples. It is all marble foyers and harbour views and contemporary art and people who grew up in fancy suburbs and went to the best schools and won prizes at university. The partners have minibars in their offices and play golf. There are waiters to make coffee and Friday night drinks are fully catered and people do coke in the toilets at the office Christmas party. It is full of queers in expensive suits.

I meet V. She is a graduate lawyer, a bit older than me. She is not out to anyone, but I suspect her.

We start hanging out, we have lunch at work, and that turns into weeknight drinks, and that turns into weekend things. I tell her I like girls but I don't let on that I have never even kissed one.

She lends me Woolf and Sackville-West and Winterson. She buys me gifts made of rare stones pulled from the earth and beautiful objects shaped from glittering metal and she writes me notes on exquisite paper that tremble in my hands when I read them.

One drunken night after office drinks, we stumble along the fringe of the Botanic Gardens. The dark limbs of Moreton Bay figs arch over us, rustling with fruit bats. We sit on a ledge of sandstone that holds the warmth of the day's sun. We look out over the city lights glinting off the surface of the water. V takes my hand and closes it between hers. Time bends and my head swims with alcohol and desire. My pores spring sweat, my blood surges and my heart bursts through my ribcage.

'Do you want me to kiss you?' she asks.

As our mouths connect, I think of all the sea creatures swimming in the harbour, breathing flagrantly through their gills as if it is the most natural of things.

Binary School

Roz Bellamy

I'm fifteen years old and I'm in love with numerous people at my Jewish high school.

One is a girl in my prayer group. In the mornings, the boys and girls are split into different rooms for *Shacharit*, the morning prayers. In the boys' room, they recite a blessing that ends with the line '*Shelo asani isha*', meaning 'Blessed are you, God, that you did not make me a woman.' In the girls' room, we substitute that line for '*She-asani Kirtzono*', meaning 'Blessed are you, God, that you made me according to your will.'

The girl I like doesn't fit the mould, and anyone who doesn't fit in at my school fascinates me. All of us, the misfits, are different in some way. She is smart and cynical, which I admire. There is much to be cynical about, which very few of my classmates seem to recognise.

My sister and I have trauma in our DNA that stems from anti-Semitism, Nazism and the Holocaust, like many others at the school – but ours is different.

My mother's parents had to flee from their home town of Odessa, Ukraine, when it was occupied by Nazi Germany and their Romanian allies. During the Holocaust in Odessa, Jewish people faced kidnappings, imprisonment, mass shootings, death marches, ghettos, starvation, concentration camps, forced labour and torture.

My grandmother and her family were starving, eating frozen earth when they could find nothing else. Decades later, after migrating to Australia, my mother's family added an 'e' to the end of their surname. They wanted to assimilate and, to do so, needed to sound less foreign.

My father's parents were British Jews who faced rations and bombing raids. My grandfather joined the British army to fight Hitler, after changing his name from Cohen to Bellamy in case he was captured by the Germans.

At Sydney airport my mother and her family had the word 'stateless' stamped on their arrival cards. My father and his family arrived as 'Ten Pound Poms' on a ship, by choice. It's a complex mix to have in your DNA: those who were forced to give up their citizenship in search of safety and those who chose to leave. Another binary alongside those I encountered at school.

As children, when we learnt about *Shabbat*, the Jewish Sabbath, the girls in my class played the role of Ima, mother, lighting the candles, preparing the food and nurturing the family, while the boys played Abba, father, reciting *Kiddush*, the blessings. At twelve, I had chosen to reject the Orthodox model of a *bat mitzvah* and instead followed the model of a *bar mitzvah* that boys have at age thirteen. This was acceptable at my family's progressive and egalitarian synagogue, but was considered unusual at my Orthodox school, where a *bat mitzvah* for a girl involved reading a speech, tucked away in the separate women's section.

Following my *bar mitzvah*, I continue to struggle with these rigid binaries. To me they are unequal, even while I have been raised in a religion and a community where they are seen as natural and are enforced constantly.

*

I don't say anything to the girl in my prayer group. I write her name in my diary and then cross it out. I do not ever write about what the crushes on girls might mean.

My school doesn't talk about homosexuality, apart from some kids using the terms 'homo', 'dyke', 'fag' and 'lezzie' out of the teachers' earshot. I learnt to keep my attraction to girls a secret years earlier, when I came out to myself in my diary without even realising it.

The first sign that something was up was when I stuck both the Mulder and Scully stickers from *TV Hits* in my diary. I was ten years old and found both actors incredibly sexy.

At fifteen, I am more aware of my sexuality, even though I don't know the words to use. I watch *The X-Files* with my father, discussing extraterrestrial life and conspiracy theories, but keeping the other new, strange – dare I say 'alien' – world to myself.

We learn about sex in PE and Health. This is a particularly cruel turn of events for someone who already finds PE teachers terrifying. In Health, we are taught an abstinence-focussed curriculum with no mention of sexual or gender diversity. Nothing in the classes is useful to me, including the biological information and an awkward session about condom use, which I have already learnt from Judy Blume books.

Books are a respite from a world that is otherwise quite lonely. I pick up a young adult novel at my local library and discover that it is about two girls falling in love. Reading it, I am wide-eyed with disbelief and I feel a growing sense of longing. I don't know what 'gay' looks like, apart from a few outdated stereotypes on TV, but the book helps me start to figure it out.

A year later, I watch the TV broadcast of the Sydney Gay and Lesbian Mardi Gras parade. I love the fierce Dykes on Bikes, the spectacular drag queens and the roar of the supportive crowd. I turn it to the lowest volume level, fearful at the prospect of being caught. Not that my parents have an issue with the parade, but being caught watching it alone might reveal something.

It is the '90s before TV has any queer characters that grab my interest, before the internet is suddenly available as a private agony aunt, and I am on my own.

One day, my parents take me and my sister to see the musical *RENT.* I am riveted by the confident and feisty bisexual character, Maureen. I barely know the word 'bisexual', apart from when the word 'bi' gets dropped around the playground, accompanied by a sneer. When Maureen sings to Joanne, 'Ever since puberty, everybody stares at me! Boys, girls, I can't help it baby,' my heartbeat quickens. Not because boys and girls notice me, but because I notice them.

In Year 11 my school participates in a community ball. We do a certain number of community service hours and then we are rewarded with a party. My best friend and I decide to do the community service without attending the ball. Our official stance is that we shouldn't need a bribe to do community service. My personal reasons are more complex: I don't date, being too confused, shy and unconfident for that.

One of my close male friends calls me in the lead up to the ball.

'Um, hey,' he says, 'I was wondering if you want to go to the ball together.'

I don't know how to respond. It is the first time someone has asked me out. After an awkward pause, I remember my official stance about the ball.

'I'm not going to the dance,' I reply, and tell him that my friend and I are boycotting it. 'We're going to stay home and watch *Buffy*.'

'Oh, okay,' he says, sounding embarrassed. 'No problem.'

I stay home but, even during the magic of *Buffy*-watching, I wonder if I should have gone.

In Year 12 I am preoccupied with my studies but spend a significant part of the year with crushes on males and females. I only tell my best friend about my heterosexual crushes. When I mention one of the boys I am most attracted to, she scoffs. 'He's so boring!' she says. 'And he's dumb.' We have never seen eye to eye on boys. Whenever I swoon over video clips of Taylor Hanson, she says, 'but he looks like a girl!'

During the first year of uni two close male friends come out. One is the friend who invited me to the community ball. It turns out that he had wanted me there as his beard. When I find this out, I wish I had agreed. How cool would that have been? Two questioning teens being beards for each other at a Jewish community dance.

I don't tell my gay friends about my sexuality. Being romantically and sexually attracted to men makes me decide against it. Maybe I will end up with a guy, I think. Nobody needs to know about my big gay feelings.

I feel fortunate to pass as cisgender and heterosexual, even if I'm isolated and unhappy.

I start going to gay clubs and bars on Oxford Street with my friends. They assume I am there for fun, like the other women in our group, who put on dresses and heels and join them for a night out free of unwanted male attention.

I dance, nod appreciatively when they point out various men they are pursuing, and drink. I notice butch and androgynous women or gender diverse people with short hair, piercings and tattoos, who move around the room with a confidence I can't imagine possessing. Sometimes we make eye contact from afar – mine tentative, theirs flirty and bold – but I am too afraid to approach. I settle for being complimented by a drag queen. 'You're dancing in such high heels,' she says. 'Bless your heart!'

The only time I feel I can explore my attraction to women is on my own, not at the clubs with my friends. University offers anonymity and freedom, but I'm unable to do much more than walk past the queer space or fantasise about the Scandinavian exchange students.

I'm not concerned about being attracted to people of all genders. It feels like a naughty secret. I walk the hallways propelled by a rush of hormones and adrenaline; I am attracted to a ridiculous number of people. I don't feel the need to talk to friends about it, or label it.

*

Only years later do I realise that gender is irrelevant to my attractions, because sexuality and gender are not binaries for me, and I do not fit into binaries. I am sexually attracted to people, not to the specific and sometimes arbitrary categories we classify them with. Not to one type of genitalia. Not to a particular ratio of sex hormones. Gender may or may not have anything to do with sexual attraction for me.

My own gender varies depending on the day, my mood, my hormones, my feelings. Sometimes I am male *or* female, sometimes I am both, and sometimes I am neither. Sometimes what I am is undefinable, but when I first hear the words 'genderqueer' and 'gender non-binary', I feel a sense of peace. They fit. They make me feel less alone.

I talk to my parents about gender. I discover that if I had been assigned male at birth my name would have been Richard. Dick. I find this quite funny and hard to comprehend at first, but later, I am perplexed. What would Dick's life have been like at my school? If the kids were so nasty to me – that a little, closeted, cis-appearing girl – what would they have done to him? They likened my curly hair to pubes, so what would have happened to Dick? Would he still be here?

A lot has changed since the '90s. I'm out and proud, and publish writing in which I am vocal about identifying as queer, bisexual and non-binary. I am married to a woman, Rachel, and have overshared in the public domain about her and our marriage.

If I want to understand more about my family history, I can choose when I wish to learn about the trauma that took place in my family over multiple generations, rather than being tested on pogroms and concentration camps as though they are algebra or spelling.

If I want to explore my faith, I can do so without being restricted by gender or sexuality, like I was constantly at school. I don't have to thank God for anything if I don't want to.

It's my choice if I want to say '*Baruch Hashem*', or 'Blessed is our God', for making me queer and non-binary, because now I wouldn't have it any other way.

Why I've Stopped Coming Out to My Mum

Vivian Quynh Pham

'Liz thought you were the one.'

Maureen had just told me her daughter, Liz, had died. Liz was upstairs in her bedroom, my feet were stuck in the kitchen. I fought back sobs as Maureen said that Liz bragged about me while delirious from palliative care, that she was so proud of who I was.

I gave Maureen a pink box that I had made for Liz. It was the reason I had visited the house that day. I had no idea Liz was gone. Inside the pink box were my hand-made paper gardenias, flowers that thrived in coffee grounds representing Liz's love for coffee. The box was pink so that Liz would say, 'What's wrong with you, Viv? I hate pink!'

This vanished reaction ran through my head as I drove home, wailing.

That evening was the first time I came out to my parents. I had to explain to them that I would be away, dealing with my grief because my girlfriend had died, but there isn't really a word in Vietnamese for girl-that-is-my-romantic-partner, so I used the literal translation of girl-friend: bạn gái.

'So, this is a friend that you love dearly?'

'Yes …'

'Okay.'

*

My Vietnamese parents wanted me to fit into white Australia. I was named Vivian, after Julia Roberts' character in *Pretty Woman*. A hooker with a heart of gold. Head and heart in the right place, but wrong position in space and time.

Growing up, depression robbed my vision of colour. Even while dreaming, I couldn't make out the colours of the world. I didn't see a psychologist (what Vietnamese parent would allow that?), so this is all retrospective self-diagnosis, but colour and mood have always been linked for me, and when I was young the world was grey.

What coloured my world in was fiction and sports and girls. The first two were acceptable, the third was not. Homosexuality had been illegal in New South Wales until 1983, and for a Catholic child it may as well have still been.

By fifteen, I had become a textbook, first-generation academic overachiever. I gave up on fiction and sports and girls, and tried to 'pray away the gay'. I would be a doctor, I would be straight, I would be acceptable to both white Australia and my Vietnamese parents. My world turned grey again.

By sixteen, well, I can't remember sixteen. I know from what I've been told that I tried to commit suicide a few times. But by the end of that year, I had reconciled my relationship with god with my sexuality. Which meant that I stopped praying and started to see a counsellor. I become every Asian stereotype you can think of. Instead of dealing with my sexuality via religious shame, I distracted myself from it by staying busy. I was musical, academic, a leader in my high school – a long list of high-achievement things rather than 'that Gay Asian'.

*

Liz made it impossible to remain in this state of distraction.

We first met at Galentine's Day, a *Parks and Recreation*–inspired annual celebration of female solidarity held by Liz's cousin. I didn't have a type before Liz, but Liz was my type: tall, blonde, ambivert, drama-seeker, nosy, eloquent, articulate, bold. I saw so many colours. Most of all, gold.

Despite being inspired by her fierce feminism (at a time when feminist ideals hadn't quite diffused into Australia), I daydreamed about being her housewife – an urge I had never felt before, or since. I wanted to back this brilliant woman as she conquered the world, to become a power couple in black cocktail dresses staring down the patriarchy with middle fingers raised.

I first kissed Liz in the club while the rest of the group danced. She kissed back. The hetero attention was ruining our moment, so we walked along the beach back to her car, where Liz told me about her cancer remission.

'You are not your disease.'

I later discovered that this drunken but heartfelt response was the moment Liz decided that I was extraordinary. I didn't see her as a 'cancer survivor', I just saw Liz: strong, golden Liz. (That she continued to feel this way despite me throwing up moments later is a testament to her generosity.)

I also later discovered that she was re-diagnosed the next day. She never told me, so our future remained colourful in my mind right up to the moment I delivered the pink box. According to the blog she was keeping, her scans showed that she 'lit up like a Christmas tree'.

*

The second time I came out to my mum, I was on my way to visit Liz. She's at Scarborough Cemetery, a few rows from my maternal grandmother.

'You are going to see your friend?'

'She's actually my girlfriend.'

Movies and TV don't much show what it's like coming out to a non-white mum. There was no sympathy or an 'everything is going to be okay' moment. There was shock, confusion and denial.

Shock was standing in the kitchen and telling your daughter everything you can think of to erase her queer identity.

'No, you're not.' 'You're young, you don't even know what this means.' 'It's just a phase.' 'I liked my female friends too. Maybe you like them too.' 'You just haven't found the right man.'

Confusion was saying the words 'you're not gay'.

Pê-đê is the Vietnamese word for gay. Like the French word pede, it is also derogatory slang, closer to the word 'tranny'. My arsenal of queer theory, which in English allowed me to argue fiercely against such words (channelling my inner-Liz), didn't exist in Vietnamese. There was no shared cultural narrative for being gay and Vietnamese, no celebrities that had been embraced by the straight mainstream, nothing I could lean on for sympathy or understanding.

65

I rejected *pê-đê* and told her I just liked people for who they were, in the hope it would provide my mother with some kind of a concept of her daughter that wasn't derogatory slang – something that didn't mean that she had failed me.

As for denial, that was how she chose to cope. I should have left it there.

When I told my friends, who were white, what had happened, the cultural barrier between us became obvious. They encouraged me to try again. They insisted. 'Your parents will accept you, of course they will.' 'It's their duty to love you.' 'She just needs time.' 'Next time they will understand'. No. Next time was even worse.

*

By the time I was with Liz, my psychologist had helped me understand the relationship between my mood and my perception of colour.

Liz looked bronze as she hopped the fence to the mountain trail, which I wouldn't have had the guts to tackle at night if I wasn't with her. Bronze is a colour I associate with fearlessness, and she made me feel bronze too as we began our hike, torches in hand, a bubble of bravery in the darkness.

In classic Liz fashion, the only hint she gave me about where we were going was 'wear comfortable shoes'. I became suspicious as she drove us up the mountain, a drive she said she sometimes took when she needed to think. I imagine she drove there a lot during her first round of cancer – a habit I inherited.

At the top was a view over the city, its lights rippling against the black backdrop of the South Pacific Ocean. The oil rigs on the horizon looked like they were floating on the clouds. Liz brought chocolate and a picnic mat for us to enjoy the view. We kissed with the city behind us.

This sumptuous moment under the moon became so embedded in my memory that I would know the location of the mountain no matter where I was.

Only on our way back to the car did she tell me that she hadn't been sure she would be up for the mountain trail at night. The same way she had given me bronze bravery, I had given it to her. On the drive home she mentioned we would be able to spend more time together as her graduate job had given her time off. In reality she had quit to undergo treatment.

*

The last time I came out to my mum, I wish her only reaction was denial.

Coming out seems to be the foundational gay rite of passage. It's supposed to be a punctuation of your life, an empowering political act, a personal duty to your gay forebears who didn't enjoy the privileges of a queer-friendly place and time. And so, as a young queer adult, it was imperative for me to come out in all areas of my life. Or so it seemed. Back then, I had never considered an alternative to the linear journey. It seemed like there was only one path, from 'closet' to 'out', and I was delaying the inevitable.

In 1997, Sears and Williams wrote that one-on-one contact is the single most effective way to change homophobic attitudes. And it works. Media representation is on the rise, and prejudice against LGBTIQA+ individuals is on the decline. However, Sears and Williams also said that 'many tenured full professors who are gay or lesbian continue to cower cowardly in the closet'. This image resonated with me. This idea that the closet is a space of suffering, shame and failure. If I didn't come out of it to my parents, it would mean that I was ashamed. No one ever said this to me, but it's what I had absorbed, and the recent legalisation of same-sex marriage had inspired me to be the best queer person I could be. I would 'come out' to my mother, love would conquer all, and I would never have to return to the closet again. I would be stronger for challenging her closed-mindedness, and she would be opened up to a rich new queer culture.

Wouldn't that be what Liz wanted of me? To be a strong, confident, bronze, queer person – like her?

But this white, Western LGBTIQA+ discourse didn't anticipate the reaction of a Catholic Vietnamese woman. It didn't anticipate that, for some minorities, the closet might be the better place to be. That the closet is a safe space, a tactical move, and even a powerful, fluid space for some. That the imposing of Western queer values on a person whose non-white culture left them unprepared for the coming-out ritual can cause pain rather than liberation.

67

The night I came out to my mother for the third time, she wanted to kill herself. The next day, so did I.

*

My next date with Liz was at a friend's party. Liz couldn't drive so I offered to take us out to dinner at her favourite Mediterranean restaurant before heading to the party. Afterwards, we went to a cocktail bar and I showed her how to salsa. Her friends pulled me aside and drunkenly told me that they've never seen her so happy. That was also our last date. It didn't feel like it. There were no goodbyes.

But our relationship didn't end with her death. I had lent Liz *Why I Write* by George Orwell. After she died, I retrieved it from her bedside table. It was filled with underlinings, paperclip bookmarks (she knew I hated dog-earring books) and angry feminist book graffiti.

'Woe is me George.' 'Who does this man think he is?' 'Get off your high horse, George!'

Her defiant defacing of the literary canon is one of the many times she showed me – in life and after – that I don't have to accept what people say, whether they're hallowed white male authors or allies in the queer discourse.

I put this principle into action daily. From responding to cat-callers, disagreeing with classmates in tutorials, or opening discussions with soccer teammates at the pub.

'I think that who you end up with determines your sexuality.' Cue me opening a discussion on romantic, sexual and gender spectrums. 'We don't need feminism anymore'. Well, let me introduce you to intersectional feminism and modern toxic masculinity. 'I'm all for equality, but like, I'm not a feminist'. So, you examine and repair people's dental crowns, but refuse to call yourself a dentist?

'You should be ashamed for not coming out in all aspects of your life,' I told myself. But what right did cultural expectations, or anyone else, have to determine what would make me happy? After all, one of the things Liz loved about me is how I am unapologetically Vivian.

*

I've decided to never come out to my mum again.

Professor Mary Lou Rasmussen at the Australian National University writes that 'when coming out discourses are privileged, the act of not coming out may be read as an abdication of responsibility, or the act of somebody who is disempowered or somehow ashamed of their inherent gayness.' Today, I am selectively 'out' to certain people and some situations – and I am not ashamed. The flexibility of the queer closet has allowed me to build a stronger relationship with my mother. We're currently a hemisphere apart, but she calls me every weekend. She still questions my antidepressant prescriptions, and she did vote 'No' on the postal survey, but I love her dearly.

When I forgot to buy ingredients for dinner, she would cook for me or buy my groceries, knowing I was low on money. When I was stuck at university in the cold rain, with all my gear, she would drive to pick me up. When I had tonsillitis, she let me sleep in the same bed as her while I sweated and shivered through the nights. I know she loves me.

Developing my ethnic identity means maintaining this loving relationship with my mother. I'm out to my father (a Buddhist) and my two brothers, while never telling my extended family.

Developing my queer identity means being involved in queer literature, in political conversations, and making queer discourse accessible to everyone.

Developing my personal identity only requires remembering Liz.

I've never regretted our time together. Sometimes I wish I'd had the chance to say goodbye, but I know you wanted me to remember you with a full head of hair – to remember you gold. Thank you for being vulnerable with me. I know how hard that was for you. Thank you for not letting me go when treatment was getting rough. Thank you, Elizabeth, for reminding me, every day, how to be bronze.

Training to Be Me

Cindy Zhou

i. In preparation for gruelling physical activity, one should practise the movements needed for the journey ahead.

Every Monday after school, for two hours or so, I would stay behind for rowing practice. It was winter, and we weren't at the point of wearing spandex yet. Those months were purely for training 'off-water' – rotations on the three ergometers on the mezzanine above the school gym. I studied the theory, the anatomy of a stroke: catch, extraction, drive, recovery and settle. Rowing is about coordination and focus, trust and teamwork. It builds resilience and it would make me strong.

Well, at least that's what I led my mother to believe.

Once the permission slip was signed, it quickly met with the guts of one of the rubbish bins at the school's unfenced perimeters the next day. I had (and still have) wiry, noodle arms that can't tear open most forms of plastic packaging, let alone wield oars against resistance to transport a carbon-fibre shell full of humans down a river. The whole rowing thing was an elaborate ruse. I had zero interest in this kind of sport, but it was the decoy I selected, a plausible front.

I was actually making weekly excursions down the Frankston line to a secret house tucked away two blocks from Edithvale Beach. It was double-storey, corrugated-iron shed meets '70s-style brick beach house. Our hideaway. *Click-clack, click-clack*. Always a stopping-all-stations train. It would take over an hour from the clang of the final school bell before we arrived and put the key in the door. Not an actual front door, but a sliding door with a rusted locking mechanism that would stick, and threaten to snap the key. Sometimes we would spend ten minutes trying to get in.

Inside it smelt of old mothballs, and there were racquets, balls, towels, chairs and mattresses shelved in the corners. There was a great stillness about the place, as if it were suspended in time. The contents of each room told the story of a large extended family, lots of cousins around the same age coming together over the summer. Very Tim Winton.

It was very unfamiliar for someone with only a theoretical knowledge of holiday houses. My own family moved around a lot, and so the concept of feeling *at home* would constantly and often abruptly shift. My parents came to Australia in the midst of the Tiananmen Square massacre, granted humanitarian visas by Bob Hawke in the late '80s. Like many other first-generation migrants, they had to rebuild their life on new territory from nothing. Dad went from being a trained doctor in China to twisting lids onto toothpaste bottles in a factory. Mum was a chemical scientist, but now she couldn't read the labels in shops. The notion of holiday houses just seemed to me like props, decorations for the coastline, glossy images in magazines. During school holidays my dad would 'treat' my sisters and me by driving us to St Georges Road in Toorak to stare at the mansions from our car windows, crawling along at ten kilometres per hour.

The Edithvale hideaway was a parallel universe, a room of our own away from the prying eyes of the rest of the world. Sixty minutes on the timer before we had to leave to meet curfew. One hour stripped of self-consciousness, knowing it was just us. No labels, fear or danger. Just two fifteen-year-olds falling in love, deeply, and for the first time. Most weeks, we would make this journey on Mondays. She would find a strategy to obtain the key from family members, and I would talk to my mum about rowing techniques to keep up the ruse. We knew this couldn't last, though we never said it out loud. The illusion would have to shatter, but not yet. Canaries in a crystal cage.

ii. The *catch* is where the blade of the oar slices into the water.

When I was twelve, I would press my nose up against the bathroom mirror, willing the black beads of my pupils to fix on their reflection. *Look at yourself and say it. I dare you.* I eyed myself like an opponent, locked in a stare, perfectly still. I realised I couldn't say it out loud. Up to that point, I had definitely never used the word for *it* before. Let alone put it into a sentence.

Lesbian. *Lezzz … bee-yan.* I knew at a gut level that in the Chinese vernacular translation, *tong xing lian*, were connotations of eroticism, moral offence and pathology. I'd say it on the count of *one … two …* even as a muted thought, it seemed both dangerous and wild. It did not feel like a safe word to say. My throat clamped around the 'le-' and my tongue curled away from the next syllable into silence. In the end I scrawled 'I am a lesbian' onto a piece of scrap paper. It was barely legible, shrunken and looked like it was trying not to take up space. I ripped that piece of paper into tiny square pieces.

I've always felt different, like I was in hand-me-down clothes that never seemed to fit just right. The more I learnt about myself, the more I realised that who I was did not fit into the conventional moulds. Female, Chinese, a bit of a tomboy, painfully shy, not very popular, and now queer – albeit closeted. There's a saying in East Asian societies: *the nail that sticks out gets hammered in.*

During break times at school, my best and only friend, Ava, and I would roam the yard, pretending to be the hosts of a TV show. *The Cindy and Ava Show.* It had its own theme tune and featured special guests (any unsuspecting passer-by who we could interrogate). He played the role of the bombastic, extravagant host, and I would nod along and record sound reels on my portable tape recorder. We didn't really belong in any spaces in the yard – the playground, sandpit, sports courts and oval consisted of impervious cliques, friendship circles that were closed off to outsiders. We were outcasts through no fault of our own. We hung out in the narrow gap behind the tin sports shed and the metal wiring, literally sitting in the gutter. We talked about everything under the sun: books, music, philosophy, science – everything except for sexuality. He was different too. It's funny how it sometimes works out that way. At the time, it just felt like we didn't have the words for it. Funny, also, since we seemed to have the words for everything else. I remember wondering why that was.

iii. The *extraction* is the release of the oar as it resurfaces.

'Your mother and I want to talk to you.'

My dad closes the door behind me, motioning for me to sit across the table from him in the 'office', which is really just a table and chairs in the middle of my sisters' shared bedroom. Its bright-red three-legged vinyl chairs have been carted from house to house, and nobody ever sits in them. The backing stops halfway up the spine and imprints red marks onto my back. I hate these chairs, though I don't dare move to relieve my discomfort, especially when I see Leviticus 18:22 from the Old Testament laid out on the table.

Dad clears his throat to make way for the Gospel, his finger trailing along like it's finding a pulse: 'You shall not lie with a male as with a woman; it is an abomination. If a man lies with a male as with a woman, both of them have committed an abomination; they shall surely be put to death; their blood is upon them.'

I'm numb, grinding my spine against the chair as the deluge continues. I know better than to break the torrent of abuse, so I absorb it, letting their vitriol and my shame drown me.

'We know what you've been doing and it's evil … It is a sin … You are not our daughter … Disgusting and a disgrace … Whatever "it" is, it is not normal …'

I wonder how they found out, whether they stalked us or pried into my diary. Maybe they read my text messages, or listened in to our phone calls.

'… go to hell. She's the devil and she's brainwashing you … You will have no future … It's sick … It's just a phase …'

Two weeks after this interrogation I will come home to find that our two pet budgerigars have been pecked to death through their cage by a hawk that has been attacking wildlife in the area. My father will blame me, using the same language – will say that I am sent from the devil and that I am truly evil.

'Nobody can know that this has ever happened. What will they think at school? What kind of life are you going to have? You know what they call people like that? Like her?'

They will never say her name out loud. They malign it, twist it, and then, they expect the unthinkable: 'You are to break it off with her.'

'How could you?' That's all my mum can say. During what ends up being a two-hour ordeal, she doesn't look at me once. So much for their precious little girl. I am Medusa, with writhing snakes sprouting from my head, my skin putrid green. I hear only static; it feels like the roof is collapsing. Will they disown me? Where would I go? My mouth is viced shut. I have been plunged into a cave with bats circling above, ready to swoop.

They instruct me to end the relationship the next day, and not to speak to her again. Not to tell anybody. Put on a happy face. After all, it is my youngest sister's ninth birthday that day.

When their scare campaign fails, my dad confronts me again. He slams down some paper and demands I write a letter telling her that I hate her, that I hate us being together, and that our relationship means nothing. He will stamp this declaration of renunciation and then there is to be nothing further. Also, I am moving back to my previous school, effective from the next week. Tomorrow I am to ask for the exit form. We aren't waiting until the end of the term. I will not tell anyone the reason, and no one shall know I am leaving until after the matter has been wrapped up and tied together with a nice neat bow. I will disappear. Total erasure. I will love going back to my old school. I will not leave my room without permission out of school hours or over the holidays. My parents will bolt-lock my windows to ensure I can't leave.

These are the commands. Act like it never happened. If I don't comply, there will be trouble: he knows where she lives; he isn't afraid to tell her parents what has been going on. We aren't going to be 'just friends'; we are going to be 'strangers'. I don't know what might be real and what is a hollow threat aimed at bending me back into the mould they had intended for me.

iv. The *drive* is the sweeping of the oar as it skims just under the skin the water, until it breaks and resurfaces.

> there's a bluebird in my heart that
> wants to get out
> but I'm too clever, I only let him out
> at night sometimes
> when everybody's asleep.

I say, I know that you're there,
so don't be
sad.
then I put him back,
but he's singing a little
in there, I haven't quite let him
die
and we sleep together like
that
with our
secret pact

Charles Bukowski

After my parents found me out, it took almost two years before I started coming out, this time on my own terms. First to the school counsellor concerned friends and teachers frogmarched me to see. *What's happened to you?* I had turned zombie-like. They didn't know the reason – that's how calculatedly I had constructed and maintained my facade – but they definitely knew something was up. Thus began the first formal wave of support that helped me surface from being so soaked in shame.

On the walls of the counsellor's office were empathic Leunig cartoons and sparks of Buddhist wisdom about self-compassion; there were also dreamcatchers hanging from the ceiling, mood flipcharts, self-help booklets and lots of tissue boxes. We'd meet regularly, and she'd make me hot Milos and let me lie in a foetal position on the couch in her office when I wanted, bundled up with soft toys and throw blankets. Gradually, we started to undo the knot that had tightened on itself.

Coming out for the first time – unforced, having to say *it* out loud to someone I cared about – was, quite frankly, terrifying. I instructed my new best friend to wash the dishes as loudly as she could while I lay supine on the floor of the living room, just hidden away under the kitchen counter.

'I have something to tell you ...' The clamping-up process began, that sick feeling climbing my oesophagus. All of that internalised self-hatred – but with resolve, I began to fight it. 'You know how I left my old school?' I clenched my fists and stared at the fan.

75

How do I say this?

'What? Did you actually get kicked out? Did you set something on fire? Did you set the school on fire?' Okay, she had no idea.

It took a few goes, and a lot of patience and fake dish-washing on her part, but I was able to get it out in a garble of words. 'I was in a relationship ... with a girl.' I heard her pause and digest the information.

'So ... you're a lesbian?'

'I guess so.' Another pause. My heartbeat was roaring in my ears.

'But wait ... we've known each other for five years, right?'

'Yeah?'

'And if you're a lesbian ...'

'Yes?'

'Well, I'm pretty attractive. So, how come you never had a crush on *me*?'

I was stunned. 'Um ... you're not really my type.'

And so the gates were opened for many confessions about who I really *did* have a crush on – whether I like-liked Arizona Robbins from *Grey's Anatomy*, or whether I wanted to *be with* rather than *be* Ellen Page. And always, the exaggerated raising of her eyebrows at me every single time Katy Perry's 'I Kissed a Girl' came on.

It was this same best friend with whom, when we had both saved enough money, I embarked on the middle-class rite-of-passage trip to Europe a few years later. My uncle, who lives in Shenzhen, China, gushed, 'You're the first to be born overseas, the first to travel to Europe. Who cares about your cousin who's a college professor? *You're* the real winner!' This was the first time I had the space to exercise my economic freedom, away from home. With sixty-five kilograms of belongings strapped to my back, I was ready to get away. Taking control of the itinerary, my best friend had a very 'queer' surprise. We were going to Amsterdam in the first week of August, during Europe's biggest pride week.

Throngs of people in pink, brownstone buildings draped in rainbow flags, streams of boats and floats down the Amstel river into the harbour – this was Queer with a capital Q. Dykes on Bikes, the Gay Games, Drags on the Drag. *Reguliersdwarsstraat*, Amsterdam's renowned gay strip, and the streets and canals that stretch out from it form a gaybourhood. As a baby queer, I was simultaneously thrilled and overwhelmed. I felt like I had been dunked into an episode of *The L Word* without being given the script. Should I wear leather? Did I need to cut my hair? How do I walk? I oozed so much awkwardness that a woman I was dancing with asked me, 'So, are you a lesbian, or ... ?' Yes, I am. Just a very shy one.

v. Then there is the *recovery* phase, where the rower pulls their body back and resets for the next stroke.

The Australian Marriage Law Postal Survey, held from September to November 2017, coincided with my second year as a high-school teacher in Victoria's wheat belt, in a rural town 400 kilometres from Melbourne. While I was just a 'blow-in', one of the countless transients who passed through, the townspeople were kind. People looked out for each other and had a common understanding forged through experiences of family connectedness, acute weather conditions from droughts to floods, and a passion for local competitions. I felt included but, also, always on high alert. My neighbours offered to set me up with a farmer (like the TV show!), and I had to invent pre-prepared lines to correct the constant misgendering of my 'partner'. With a handful of people there was an unspoken 'don't ask, don't tell' policy. To my surprise, this applied to my race *and* my sexuality. Among others, there was open handshaking: 'You're the fifth Chinese person to come to town. *Ni hao!*' It was paradoxical and complex. My presence as a twofold minority allowed for more conversations – and a tangible movement towards compassion. At the same time, we were living in a political environment in which our federal member had the effrontery to liken same-sex relationships to rams in paddocks; every day I would take a deep breath before opening the local *Herald* and scanning for homophobic or transphobic tirades from 'concerned' community members. Mostly, I worried about the kids.

Every newspaper, pamphlet, interview, advertisement, poster, discussion, argument – either 'for' or 'against' – stung. Closeted and out teens in my classrooms were visibly burdened by the national debate, which they could neither escape nor cast a vote in; just below legal voting age, they were forced to watch the horror show unfold in all its grisly glory. They cried for help with desperate scrawlings in the margins of their workbooks, their bodies slumped as they circled the yard, their feet kicking at the concrete. I worried most on the days they weren't there. Everyone had an opinion, but very rarely did the debate focus on the people whose lives were going to be most affected by it. Living rurally, these kids had a shortage of support options. The nearest queer-friendly doctor was at least sixty kilometres away. Some were without phones to make emergency calls or find assistance on the internet. Driving to the next town wasn't always an option. I think of the ones who haven't made it, and it's a hurt that will never go away.

In nearby towns, my fellow queer teachers were chalking up the footpaths with hearts and affirmations: 'You are not alone', 'Love will always win'. It is our turn, the ones who have managed to pull through, to pass on the baton. How could we convey to these young people that things *were* going to be okay? That it would actually get better? In Horsham, the Wimmera Pride Project was firing up a compassionate response: offering young people spaces to attend meet-ups and seek counselling, and creating a roadshow to spread awareness about the importance of inclusion. The Horsham Arts Council production that year was *RENT*; audiences gasped, then whooped and cheered when Collins and Angel kissed. I realise now how much work educators do to form a silent safety net around vulnerable children, to keep them safe. Without them, I myself might not be here.

There is a mingling of pain and pride in being queer, and the former can still take hold. I think about how I, now twenty-four, have felt unable to ask my parents how they voted in that survey because I'm scared to hear the answer. My mum has come to accept that me being a lesbian is much like my youngest sister being left-handed: you seem to be born with it; it's difficult, if not impossible, to change, and so why bother if that's going to make you unhappy? With my father, things are silent on that front, I'm not going to lie; and yet, rather than seeing me as demonic, I'm pretty sure he just thinks of me as different, and he can accept that much. I can understand what it feels like to be scared, unsure, and in the dark.

I came out to my youngest sister last. Her response was simple: 'Oh, why would I care? That would be so silly. Lots of people are gay!' And then, in the next breath: 'So, what subjects did you do in

Year 9? I need help choosing.' I now see students *putting up* rather than tearing down posters on acceptance and inclusion; these kids are driving all of us towards a better future. I have the privilege of a mental tally of young people who have come out to me – sooner, with so many more words than I had to say who they are. They have found ways and places to be who they are. And I know that there are those who still feel lost or alone, forging on nonetheless; I admire all of them.

So, I have actually cut my hair and it doesn't look half bad. I've decided, though, that leather doesn't really suit me. I'm okay with being a quiet lesbian. Of course, I get that lump in my throat sometimes still, but the difference is that my bluebird is out of its cage and it's singing. It's telling me: it's alright, you're okay. It's going to be okay.

vi. *Settle*. Lowering the stroke rate, but maintaining the pressure.

The Watering Hole

Samuel Leighton-Dore

Some of my earliest recollections of sexuality took place by a swimming pool, the air thick with the smell of chlorine as my peers and I undressed behind loosely held beach towels. Changing rooms, full of swinging willies and naked butts, provoked a fresh sense of anxiety and excitement – an indication of things to come as I edged cautiously towards puberty.

I experienced my first erection while lining up for a waterslide at the Sydney Olympic Park Aquatic Centre. With bare bodies pressed into a long, shivering procession, I reached the front of the queue only to have an instructor (well, the pimply seventeen-year-old who mumbled 'go') point at the misshapen lump growing in my speedos and laugh.

'Holy shit, he's got a stiffy!' he shouted. 'Gross!'

A wicked chorus of laughter followed me as I leapt feet-first down the winding blue tunnel, flipping and cracking my face against the hard plastic walls, before disappearing into the churning waters below. Mortified, I held my breath and swam as far from the waterslide's gaping exit as possible, resurfacing several metres away – covered in blood, forever changed and, truth be told, still a little hard.

The young man's laughter rang out in my head. The word 'gross' stung like salted hot chips on my split bottom lip. I hadn't noticed any girls in line, only boys, standing shoulder to shoulder, teeth chattering as drops of water ran slowly down their backs. Boys, their nipples hard and shrunken, skin prickled with goosebumps.

Boys, I thought. *Gross* ...

One of several psychological repercussions from that day was that I convinced myself erections were my body's way of expressing disgust. Whenever I saw something 'gross', such as an older male student walking topless and sweaty across the school cricket pitch, my dick would awaken and gently nudge my inner thigh *to warn me*. This made sense, I reasoned. It was a survival mechanism, albeit a highly visible and inconvenient one.

The alternative – that I was attracted to boys and slowly developing into a gay adult man – was far more daunting.

Unfortunately, my theory was soon disproven. During a lunchtime discussion with classmates about seeing family members naked, I exclaimed that the sight of my mother in the shower 'gave me a stiffy'. The group erupted into giggles, and it became sorely apparent that my use of the word 'stiffy' had, in fact, been incorrect – and that perhaps the pool instructor had been right all along.

Perhaps my body was trying to tell me something.

Despite the early warning signs, over the following years swimming pools remained the backdrop to my sexual development. Growing up in the inner western suburbs of Sydney, the local public pool was my first and only point of contact with semi-naked human bodies that were not my own. Long afternoons spent at the pool were filed away: sun-bleached, flesh-toned collages to be revisited late at night, shrouded in the secrecy of bedsheets, pillow pushed to my groin.

While these memories were undoubtedly tinted by my slow sexual awakening, they meant much more to me than that. Throughout summer, I always looked forward to Saturday morning trips to the pool: retrieving loose hairbands and twenty-cent coins from the tiled floor of the deep end, ducking between crowded lap lanes and spending my allocated two dollars at the canteen. Ears popping, bloated bellies, patterned towels and long stretches of hot concrete: these are only some of the visceral memories I look back on fondly.

Hitting puberty, the annual school swimming carnival came to resemble a low-rent, increasingly horny debutante ball. Category: swimwear. For me, the carnival was an opportunity for boys (and girls, I guess) from all year groups to gather, undress, slip into tight scraps of navy fabric and compete against one another (as well as gay, I've always been a little competitive). They were also an opportunity to manoeuvre a solid minute-long perv at Lucas Bobbin's chest or accidentally brush up against Harry Shield's bum on my way to the loo – where the full-length changing-room mirrors were angled *just right* to catch a glimpse of older guys spraying piss into the long, teal-tiled urinals.

Pubescent triumphs aside, swimming pools also set the stage for numerous very steep, very public learning curves. At my Year 6 swimming carnival, I delivered my first Valentine's Day card. I gave it to a blonde girl named Kelly after watching her win the U13 medley in a black one-piece. It was all very Cameron Diaz in *Charlie's Angels*, I thought. She was fabulous – and I was relieved. Was I actually attracted to a girl? Propelled by an unrelenting sense of denial, had I stumbled blind and desperate into the shallow waters of heterosexuality?

Spoiler alert: I had not.

Standing before what felt like a stadium of eagle-eyed spectators, Kelly chuckled, tilted her head to the side in a way that felt patronising, and informed me that she'd already agreed to be another boy's valentine. I overheard a passer-by whisper my name and laugh as I walked, dejected, back to my seat. I was more into Drew Barrymore anyway, I reminded myself in quiet consolation. No, I thought somewhere deep down, I was more into Charlie.

Coming out of the closet at sixteen, I quickly discovered that inner-city pools were the ideal place to bask in my emerging sexuality and confidence. Spending the day at Prince Alfred Park Pool – camper than Christmas, with its staggered lawns and bright yellow umbrellas – felt like stepping into the glossy pages of *DNA* magazine. Everywhere you looked there were chiselled abs and gym-built bums you could imagine bouncing on like they were trampolines.

There were more pragmatic benefits to pools, too. In a pre-Grindr world, Victoria Park Pool was the perfect casual first-date location or meeting place, particularly because it attracted the elusive and highly sought-after first-year gays from Sydney University.

However, these days, for me, swimming pools have quite simply become the great Australian equaliser.

I now live in a slightly conservative part of the Gold Coast, with my partner of five years, and our building's 25-metre pool refuses to discriminate. In the stick of summer it unites us with our neighbours: the middle-aged, crop top–wearing Russian woman with the 'cops are tops' bumper sticker; the openly homophobic 78-year-old with throat cancer; the redheaded hippy divorcee and her teenage daughter, Shania – named, of course, after the Twain. Regardless of age, sexuality or politics, we gather in the shared, inherently human discomfort of 35-degree days: air thick, as always, with the smell of chlorine.

And what could possibly be more Australian than that?

Car Windows

Tim Sinclair

'*Look at this faggot,*' the young man sneers to his mates. They're standing around his muscle car in the narrow alleyway, so there's no way not to get close as I walk past. It's two in the afternoon. I can see bright sunshine streaming in at the end of the alley.

I've been here before. I know what to do. Look away, but don't look away too obviously. Don't run; don't show fear. Just keep walking.

I walk past, hyper-aware of their distance from me, sweat prickling all over the back of my shirt. The three mates are watching me, watching their leader, waiting to see what's going to happen next.

'Faggot,' he says again as I pass, and spits on me – a huge slimy gob I can feel through my shirt as it starts to slide down my chest. I'm so shocked I don't react. It's probably the thing that saves my life.

*

Growing up queer for me was fear: fear embedded so deeply it felt natural. It's taken me years to peel back the scar tissue, to find out what was there in the first place. And I'm still scared. Do I get to belong now? Have I earned my rainbow stripes?

This is the problem of falling outside the either/or. I'm not gay. I'm not straight. I'm not alone in this, but for someone who's always felt like an outsider, belonging becomes yet another question. Or is it the central question? I can't tell anymore. I've wasted a lot of time waiting for somebody to give me the tick of approval.

*

'How much do you charge?' yells a kid out of a car window. Boys at the traffic lights. His friends are laughing and I lose my cool. I stick my middle finger up and lean over their bonnet. His face darkens and he starts to open the door, adrenaline spiking shards through my veins.

The light changes. His mates pull him in and he slams the door, bravado intact, and I fall backwards into myself, realising it's a game, it's just a fucking game. And that's it, isn't it? I've taken it too seriously. It's supposed to just wash off. It's words thrown out to test the water, and only faggots will rise to the bait, right? I've never known how to play this game.

*

I grew up in small-town Australia. Puberty in the 1980s. High school was almost entirely defined by trying to fit in, in any number of ways. Something started opening up at university in the '90s, but I was still squeezed into the conservatism of Adelaide's tightly gridded streets.

It stuns me now when I give writing workshops in high schools and hear open discussion of sexuality. I know that high school is still full of fear; I know adolescence is still an excruciating time. It's not all rainbows, but it's something.

*

My partner has a Chinese mother and an Anglo father. I learnt the term 'halfie' from her. I try hard not to map my experience over hers, because the last thing the world needs is yet another white man co-opting the story of a person of colour. But she has taught me a lot about being from neither one world nor another. She confuses a lot of people in Australia, where the mainstream expectation is whiteness, and people can't quite get a read on her otherness.

From her I finally came to understand just how offensive is the question, *So, where are you from?* Because it never means that. It means, *You're not from here*. It means, *You're not like us*. It means, *I'm the one who gets to judge, and I'm having trouble judging you, and that angers me*. It means, *What are ya?*

85

So, somewhat like her story, but mostly like my own. Her experience, gently and generously shared, has helped me understand my own. Not *a bit gay* or *mostly straight*, but something else, something other, something that can confuse and anger people. *What are ya?*

'Halfies are the prettiest people,' she says. Does that apply to queers, too? Most of my life I've wanted to hide.

But I'm not *queers*. I'm me. I'm here, I'm queer, I'm in the rainbow soup – still figuring out exactly where; still trying to be okay with being my own particular kind of crouton. And this is the heart of the matter. Because if you can't be yourself in your own way, then god help you when you die with a wallet full of fake IDs.

*

I like the word 'queer'. It's like a question, a question mark, a reminder. I've always asked questions. Have driven myself half-mad with them.

I embrace the word queer. It's a query, a reminder to ask: *Who are you? Who might you become?* I hope I don't get to the end of that question before I die.

I think it's an important word for the world right now, as political debate degenerates to Us v. Them, as the glorious grey areas of the internet become ever more black and white. Queer is middle ground, blurred boundaries, somewhere a productive discussion might be had instead of a slogan-shouting match. Come in. Let's talk. Let's try to figure something out.

Perhaps I'm being optimistic. But I like the word queer.

*

In the early days, trying to figure it out. 'Look, I just don't know,' I said. 'In a room full of gay people I feel straight. And in a room full of straight people …'

'… you feel like vomiting?' my friend finished helpfully.

She was joking, but she'd hit on something: the physical discomfort of being mistaken for something I was not, of being misread as straight, or misread as gay – neither of which I was comfortable with.

86

The boys in the supermarket car park lean out the car window, fake-coughing 'Poofter!' 'Faggot!' I walk past them, not rising but rising, hurting, ashamed, unable to embody what I'm supposed to, which is *fuck them fuck you fuck off cunt*, flash my arse in contempt, anything to show that their taunts are not getting under my skin.

*

I started seeing K. She was queer, as were most of the friends I met through her. It was a revelation to me how matter of fact she was about it. We didn't talk about it a lot because I still had so much work to do myself, but I observed her love for life and love for her friends, and marvelled at the way her sexuality was core to who she was but at the same time did not define her.

Partly, the work I had to do was in deconstructing layers of misplaced assumptions. We were walking in the city one day and fell in behind two young women holding hands, obviously lovers. This was the '90s; to hold hands in public was a political act. I thought of K as very political, and my mind started spinning with fears that I was holding her back. What was she doing with a boy when she should be sticking it to society by being with a girl? I had a long way to go.

A friend of K's saw the questions in me. We were talking about Queer Collaborations, the national tertiary-student queer conference, which was to be held in Adelaide that year.

'And what about you?' she asked, turning to me. 'Are you going?' She gave me a look that implied I probably should: part speculation, part invitation.

Who was I? How could I presume? Who did I think I was? All my old insecurities, gushing out into a new context.

I went. For one afternoon. With K, who was as smiling and outgoing as ever, complimenting the boys on their angel outfits as they walked past. I didn't know where to look. *What if they see me what if they see through me?*

I chose a panel on storytelling. Something safe, somewhere I could sit in the back row and feel like I wasn't being a total fake. In the break afterwards, K introduced me to a girl she'd met the day before and then wandered off to talk to somebody else.

'And are you here with your boyfriend?' she asked.

'Ah … no,' I stumbled. 'I'm here with K.'

A pause. 'You and she … are lovers?'

'Um. Yeah.' My face went bright red. One hour here and I'd been outed. I lurched away, I found K, I said I was going, I left.

*

Around the same time, my friend B found herself a girlfriend. She was wildly happy, but also frustrated by the simplistic conversation around her. 'My community,' she said scornfully. 'Okay, I'm gay, but they're not "my community".'

I got it. There was this idea that once you'd clicked your heels three times and come out, a unicorn would appear in a rainbow of glitter and present you with your passport, and you'd be swept away to the embrace of *your community*. I was scared to come out because I didn't know what I was coming out *as*. I was afraid of rejection, of seeming presumptuous, of having a different definition of *queer* to everybody else. Who would want to embrace me if all I was sure about was what I wasn't?

I'd spent my life feeling uncomfortable with the community I'd grown up in, so why would I join another one? To me, 'community' was just another word for a group of people to stand on the outside of.

*

'Do you take it up the arse?' says the young man in Rundle Mall as I walk past. Bully's posture: legs wide, head cocked in disdainful appraisal.

'Sure!' I say. I've started to reclaim. 'It's the only way to go.' And his bravado pours out of his gaping mouth and he sits there wordlessly, stunned. I've taken his ammunition. But I walk away quickly, not turning around. *Don't turn around. Don't make him come after you. Don't make him try to save face in front of his friends, because surely this was a performance for his friends.*

*

I'm comfortable with my gender identity. Deeply troubled by what men can be, by what society expects them to be, by what men are

88

capable of but, nevertheless, I'm a man in a man's body.

My partner is similarly comfortable with her gender identity, but she feels that inside her there's a sardonic gay New Yorker. Sometimes he's not hidden very far inside. She grew up in New York, hanging out with her uncle's group 'Asians and Friends', made up of gay Asian or Asian-American men with white partners. In the context of our relationship, she's both the Asian and the Friend.

And that's it, isn't it? We're complicated, we're multiple, we're many. All of us. It's why I find labels so problematic. It's why I like the word queer. It's a fuzzy embrace. I can wrap myself up in that rainbow blanket and be me inside its warmth. And the people I love most are the ones who feel like they can sit inside that blanket cave with me and be them. Whoever they happen to be.

*

Back in Adelaide, I signed up with some friends to take part in 'Fairies at the Bottom of the Garden', a poetry reading in the Botanic Garden that was part of Feast, the Adelaide queer arts festival. I loved how camp the name was, how poofy. It was another 'fuck you' to the taunting voices. But then the program came out, and I realised that I hadn't. My turn.

I went around to my parents' house, discovering to my relief that only my mother was home. Not that I grew up in an especially homophobic household – it was more like a 'don't ask, don't tell' policy. About everything.

'I have an announcement,' I blurted out, halfway through cup-of-tea time. I was making it more awkward for myself, and I could sense my mother's growing discomfort.

I don't remember the words I used. I'd practised a little speech, but I couldn't tell you what I actually said. A few days later I went around again and found Dad in his shed. It was him who brought it up, completing our circuitous family communication.

'Mum told me about the reading you're doing,' he said. I nodded, unable to speak. 'Good,' he said. 'That's good.' And we went back to talking about his latest creation of wood and wire and left-over pieces from the botany department he'd salvaged from the skip outside his office.

I used to think it was my parents who'd discouraged me from speaking freely, speaking emotionally. I've come to realise I'm as much a part of the pattern as they are. Hold it inside. That's what growing up queer has done to me. Hold it in. Don't let people see what's going on. Clench, shutter, cocoon. The term 'coming out' encapsulates so much, so perfectly.

My heart aches for the young people who are still dying inside their chrysalises, without ever having had the joy of flight.

*

I'm lucky. In so many ways. And the world we live in now feels a million miles from the fears of before. But there's more work to do and there are more questions to ask. All I can do is try to embody the questions, try to inhabit them in the most honest way possible. Adhere to that simplest and most difficult of truths: it's only me who gets to decide if I belong. And, maybe one day, I can find it in myself to love those terrified young men who scream their fear out of car windows.

Bent Man Running

Steve Dow

I was winning that day, a shy twelve-year-old dashing across the dewy grass of the technical school's oval. This was a surprising elevation of my stature, as elsewhere on campus my unique practical skills confounded the supply of tomorrow's carpentry and sheet-metal workforce, and my Physical Education report usually confirmed stereo-tropes of unmanly awkwardness. Australian Rules football was the religion of my fellow pimpled proletarians, but I was a short-arse who couldn't connect his foot with the will of the ball. It was true that my great-grandfather had kicked goals for Carlton in a couple of grand finals at the dawn of the twentieth century – his name was Percy, and he was a policeman – but his genetic gift appeared to have gone south, along with any familial height advantage. 'Steve tries hard, but ...' is the line I best remember from that page-long log of crimes against sport in south-suburban Frankston.

However, running simply required one foot in front of the other. It brought clarity to my spatially challenged self, a way forward. It allowed me to lose that habitual sense of difference and momentarily belong to the tribe, while averting eye contact, because eyes need to be cast forward. Thus I found myself ahead in the two-hundred-metre sprint.

I knew I was ahead, because I chose to look back, and saw my competitors at various points behind me: the usual alpha leader, with the freckles and protruding slack jaw; his beta boy chorus slugging along. That glance was the last thing I remember before I fell. As I slipped, I reached my right arm back to try to stop the fall.

The break and bend, on the lower forearm, was something to behold; my classmates closed around me and began pointing and commenting. 'Look at his arm!' said one bright spark with a nice line in the bleeding obvious. My head fuzzed as the pain connected to my synapses, and I regarded the arm with a mix of curiosity and revulsion, as though it were no longer part of my body. In one short snap I had gained my peers' rapt attention – and also validated their habit of picking me last for teams: in this race, I'd not only come last, but was doubled over on the ground unable to stand up again.

That first time I broke my arm, the PE teacher scooped me up. He had tight curly hair on his head and chest; I know this because once he had taken his shirt off during a baseball game. The Americanness of baseball had seemed exciting, although I couldn't make the bat connect with the ball there either. The teacher carried me in his arms, *An Officer and a Gentleman*–style, from the oval, past the brown-brick gymnasium and up the concrete stairs to the first-aid room. His clean-shaven face distinguished him from the moustachioed relief teacher who attended my next bone break, for I would repeat the exercise. Twice, in fact.

The next snap was on a polished gym floor during a game of basketball; and the third in the new year, when my foot became entangled in the spokes of my bicycle. I flipped over the handle-bars onto the road, and my right arm, once again, failed to take my weight.

It was not all bad news. Having my arm in a cast granted temporary respite from the sick feeling that turned my stomach when I descended the stairs to the gymnasium every Tuesday and Thursday. A plaster leave pass.

Many of the boys in the combined 7G and 7H gym class joined in the regular change-room singalong, which went – to the tune of that well-known American western ballad in trochaic meter, 'Oh My Darling, Clementine' – 'Pull your pants up, pull your pants up, pull your paaaaants up, Steven Dow.' Besides the oddity of kids at the beginning of the 1980s singing a cowboy ode popularised by Bing Crosby in the 1940s, I wondered why they focused on my regular-looking pants. They were neither loose nor required pulling up. The inference went well beyond accusations of laziness.

Was 'pants' a euphemism for 'poofter', or was I giving these guys too much credit? Why the archaic choice of tune? I should have punched the alpha leader or regaled his beta chorus with rapier wit about his inability to deviate from the same three lines, although the semitone key change had a certain admirable fluency.

Instead, I ignored them, and brooded. The bullies simply took this response as appeasement and continued. One day I cracked and walked out, leaving the singalong behind me.

'He's been busting a gut,' said the curly-haired teacher, admonishing my classmates after I had marched my allegedly baggy pants out of there. I wish he'd written *that* endorsement on my PE report. Later, the curly one would shift the blame to me by saying I didn't project myself enough to blend in. When he'd lugged a case of free chocolate Big Ms in cardboard cartons from the canteen to class, for instance, I'd *failed to take one* alongside each of my classmates. It was through this abject reluctance to drink flavoured milk that I had brought the bullying upon myself, totally undoing my work in busting a gut.

Shame shifting was also the tactic of the Year 7 coordinator, to whose office I was summoned later that day to explain my walk out. 'Do you feel close to men?' asked the nanna-looking coordinator, apropos of nothing, relevant to zilch. Her permanent wave and spectacles only accentuated her beady, quizzical eyes, searching my face for portals of potential gossip. 'No,' I replied. I wasn't going to confide anything in her even if I could name it, not even my curiosity with moustaches. I had not long before read that the hirsute Village People were sympathetic to something called 'gay liberation' and I thought that was kind of them, though it seemed an abstract concept with no application to myself.

I was nineteen before I would test my sympathy to heterosexuality. I did this by paying to lose my virginity to a female sex worker. She had long brown hair, and while I watched a physically taut straight couple have sex on stage, she slid into the bank of seats next to me and whispered, 'Would you like to come upstairs?' I don't remember the music that was playing at that moment, though I do recall a female stripper who had earlier owned the stage by unfurling herself to Peter Gabriel's melancholic 'In Your Eyes'. I must have been there a while.

Having been successfully fellated and mounted in a bedroom behind a locked metal gate, through no skill set of my own – 'There's no feeling in the world like it,' the sex worker instructed me – I dashed down Darlinghurst Road in Kings Cross through the night's thrum of people. I couldn't tell you what made me run. Maybe I was trying to catch up to the tribe. Or trying to find Oxford Street and what I really wanted – men – but this was an unnamed need which would take me a few more years to act upon.

It is 2018. I am pulling my chest to the bar at CrossFit. Pronated grip, with my palms wrapped over the top of the bar, is sometimes preferable to supinated grip – palms wrapped under the bar – due to a lingering kink from all the breaks in my right arm, which prevent complete forearm rotation. Two laps of running the laneway equals eight hundred metres, and I only occasionally remind myself not to look back to assess the advancing party. This is not a competition. I'm usually running behind most of the people in the class anyway, because many are half my age. I'm glad to just finish the workout of the day, the torturous crossover of cardio and weights, without a little vom. Functional fitness, they call it. And yet my awkwardness lingers: I can't really skip beyond a basic bounce, for the pattern of running while skipping is spatially beyond me – a brisk *foot, rope, foot, rope* rhythm becomes a sluggish *foot, foot, rope* – and I have given up trying to kick up into a handstand. The GP suggests the stiffness in my left hip and lower back might be early signs of arthritis, but clearly such a development would be unfair, because I am red in the face like a National Party water hoarder and busting a gut, as old-school PE teachers used to say.

I got an email recently from one of the guys from school. I hadn't heard his name in decades. He wrote to apologise for the bullying; said his own son was now about the age we were then, giving him pause for thought. Maybe his son was also stereotypically non-conformist on the sporting field, if you know what I'm saying. I recall cruelly retaliating at this guy one day on the grassy knoll above the gym by calling him 'Helium Head'. He did have an outsized head, though maybe he eventually grew into it. Anyway, he had responded with a punch to my nose, drawing blood. I wrote back to the email cheerily and said no, the experience hadn't affected me, and attached a drawing of a balloon with a cartoon face. Not really.

I have been living happily with the same guy, conveniently also named Steve, for almost twenty years, contentedly out as a gay man since my mid-twenties – let's say 'queer' for solidarity – yet I say little about my relationship in my CrossFit classes. For instance, whenever I mentioned our rescue dog, Oscar – who shared our lives for eleven years and four months until he breathed his last in early 2019 – he somehow, unthinkingly, became 'my dog' rather than 'our dog'. Now that I think about it, I see that I evade follow-up questions about my personal life. An old reflex.

Am I wary of being judged in this environment? Nobody in these workout classes has ever given me real cause to be cautious, save the odd incautious trainer's remark that I'm a few beats behind those who are younger and therefore fitter. The laughter is communal, and never at someone's physical or other shortcomings. Here they cheer you on, even when you're coming last. But I need to stop running now.

I need to draw breath.

The Bent Bits Are the Best Bits

Jax Jacki Brown

'Would you rather be deaf or blind?'

I hate this game. Can't she tell?

I know where it's going, and its headed straight for me and my body. I stare at the ground as I walk, watch my right foot drag with every step, careful where I put my sticks so I don't slip up in front of her. The ends of my sticks make a small *thunk* sound as I press them into the grass – right, left, right – as we slowly walk beside each other.

My toes have calluses on the tops of them from years of being pulled along the ground. The palms of my hands and my knees are callused too, from crawling everywhere, through bush tracks, over rocks, across sand. Most of the time I don't feel ashamed. I like being near to the land, knowing it close up, seeing the things others miss, feeling it with my hands, knees and toes, all at once – three parts of me where others only give their feet.

I know everyone thinks I should feel ashamed. Walking is considered better than crawling. Walking gets me praised by Mum for showing how straight I can be. Dad calls me his 'little trooper'.

Eight-year-olds shouldn't crawl. 'Only babies crawl' – that's what Chris, my brother's friend, says. It's his mum who is beside me now, so I must keep walking even though this part of the track is the best bit for crawling.

There is a small muddy creek. It's two and a half cripple steps or three crawls wide. My dad has built a little bridge over it, but the wood is dark and always burning from the sun, so I prefer to crawl or walk through the creek instead. I love feeling the cool water, the way my stick ends are sucked into the black mud so when I pull them free they make a popping sound.

Frogs live here. I've caught them with my brother, captured them in buckets and carried them to our shack. We put them on the big windows in the front room and watch their feet suction onto the glass, climbing up, up, trying to get away.

'Do you ever wish you could walk, be normal ... that you weren't handicapped?'

My whole body flinches at her question. I really want to sit down but I am determined – that's what they tell me. I don't give up. That's a good thing, right?

It will take me years to know my limits, to learn to rest when I need to, to stop pushing myself. To tell people to fuck off.

She smells of cigarettes and sunscreen – and secrets. I want to tell her I know some of hers, some things that she is so scared will spill out she gets migraines from the pressure of holding them inside. I know she has one vagina flap longer than the other – Mum told me. She's done some sex thing with the man she's having an affair with, and that's stretched it. I imagine it, that long flap, tucked up inside her swimmers, a small bulge on one side. Does it chafe as she walks, slowly, beside me?

I want to ask how her flap is going. What does she tell her husband, who drinks too much VB and yells at my father for being a 'fucking dole-bludging hippy'? How does she explain how her flap came to be? Does she feel ashamed of it? Or does she secretly feel proud? Does she pull it to make it grow? Does she wish she could just let it out?

*

'Are you a boy or a girl?'

'I ... don't know. What do you think I am?'

'You're a girrrl ... are you? Why's your hair so short?'

'I like it. Mum shaved it for me. Wanna feel it? It's all smooth.'

'You're weird. Girls have long hair, don't you know?'

We paddle on our boogie boards in the still, warm water of the lagoon and don't say anything for a bit. There are lice in my cozzie and sometimes they bite my crotch. They particularly like the crotch.

Not many kids are allowed to swim here: just me and my

brother and sometimes other kids when their parents are too drunk to care.

It's full of piss. Actual man piss. The clubhouse runs beside it and on a 'clubby night', when they are having a 'do', all the blokes duck around the side of the club and piss into this water. Mum says it's good for our immune system. 'Just try not to drink it, okay?'

'Where's your parents?' I ask.

'My mum's gone.'

She breathes in hard. 'And my dad … he shot himself in the head … my brother found him … that's why he's so angry.'

'Your brother is real scary. He chased us with a knife yesterday, just for going near your place, there was blood on it.'

'It was only tomato sauce, not real blood,' she says.

*

I am bleeding. Bleeding in my undies. In my grandpa's outdoor toilet that smells of old dog and mildew. My belly and my thighs ache.

I get home and tell Mum that I must have hurt myself somehow. Mum gets all excited and says, 'No, it's just your period, you're becoming a woman now.'

I think, *What if I don't want to become a woman? What if I want to be a person, or a boy with short hair?* I don't say this out loud. My parents didn't cope when I started writing 'I want a dick, love Jack' on all the Christmas and birthday cards to our family. I keep it inside.

Mum gets a bag of old white nappies, cut up and now used as rags, down from a hook in the laundry and shows me how to fold them over and put them inside my undies. It feels so big and bulky down there.

That afternoon, Dad takes me to my physio, where my body is pulled and stretched. It hurts, really hurts, but I never ask them to stop. I think to myself, *I'm good, and if I try hard enough I'll become normal.* I imagine myself above myself, looking down. From up here, I am safe. I can endure whatever they decide to do, whatever they declare is in my 'best interests'. This body is not mine. I will grow into something else.

Carla, the physio, gives me a present to remind me of how 'straight and tall' I can be if I just keep trying. If I keep giving my body over to the pain, I will become straighter, right? A little statue of an emperor penguin with his 'shoulders back, and legs straight, Jacki,' Carla says in her thick Polish accent. I hate her, but I push this hate down into myself.

I am exiled from my body. It will take years to come home.

*

She pushes me in my new wheelchair up the ramp and I loll my head into her breasts for the briefest of moments, letting the back of my head touch her through her red school jumper. She doesn't notice, or she thinks it's an accident. I'm nervous and sweaty. I feel like this all the time around her recently. I can't look her in the eyes anymore, and I don't know what to say when she asks me what I think about Daniel, the boy all the Year 8 girls seem to have a crush on. She keeps bugging me to ask out Mathew, the only other person in our school in a wheelchair, but I don't like him like that, and he really doesn't like me, not even as a mate, he's made that clear.

At night I lie awake and imagine her on top of me, kissing me, her thick curly hair falling in my face. I imagine touching her breasts lightly. I feel my naturally tense muscles tighten further as I touch myself. I don't know what our bodies would do together beyond this naked making out. My special school had no sex ed classes and our high school health classes don't talk about girls getting together.

Mum called me into her bedroom a few months ago and said it would take a 'special kind of man' to love me. 'If you ever get into bed with a man,' she said, 'make sure he has a condom on at all times.' I imagine a disembodied cock sliding across a bed towards me, limp condom drooping off its tip, threatening to fall off.

*

I'm immobilised. I can't move. I don't know how I am going to get up and make it to the car to head home. I'm trying really hard not to look at her breasts but they are so close to her face and I'm trying to avoid looking at her lips. so I keep looking down … Why do breasts have to be so close to faces? And why do I always have to be at breast height in this wheelchair? It's a cruel trick.

I shouldn't have had any puffs on this joint. Damn it! I was just

99

trying to be cool, to relax so I could talk to her, but now there are big gaps between what she says and me trying to find words to respond and she is so close to me … and so damn beautiful … she's showing me her stoner artwork and wanting to know about my art, but my mouth is so dry and my hands are so sweaty … and I … don't know what to say and I'm sure if I speak I'll just say 'I want you.'

Mum and Dad come and pick me up and I talk about her all the way home, about how cool she is, and how rad her artwork is. Mum says, 'It's good you have a friend, darling, you seem to really like her.' I blush and fall silent. I try to stop the shaking in my legs, pressing down hard on my knees, Mum can read my body in a way that others can't; she knows shaking legs means I'm feeling emotional. I hope she doesn't work out why.

*

It's dawn. I can see the light around the edges of the thick motel blind. I'm wearing my blue winter PJs, the ones Mum got me for Christmas with the tiny sheep on them that say 'baaah, bedtime' in big black font.

I roll over and can see her silhouette; she is turned away from me, lying on her side, snoring softly. I wiggle over until I am almost touching her, almost spooning her. 'Are you awake?' I whisper into the centimetre of air between me and her neck. Nothing. I reach up and run a finger over her shoulder and down her back to where her tank top starts. This. This is the bravest, most exhilarating thing I have ever done. She stirs, and I ask again softly, 'Are you awake?' 'I am now,' she says, and I slide my arm around her and stroke her belly.

We stay in that bed, in that room, for a week, watching midday cooking shows turned up loud and having sex softly and awkwardly.

When she has to go home to Sydney and I have to return home because my parents are getting back from holidays, she gives me the cassette tape she made for our week together and has a dozen red roses and chocolates delivered to my door. Mum comes into my room with them and says, 'Well, you haven't been seeing a man, because a man wouldn't think to do this.' I say, 'No, it's this girl I met online.' Mum tells me not to make my life harder than it already is, and to not tell anyone because it's probably just a phase. 'Everyone's experimented at some point, Jack.'

*

I'm in love with her from the first time she kisses me. We kissed for about five hours that night. She invites me over for dinner a few days later and we end up in her bed. When I eventually get the courage to remove my clothes, she says, 'This is not what I was expecting ...' 'What?' I reply. 'You ... you carry yourself like you're hiding something under your clothes, like you're ashamed ... but you're beautiful, do you know that?'

I don't know that. But I know she is beautiful, and I know I can't disconnect from my body with her. She calls me into it, slowly and gently. I catch glimpses of myself under her hands and under her mouth, and I am not 'wrong' or 'strange' but desired, *just as I am.*

In the early hours of the morning she brings her guitar to bed, and in the soft candlelight plays me Mazzy Star's 'Fade into You'. 'I want to hold the hand inside you', and I know this night will stay with me for a lifetime.

Healing is found in this moment. Healing from all the shame that was placed on me and my body by all the doctors and therapists who treated me as fundamentally 'wrong' and needing to be 'fixed', who tried to push me closer to some elusive idea of 'normal', to unbend me, make me straighter. Those treatments were done to my body throughout my childhood in the name of 'normalisation' and my supposed 'best interests'.

She holds me as we fall asleep, and healing finds me; it seeps into my muscles, whispering, 'You are enough, you are whole.'

I find all the beautiful things our small town has to offer – flowers, chocolates, a hand-made waistcoat – and pile them on my bed for her, to say, 'I love you, and thank you.' But it is too much, too soon, and she says she doesn't feel the same way back, and leaves.

I cannot listen to Mazzy Star for five years without aching.

*

I discover disability pride in books long before I find a disability-rights community in person. It finds me first in the small TAFE library, as I wheel past an even smaller LGBTIQA+ collection titled (I kid you not) 'Deviance'. A book called *Exploring Disability: A Sociological Introduction* describes the disability rights movement and introduces me to the social model of disability, which argues that disability is not a personal problem but a social issue of entrenched systematic discrimination and exclusion of people with non-normative bodies and minds. This radical reframing of the 'problem' of disability not as a personal issue but as a political one transforms my thinking about myself and the world. Slowly I work through my internalised ableism and begin to seek out other people with disabilities – they are *my* people, and together we can advocate for change!

Queer sex and masturbation become a way to reconnect with my body, to breathe into it, and to fully experience it, to love it.

*

I am curled around my partner, her fingers lovingly tracing the bend of my legs. I am breathing in this moment, letting it settle into my muscle memory, letting healing find me.

I am calling my body home. I am reclaiming it. I am naming it as mine. Reconnection is found in these quite moments, pride nurtured.

There is lightning in my legs; big jolts like electricity run up me. I can feel them building before they strike. I love how my body moves, how my emotions and my muscles are intertwined, how I wear my feelings on the surface.

Our baby wriggles inside Anne's belly in response to my jumps. Our little being will be here soon, and it feels like the most terrifying and hopeful thing I have ever done.

I lie my hand on our tiny moving human and think about all the things I want to teach her. I imagine her learning to say 'My body, my choice!' and the power of this –particularly if she happens to have a disability.

I feel a big spasm building in my left leg. I close my eyes and breathe myself into it, breathe my pride and politics and all that I know now, breathe it all into that electric feeling in my body.

And as it moves, I send this energy back: back to that kid I was, who was taught only shame. I send pride, love, community. I tell her the bent bits are the best bits.

The baby kicks, Anne sleeps.

Reunion

Kelly Parry

I never thought I would make it to a fortieth school reunion. Yet here I am.

After a couple more drinks, the big questions begin. 'You weren't always gay, though, were you? Not while you were at school?' 'We shared a bed so many times, how come you never made a move on me? You never even tried to kiss me.'

What do I say? We were teenagers, we went to an all-girl Catholic school, you had a boyfriend. And *you* were juggling so many dicks you could have been hired by a circus. Me? I was still trying to work out who I was or might one day become. And after all, it was *forty years ago.*

In 1978 girls were divided into categories: 'frigid', and two kinds of 'mole' – 'slack-arsed' or 'regular'. Confusingly, you could be a 'frigid mole', but only if you were a prick-tease. Guys were 'spunkrats' or 'deadshits'. Deadshits got dropped if they told their mates they'd rooted you when you'd only been fingered. When life was good it was 'bitching'; when things were rough it was 'bullshit'.

Many remember it as a golden time to have been young. The second wave of feminism, free love, readily available contraception and *Cosmo* magazine offering step-by-step instructions on how to give the best blow jobs meant that as young women we were encouraged to push the traditional boundaries when it came to sex and relationships. Just so long as it was heterosexual and it was what the guys wanted. There was no mention of queer.

My earliest memories as a kid growing up in the suburbs of Brisbane are of being aware that I was breaking unspoken, unnamed or unknown rules. It wasn't just the summer heat that was stifling. A man was king of his castle, a woman's place was in the home, and children should be seen and not heard. Gender roles and social constructs were as tight and twisted as old Aunty May's corset.

Each time I was offered a doll I asked for a book; when they gave me the doll instead, I shaved her hair and turned her into a nun. At that stage I was an only child, so my quirks and peculiarities were attributed to my lack of siblings. They hoped I'd grow out of it. But I knew the truth. I knew I could never grow out of being myself.

There's a photo of me. I'm dressed in a white singlet and big white undies. I am standing in my grandparents' backyard, honey brown, squinting up into the sun, smiling. My curly blonde hair is done up in rollers and I'm pushing a huge old lawnmower. I was a little girl who looked like a Barbie and behaved like a Ken.

The backyard, under the cool of the mulberry tree, was my favourite place. Bloated blowflies fresh from the bin jostled for space on my toes and nose. While my family got drunk on cold glasses of beer, the bees got drunk on the delicious nectar of passionfruit flowers. It was here I could ponder in peace how it was possible to feel the things I felt for Rhonda. When I would see her floating by on her perfect powder-blue Malvern Star bike, I wanted to run inside and tell my family that she made me smell frangipani and taste vanilla paddle-pop. But I didn't. My instincts for self-preservation were strong – I've always been part cockroach.

I found I was another kind of animal when my teen hormones and natural curiosity kicked in, right around the time I found my father's hidden stash of soft-porn magazines. He had brought them back from a trip to the United States. God bless America. It was in one of these magazines that I met Busty Barb and her friend Suzie the Swinger. It was the first time I had read the terms 'hot lesbo', 'sexy bi bitch' and 'split wet beaver'. And there were pictures to go with them. Unrealistic porn fantasy it may have been, but I was like Alice diving down the rabbit hole. I was falling fast into an unknown world and I wasn't going to stop myself.

Although my old schoolfriends may be miffed that I hadn't wanted muff in my teens, at that time in my youth I still enjoyed playing with boys. I was even trying desperately to fall in love with them. I said and did all the right things, but it still felt very wrong.

At age twenty I escaped Brisbane and moved to Sydney to study acting. To support myself I worked as a tea lady at a private hospital that specialised in late-term abortions and the removal of anal warts. I was living the dream. My share house was filled with people and drugs and music and art and fucking and parties that were full of people fucking while making music, taking drugs and calling it art. Everyone was gay or straight, or gay and straight, or bisexual, or adventuring. It was a perfect time to spread those wings and fly. When I landed, I was in love with another woman. It was an easy feeling. I didn't feel pressured to love more or feel guilty that I loved less, like I had when I'd tried to love boys.

That first time being in love with a woman wasn't perfect and it didn't last, but it was right. Not right enough to tell my family, but right enough to tell my friends. On the coming-out-o-meter, they were varying degrees of cool acceptance to fulsome embrace. The early 1980s were a magic time in the land of gay. Before AIDS arrived to devastate us and change our world, the boys were having the time of their lives and I was happy to hag along.

But not as 'a lesbian', oh gosh no. I was a woman who fell in love with other women. And slept with them. A lot. But lesbian? Although not yet ready to acknowledge my internal homophobe, homophobia and I were quickly becoming acquainted. People who happily gave me acting roles before they knew that I pounded the mound, munched the minge, scissored the sisters – or whatever they imagined my sex life to include – were now 'casting their net more widely'. Don't call us and we will conveniently forget to call you. Becoming myself meant I was compelled to choose between a closet and a hard place. I went to the hairdresser and told him I wanted to look like Annie Lennox, the most lesbian thing I could think of to do. The second most lesbian thing was to grab a girlfriend, buy a car and drive to Perth. So I did that too. I chose the terror and wonder of freedom.

I didn't come out to my parents until I was twenty-six and living in Melbourne, safe in the knowledge I was two states away from them. I didn't expect it to go well and I wasn't surprised by their reactions. Banned from attending family weddings, funerals or Christmas in case I said anything about having a girlfriend to any extended family members, my circulation was reduced to inner-circle family members only. My parents would never be ready to come out.

I, on the other hand, was becoming a whiz at it. I met my current partner at an early morning work meeting and fell Hollywood-style in love at first sight. I had never wanted kids; I felt mine was a genetic pool not to be tapped. She insisted otherwise, and in the days when the internet was in its infancy we searched for ways to make our own babies. This involved endless comings out to potential sperm donors, including our favourite waiter, who immediately offered his semen along with our café lattes.

Romance and baby-making for same-sex couples are not necessarily connected. We used to pick up the semen from our lovely donor, swing by and grab a pizza and come home and inseminate. We told everyone, including the pizza guy what was going on, in graphic detail. In the end, I used to explain it as if it was a veterinary procedure: take one small round furry hole, one jar of yucky smelling liquid, fill a syringe with said liquid, place in hole and squirt. Less like hot sex, more like worming the cat. But it did get the job done. Twice.

I'm not sure what was more stressful – coming out to my family as a lesbian or as pregnant.

Once you have kids your identity changes, you are no longer a red-hot sex-bitch lesbian; you are a parent in a very straight world. When we enrolled the kids in preschool, we said that we were a two-mummy family. The worker wrote that we were Mormon. Somehow that was a more logical leap than lesbians.

Although it could have gone either way, having children did build a bridge to my parents that I hadn't anticipated. We were a family – unnatural and ungodly, but a family none the less. Over the years my parents mellowed, slightly; they love their grandkids and they certainly like my girlfriend more than they like me. Ironically, when Australia was subjected to the cowardly plebiscite on marriage equality, I called Mum and Dad to do my weekly check-in and the first thing my super-conservative, Pauline Hanson–loving Catholic mother said was, 'We'll be voting "Yes" in the marriage equality thing. Everyone deserves an equal chance to be miserable.'

I never thought I would make it to a fortieth school reunion. Yet here I am: clean, sober and queer, answering coming-out questions, hearing stories from parents with queer kids and sharing photos of my own family.

I scroll through my phone, surrounded by delighted faces. 'Here's my partner of twenty-four years – that's at least twelve hundred straight years. This is our daughter, she's just started at uni; here is our son, he's in Year 11; this is our eldest daughter, she adopted us when she got kicked out of home at fifteen when her parents found out she was gay. She's now a psychologist. And this adorable little Sudanese guy is a new addition. He comes for weekends with white people while his mum works.'

Queer connections run deep and wide – not only through choice, but also through necessity. Although this was not supposed to be a coming-out story, it always ends up that way. We lose family, friends and former lives when we begin the process of showing the world the truth of ourselves. This is why the family we create is expansive and welcoming and safe. We are bonded together by oppression and revolution, radical acts and the comfort of the ordinary, love bites and battle scars, addiction and sobriety, fear and courage, birth and death. Blood and genetics are a minor part of what true family is for me. Love and tears plus laughter and kindness, minus fuckery, multiplied by time equals family. It's not a perfect formula, but it works for me.

You Can Take the Queer Out of the Country

M'ck McKeague

I never feel too far away from my childhood – my coming out story and the journey that led to it is a well-rehearsed script. At thirty, I've had enough audiences now to know which parts land easily and which parts hang uncomfortably in the air between us. I've learnt how to gloss over the uncomfortable parts, and how to emphasise the parts that affirm people's preconceived ideas about trans people. It's a skill most of us learn the hard way.

By 2015, I was tired of the edited version of my story, so I decided to painstakingly recreate my teenage bedroom – every Placebo poster, every never-sent love letter, every tortured diary entry, every life-saving CD, every incomprehensible MSN conversation – and invited strangers to walk in, make themselves at home and dig through the uncensored detritus of my adolescent existence in early 2000s Rockhampton. The installation, titled *NEVERLAND (well, this is embarrassing)* was an attempt at exposing some of the complexities and contradictions that are so frequently erased in dominant queer and trans narratives. As I dug into the relics of my past I found 'born this way' thoroughly tangled up with 'doing a really convincing job of trying desperately not to be this way'. I remembered that my first experiences of having my queerness being seen and understood were bound up in the fabric of my (ostensibly) cis-straight first love.

Making and presenting this work was scary, uncomfortable and, living up to its title, quite embarrassing. It made me reflect a lot on the cost of the curatorial process we often feel pressured into when we retell our histories in the endless quest to prove our identities legitimate.

We relive our histories to rewrite them and too often, in the drafting process, erase ourselves altogether. All that remains is a half-sentence from our diary that matches what a trans kid on *Four Corners* said, the sick feeling in the pit of our stomach when we went shopping for our high-school formal, the angsty crush we had on our best friend. Supposedly these memories legitimise us. We are certified, stamped and filed. The more of these memories we can gather from our histories, and the better we get at erasing what was once in between, the easier it is to find acceptance and community.

In Brisbane and Melbourne, I am extremely privileged to have found queer and arts communities where I generally feel valued, understood and cared for. However, thirteen years after flying the coop it still baffles me that when I say I'm from Central Queensland responses usually range from subtle disgust to mild fear to the most patronising sympathy. I can only imagine how this intensifies for my friends from much further north or further west than where I'm from.

When I moved to Brisbane from Rockhampton as a seventeen-year-old, I was a bottle of Passion Pop that had been shaken too long and too hard. I didn't know that non-binary trans people even existed, let alone that I could be one. I didn't know that I was living with bipolar. I didn't know that my best friends from high school were all silently dealing with their own, freakishly similar, internal-ised nightmares. All I knew was that by age twelve I'd made the decision to leave Rocky, and at age fourteen I got a job so I could start saving to leave. Basically, as soon as they let me out of the gate with my Year 12 certificate, I packed up to start a new life in the Big Smoke.

This is the story we all know and love: angsty artsy/alternative/ queer kid escapes oppressive country town and lives happily ever after in a progressive metropolitan wonderland. It *does* get better! Thank goodness.

This is the story I told others (and myself) for years. I learnt quickly from the disgust–fear–sympathy trifecta reaction that the shame I felt about coming from the ~~bogan~~ beef capital was pre-cisely what I *should* feel. I learnt that distancing myself from my history as much as possible, and as fast as possible, was the only way to be taken seriously in the 'progressive' landscape I now occupied. And, without questioning it, I got out my eraser and set to work.

In 2006, my first year living in Brisbane, I became acutely aware of the parts of myself that were unpalatable to queers who grew up in the city. My penchant for XXXX Bitters and low-brow nu metal was reason for ridicule. My central Queensland accent was cause for humiliation. This might seem harmless at first, but the process of attempting to remove them from my history and my sense of self, or at the very least trivialise them, did more damage than you might imagine. How do you change your accent when it comes back stronger in every conversation with your family and oldest friends? How can you hold space in your life for the people who are embedded in it when you're ashamed of your own story? How can you feel whole when the validation of your gender or sexual orientation comes at the cost of the place you've called home for most of your life?

There are two main, acceptable versions of your story: 1. It is awful here; I'm really struggling; please help me get out of here because I obviously couldn't do it without your incredible, glitter-shitting self. And 2. It was awful there. I really struggled. I'm so glad I am out now and that I'm allowed to shit glitter almost any-time I want.

These stories are not necessarily lies. They're just oversimpli-fied. When the only card you have to play in your hand is to tell your story the way people expect to hear it, you end up feeling – at least partially – erased. Reduced, condensed, disavowed.

Of course, when someone manages to extricate themselves from an abusive or oppressive environment, it is cause for celebration. For me, leaving Rockhampton was a huge and important decision. But when metropolitan queer communities make it mandatory that you escape (or literally die trying) in order to legitimise who you are, we contribute further to a dangerous isolation that spans more than the number of kilometres to the nearest major city. The much vaunted 'escape' is contingent on a myriad of privileges. What would my story look like if I had needed to financially support my family when I got that job at fourteen? What would my story look like if I wasn't white? The unqualified celebration of those queers who leave comes overwhelmingly at the expense of the complex reasons some might need – or, as shocking as this sounds, want – to stay, and implicitly contributes to the intersecting oppressions that are bound up in that choice.

And okay, I get it. When you think of regional and rural Queensland, there are very real reasons you think of Bob Katter and Pauline Hanson and a homogenous mass of aggressive, bigoted, white, uneducated cis dudes that you believe make up the entire Australian population outside of the south-east corner. But aside from how reductive and classist these assumptions are, they render invisible every marginalised person whose life is materially affected by the Pauline Hansons and Bob Katters of those areas. These conversations are centred on the oppressors and forget the survivors altogether – unless of course they have successfully escaped (yay for them!) or are too young to move (don't worry, it gets better!).

What about the people who stay? And what about the people who leave but return later as adults? Whether these life decisions happen by 'choice' (see also: false dichotomies), necessity, or through lack of access, queers who remain in the country are treated as less than those who don't. It is assumed they are stupid, that they brought it on themselves, that they 'chose' geographical isolation and therefore deserve social isolation. Or you assume they simply don't exist.

In my own desperate need to rid myself of all things Rocky, I treated good people like shit. I had no compassion for myself, so I had very little sympathy for my loved ones who were all deeply affected by their own regional and rural histories. I felt ashamed, afraid that the people from my past would expose me for the imposter I felt I was in my newfound city community. I had learnt how to talk the talk – or so I thought – and so if you didn't sound like a bona fide left-wing, urban arts undergrad I no longer had time for you. Never mind the actual substance of what you were saying.

Since recognising my own internalised stigma, I've come to see how often people dismiss the experiences of people from regional and rural backgrounds. These dismissers are often Good People – critical thinkers, people with a good grasp of classism, sexism, racism, ableism, and so on. But, somehow, once the obligatory 'please remember that not everyone can come out safely' memo is posted into the Facebook void for International Coming Out Day, country queers are either forgotten or explicitly considered inferior. This forgetting, this unchecked conflation of boganism with bigotry, and the many other ways, both subtle and overt, that people from regional and rural areas are stigmatised, is getting old. It's high time that we acknowledge the complexity of the lives of those who don't, or didn't always, live in a major city. And when we do this, it needs to be with absolute care for those who have sustained trauma through living in regional, rural and/or isolated areas, regardless of whether or not they have relocated to a major city. We need to acknowledge our privileges and listen deeply and carefully to one another's stories, to hear beyond the slang or inflection or personal circumstances that we might be conditioned to cringe at. We need to make space for stories to be told with depth, nuance and in brash, twangy, to-the-point short sentences.

Because you can take the queer out of the country*, but you can't take the country out of our queer histories. Believe me, I tried.

* Usually I would only use the word 'country' to describe specifically rural areas, because life and amenities and access to the privileges of community are different for people in these places than for those living in relatively large regional towns. However it was snappier than saying 'You can take the queer out of the regional, rural and/or isolated geographical area but ...' I hope my friends from the actual country will forgive me for this.

The Risk

Thom Mitchell

Few people *grow up* queer in Australia: we're not allowed to. Heterosexuality guards its supremacy. I used to sleep with a guy whose parents attempted to exorcise him. It wasn't like in the movies – ambush and surprise. It was planned. He let them try it. They had raised him, after all. Besides, what would it change? Straight culture makes exorcists of us all.

I grew up in a beautiful house on an emerald hill at a place called The Risk, deep dairy country, in the Northern Rivers of New South Wales. Our gravel driveway was a kilometre long and edged into the paddocks after big rain. When my mother turned off the highway she'd cross the first of three cattle grids and the red flash of her car would kick up a cloud of streaming dust. Attuned to her movements, I sometimes heard her car thrum across the second grid, which gave me about a minute to shut down the computer and disappear into my bedroom. The desktop was in the kitchen, next to the landline ran Dodo dial-up that whirred with the effort of loading porn. Sometimes the old Windows 98 froze. Never me.

Often I didn't hear Mum's approach until she crossed the third grid, breaching the border of our five-acre property. She took the bend fast, past the Moreton Bay fig and the stables and into the garage, where she always stopped abruptly and close to the wall. Our border collie, Bear, had a special yodel for greeting. If I was lucky, Mum would lean down to pat her or pause to gather up groceries. I never got caught but would often slip out of the kitchen just at the moment she entered. For any adolescent, these stakes would be high. For me, they were higher.

In Year 7 I had a close friend who lived in a flood-plain house with a lower storey that was forever half built. Upstairs we ate plain rice with his parents. They never ventured below. Down there the floor was in place, but the walls were just frames with fabric stretched taut: thin membranes between us and the world, flimsy partitions that threatened osmosis. Down there, my friend and I palpitated on his brother's bed. Our fingers felt for warm flesh in hushed, furtive stages that grew like raised stakes in a gambler's bet. It was only a hand job. It didn't take long and remorse came with release. 'Disgusting,' we said. 'Dirty.' We were thirteen. That was my first sexual experience. We went back upstairs and I couldn't meet anyone's eyes. It was never mentioned again.

I can't tell you his name, because it's uncommon. I don't want to out him, embarrass him, or bring on retribution – from where, I don't know. Often it's enough just to speak or be seen. I can't explain the shame either. It was the kind that makes you wish you would vanish. To be 'gay' was to be the butt of a joke that you too were making; to accept yourself was self-destructive. I don't know how much of that loathing I still bear within me, or how much silence.

Around that time I watched *Brokeback Mountain*. There's a violence in the way the two men kiss and fuck that reflects the hostility of their environment. Ennis is haunted by the spectre of two faggots who were tortured and murdered. He's never able to meet Jack's yearning. Love is not love – it's a 'fishing trip'. Only when Jack dies does Ennis realise: that which is suppressed and left unspoken proves the most painful.

I lay on a mattress in front of the TV, Mum and her boyfriend, Bill, behind me on the couch. My body sensed the sex scene coming. The satin of adolescent boxers is so loose and thin. When it began I rolled over onto my belly.

'Ugh. Come on,' said Bill. 'That's a bit much. Do we have to watch this?' He was also shifting in his seat, sounding off little grunts of discomfort. 'It's just a bit off.'

Bill was fond of saying, 'Children should be seen and not heard,' and so I said nothing.

The film was especially apposite because at the time I was a cowboy, of sorts. I grew up on horseback and couldn't wait to go droving. My mentor was an old-timer named Roy – a farrier, drover and dealer in horses. He had the lease on the Wiangaree Rodeo Ground and used to break in horses there at the yards. Roy had a hawkish nose, a hernia and a bung knee; was a self-proclaimed geriatric. He grinned 'like a rat with a gold tooth', to use a phrase he loved. He was a kind man, but racist, sexist and homophobic. Even for that part of the world he was anachronistic. A nasty divorce had left him with no car, so for a while he got around on his huge gelding, Hank, riding the back roads. When he did get a car, he drove very slowly. He'd begin trips by declaring: 'And we're off with the speed of a thousand startled turtles.' I used to look forward to hearing his car cross the third grid, beginning those jamboree nights when Mum and I would sing country music with him in the kitchen. Roy inspired me, gave me shots of rum in my coffee, taught me to build fences and to connect with the landscape I lived in. He was good to me and for a few years I loved him; but after I left Mum's, I totally ghosted him. What choice did I have? The facts of my life would have broken his heart.

*

When I was fourteen Mum kicked me out, to live in Wollongong with my father. When I was sixteen, I showed a Centrelink social worker my grades and convinced her it would be best for my father, his partner, my mother and me if my last two years of schooling were spent living alone. So I moved into the ground floor of a duplex under another family's house. The roof was so low I couldn't stand up, but there was space there, seclusion, to grow in new ways.

Grades weren't the issue. I graduated with a scholarship to study law and media at the University of New South Wales. Two years later I got a job as a journalist at *New Matilda*, on the environment beat. In December 2015 I covered the UN climate-change conference in Paris. The global response felt grimly absurd – I stood around with other journalists, negotiators and spectators, buying pre-poured, tin foil–capped wine in a converted aircraft hangar that felt like IKEA. I moved to Melbourne in July the next year.

I started gardening at my rental in Preston, a listless search for life. I brought in a truckload of soil, a ute tray of manure, and scattered seeds. I got stoned and wandered around in the flamboyant satin robe that a friend made me. High, screeching at birds, scratching at mulch, pretending I knew what I was doing. Mostly, though, I stayed in bed. I rarely left home. I didn't study or work. A good friend dubbed it my dark night of the soul. It was the time when I really started to grow up as a queer.

The only spaces that enlivened me were the queer clubs, which, by their liminal nature, grant us permission; inhibition is shaken loose and with our movement we speak of community. There was restoration in this euphoria for me, but it was fleeting and could not endure the day. The flesh and beat of a club would whisk me to a humid peak, and often I'd bring someone home; but when they left, a terrible nothing would climb into my bed to lie with me for the rest of the day. If I got to the previous night's dishes, I'd stare detachedly out the window and mark the progress of a noxious vine as it strangled our fence.

The time at clubs cost money and I often ran out. One day I couldn't make rent. I had to ask Mum. Dialling, I watched a bee dance with the violet flowers of the borage plants taking over the garden. I'd hardly asked anything of my parents since moving out years before. Since the days when we'd canter down straight stretches of flat road up Grady's Creek, I'd barely spoken to Mum. She agreed to cover the rent so long as I went to see a psychologist.

'Why don't you come on this trip with me?' Mum asked. She was going to Gundabooka National Park, near Bourke in inland New South Wales. 'If you're not doing anything, anyway. A change of scene might do you good.'

When I got off the phone I checked the book I'd been reading – Bruce Pascoe's *Dark Emu*. I wondered if the trip might take in the Ngunnhu, the Ngemba people's fish traps on the Barwon River. You can still see them in Brewarrina. They're thought to be the oldest enduring human constructions. I'd been outraged to learn how these marvels, about which we're not taught at school, have been all but erased from the rivers. Yes, Mum would be going right past the traps at Bre. The next day I called to tell her I'd come.

*

Mum picks me up in her red Subaru and we exit by the looping roads at Gold Coast Airport. She's not good at driving in cities. I give directions in what I hope is a patient voice, and feel panic rising. It's just us two and the few hundred kilometres to Bourke, on the edge of the desert, where we will see the last of the wildflowers. There's a lot of space for things to go wrong.

We stop at a small-town cafe named after its owner, Narelle. The kind of place where big brekkies are huge and a large cap is a muggaccino. We sit on the deck, watching big rigs roll by. Mum chatters cheerfully, glad to be clear of the city. Narelle appears to take our order.

'Mind if I smoke out here?' I ask her, gesturing at the deck.

'Fine,' she says, heading inside.

Then Mum starts. '*Oh darling*, please don't—'

'Trust me, Ma, it's better for both of us—'

'But not in front of me!'

'Come on, you know I smoke ... and you don't want to deal with me in withdrawal.'

This trip will be hard enough. We'll be together all day, every day for a week, driving, walking, camping, talking – which hasn't happened in at least five years. It's the start and I'm already burnt to the filter.

I'm exhausted from my time working at *New Matilda*. In the months after returning from Paris, I'd sit and smoke at the desk in my bedroom in Glebe, having given up on going into the office; drinking coffee like water and watching people pass by on the street with the feeling they were actors onscreen. Life narrowed down to this frame. I'd been so zealous before, so certain my witnessing mattered. In May 2016 I'd covered a blockade of coal ships at the Port of Newcastle and became infatuated with a dark, handsome boy. I'd pursued him to Melbourne, reported on the federal election, but resigned from *New Matilda* shortly thereafter. My romance had quickly gone stale and I'd done little since.

Mum and I cross the Darling Downs, drive through towns like Karara, Oman Ama, Yelarbon, Goondiwindi and Boggabilla. These places remind me of where I grew up. Country pubs, flat plains, monocrops and livestock; the quaint, invented points of interest that country people mark with homemade signs to stake a claim on the map. *We are here!* As a child these things interested me; they'd been shared ground with my mother.

We stop at a shed in the scrub with a sign on the fence that says 'Shop'. I order coffee (Nescafé Blend 43). Mum orders tea. I know now I don't belong in the country. How could I? But I hope these places will point back to some vestige of me – the part that still lives at The Risk, or else died when I left. Mum's not the only one who doesn't know where her little man went.

On the second night we stop at Moree, a popular retiree destination where the Great Artesian Basin burbles up through the earth and tourists berth their caravans and prune in hot water. I'd visited once before on a school trip, en route to Warrumbungle National Park, and learnt that people float more easily in the mineralised water. Tonight the 'grey nomads', as my mother affectionately calls them, wrinkle the pool. They grip the island at its centre and let their legs float behind them, occasionally kicking. After the pool closes I break back in and paddle lonely circles in the dark. What in God's name am I doing here?

The next day is a bad one. It's a long straight road between Moree and Bourke. Mum puts on country music and I jam in my earphones. I re-read Pascoe's book. I want to be alone, to not be. The road unspools like an endless black ribbon. My phone dies and I pull out my earbuds.

'Gosh, it's so beautiful out here,' Mum says, seizing her chance at conversation. 'The land is so flat. You can see forever.' She gestures at the grazing paddocks giving way to a crop. 'What do you think that is?'

'I don't know, Mum – maybe sorghum.' Then I charge in. 'Can you imagine what it would have been like before the invasion?' It's an accusation, somewhat rhetorical. 'It's so fucked that it's all been clear-felled – *that's* why you can see so far.' I open my window a crack and the wind makes that shrill noise it does when only one side is down.

Brewarrina is the next town we come to, but the information centre's closed. There will be no guide. We decide to wait until our return journey to see the traps.

'Oh well, darling. Let's go look at the old mission,' Mum says, consulting a pamphlet. 'It's just a few kilometres out.'

'Sure.' I shove in my earphones, even though my phone's dead, and peer through the window at the dirt road running red. I spot a mob of emus off in the mulga but say nothing. Mum struggles on alone to find the site. We come to a locked gate and she stops the car. It's obvious we've gone too far. Exasperated, she breaks the silence.

'What's wrong? What have I done?'

I take a long time to answer. 'Nothing.'

'Oh come on, Thom, it can't be nothing. You're ignoring me. What have I done to you?'

'It's not you, Mum. I'm just flat is all.'

'No, you suddenly went like this. What have I done? Do you want to come on this trip or not? I can turn the car around—'

'It doesn't work like that, Mum. It's not linear, causative. I'm just flat. I don't know ... *I want to kill myself.*' The beaded seat cover squeals as I face her. 'I'm really not sure what else to say; and if you don't get that – that it's not about you – I'm definitely not going to say anything else. Trust me, if I knew what the problem was I'd tell you. I'd fix it myself. I wouldn't be here. Can you just leave me alone?'

'Do you want to go back, is that it?' She's using her school-teacher voice.

I don't answer. I don't know. It doesn't seem to matter much either way.

We don't find the mission, but carry on in silence to Bourke. The hotel has a poky pool and two single beds that regard each other suspiciously across the small room. I throw my bag down and grab some beers, tell Mum I'm going for a walk.

I'd been to Bourke a few months earlier, just before moving to Melbourne, to report on a Fred Hollows Foundation reunion. I loved the place. Utes and trucks drift down its wide streets like tumbleweed. Groups of kids ride up to you on bikes to say hello. Graffiti on the courthouse reads: 'Shiela is a single sexy babe Brie chick', 'Clayton is a big sexy cunt in Bourke, he got sexy body and legs.' At the north edge of town, the slow, brown Darling River is beautiful – you can walk among fallen limbs and flitting birds and rarely spot another person. I climb up a water-monitoring tower and cry, chain-smoking ciggies. I imagine that the half-submerged gum logs bobbing by might be crocs.

I have always been filled with horror and smallness when I imagine crocodiles. Though I've never seen them in the wild, their spectres come for me at rivers and creeks. I'm terrified of their quiet way of secreting themselves and striking before you even know they are there; then, after the death roll, waters smooth over, more logs float by and the body decays in a cave. There are no crocs at Bourke, nor where I grew up, but to me these murky rivers look similar to the ones that I know do conceal them. Slow and gentle on the surface, there is turbulence underneath.

I climb down to the bank and start gathering rocks. Among the vegetation the air sings with insect frenzy. The sun is dipping. I hunt for just the right rocks. Throwing rocks, which I peg down at logs from the tower's serrated-steel platform. I remember something. I was watching for crocs one day as a child while my mother's boyfriend Bill and I watered our horses at Grady's Creek. We'd been working cattle in his yards, vaccinating heifers that were due to calve. In that moment, among the roiled dust, wooden fences and cowboy camaraderie, Bill seemed okay. I would cut a cow from the herd. He would open the gate and drive her into a corral that led to the crush. There, with the heifer securely wedged, he would look her over. From an old fridge in one yard I pulled out the supplies: medicine, a long pink glove. We rode to get more cattle from down by the creek.

'Hey,' Bill said. 'Thanks for your help today. Real help. You done good. Worked like a man.' He reefed his green mare's mouth away from the water, making to leave. 'Listen,' he added slowly. 'If you're gay, just don't ever tell anyone.'

I stayed there as he rode off and let my horse drink. My body was trussed up in a cave. I went home. It was never mentioned again.

*

Next morning, Mum and I drive into the national park. The plains are fat with the last of the rain. The car lolls like a big red tongue into Yanda Campground, on a swollen river's brink. It's hot but half-submerged trees stretch into the distance. There's no way to tell where the wildflower plains end and the river begins. We eat lunch at the picnic tables, under little roofs with swallows' nests in the corners, before I go fishing in the sun-warmed shallows. I want some time alone, to feel the heat of the almost-desert sun. Mum reminds me about snakes and insists I wear shoes, take a first-aid kit.

I photograph dragonflies at the water's edge, wondering why some flooded trees survive and others die. I photograph one tree up close. Its bark looks just like cracked mud. Only one species of wildflower seems to grow on the brink of this receding tide; it's pale blue and jumps off the red dirt and right down the lens, as if to say: *take me with you.*

I return to the campground empty-handed, having caught nothing.

'Let's camp at Dry Tank,' Mum says. 'Too many insects here, so close to the water.'

We sit reading that night at Dry Tank and the bugs are enormous. They wing in on the night sound and land on my brochure: a Christmas beetle, slick with oil-sheen; some armoured, pincered thing; a vampiric cicada so translucent I can read through its body. I take a photo of it, perched between Medical Services and Police. In the fluorescent glow of the camp light I spark a joint I'd picked up in Bourke. Mum doesn't say anything. Later, before bed, she explains how mosquitoes are not, as many people think, attracted to light. Actually, she says, they're drawn by carbon dioxide in our exhalations.

We break camp early to hike up Mount Gunderbooka, following the Valley of the Eagle track from Bennett's Gorge. The path to the base is hemmed in by scrub, spindly wattle that disorientates my senses. Occasionally the bush breaks open and thin, paper-leaved flowers churn like butter across drying flats. Then the vegetation recedes as we approach the mountain, brush yielding to grass, stone and squat, genuflecting shrubs. The summit is only 500 metres high, but the surrounding plains imbue the mountain with a turbulent and brooding power. It's as though in the beginning the syncline drew up all the energy this land had for rising. It's abrupt, but less stern than it seems; the hard, ancient sandstone forms a horseshoe shape to funnel water into the creeks and rivers that vein the endless lowlands.

We turn a bend and can see, suddenly, across a ravine. It's so wild; we pause to take it in. Rock folds in on itself in layers of time.

Tenacious trees with roots sunk between eons add to the palette of yellows and browns. There are eagles, too, little metal ones marking our track, and giant ones above, coasting on the currents of hot air that circulate the gorges. We're almost at the top, the rocks loose and sliding underfoot.

'I can't go all the way,' Mum says, doubled over. 'I'm fine walking uphill but, with my knee, I'm worried I won't be able to come back down.' She takes a long slug of water. 'You go up, if you want to.'

'Come on, Mum,' I say. 'I'll go slow with you.'

She shakes her head.

'Are you sure?'

'Yes. I'll wait for you here.'

*

Space is never neutral; cartographies of power and memory are always at play. In telling this story I've remembered so many little details, events, things that were said; a childhood of moments caught in my throat. That feeling of wanting the earth to swallow me up – I pushed it into my stomach, trying, always, to forget who I am. And it hurts to remember, because I feel the keening again in my guts; memories like oesophageal cancer, spreading and hard to control; the rawness of words, misshapen and wailing, that were never said. They belong to a child the world told to be mute. My throat caught on the soccer field – that joke about a loose anus. I think someone else farted, not me. I don't remember. But I can still feel the terror that I'd been found out, the panic he'd seen something in my gaze while he slept on the couch and I thought it was safe. He was my best friend at the Kyogle soccer club, for which I played every primary-school season. So many trivial moments, like that, refusing to pass. They count their own time. Repression has its own style of reason; does not follow the logic of our conscious minds. It's an adult's work, handling bile.

Without a shared experience of place, it's easy for queers to forget we're not alone. My experience is that country people fill up the vast spaces with silence. As a child I learnt to do likewise and that has robbed me of so many stories. Mum's now sold her place at The Risk. I can never go back to the verandah where we ate in the summers, overlooking the Wilsons' paddocks and the Lions Road; it snakes past The Risk Hall, where our school put on plays, into the Border Ranges and Queensland. I shared that place with my sisters, Jess and Holly, and Mum; share with Jess the memory of when Holly peed on our heads, from above in a tree she'd climbed up to escape, after we'd induced one of the laughing fits that made veins in her neck bulge. We just circled the tree, chanting: 'Now who's laughing! Now who's laughing?'

Those are the stories I've shared. I've never shared how Bill advised me to hide. I'd forgotten it until that day in Bourke, but in retrospect, it was the first moment in which I knew for sure someone else understood I was queer. Did Bill see something revolting? Or was he trying, perversely, to help, knowing there were more brutal silencers than him in the paddocks and pubs, and that if I made myself visible they'd do me a violence I would not forget? Because the truth is silence *can* offer protection. Invisibility can offer safety, and sometimes hiding is wise.

I am non-binary, as well as gay, and every day when I wake up, get dressed and do my face, I evaluate the risks of being seen. I am bold and I am loud, but some mornings I try on every skirt and dress and pass judgement on each: absurd, laughable, just a bit off. I stand back to appraise myself in the mirror's full length. Its face rests on hinges that creak to reveal a compartment concealing earrings and make-up. These hinges are busted. Unless I hold the thing up when it's open, it will fall down and shatter. It's often easier just to wear pants, a shroud for the body, to shelter the brain.

My body and brain are non-compliant – deviant, as I'm reminded daily by forms and toilets and slips of the tongue. This morning, I was reminded by an old woman. As I boarded the bus to Footscray, she reached for her rosary, muttering, glaring, beginning to count. I was wearing a skirt of thick, sweatpant fabric, white skivvy, eye shadow and chunky hoops. Well, Glory Be. To hell with you, lady.

Invisibility can offer safety, but at costs of healing and growth. Silence can protect, but also disempower. I saw a eulogy for Roy, my childhood mentor, on Facebook a while ago. At least that's what it looked like, saying something about him having loved a jamboree. I didn't click through. In fact, I scrolled even faster. I felt a shock of recognition. It wasn't only that Roy had died – I hadn't spoken to him for over a decade, although I'd felt guilty about that often enough – it was realising I'd now never know how he would have received me. The hurt and rejection I'd feared as a child will live on – indeterminate, spectral – and he will never see me in power, as an unafraid adult. I used to think vulnerability was power's antithesis. Now I see silence is. I'm still growing up as a queer person, still unlearning things I absorbed as a child.

*

On the last night of my road trip with Mum, we talked for the first time about why she kicked me out. It went like the last light of the sun, all in a blaze. Neither of us was able to offer more than raw sides of pain, but at least those cuts gave some things form; it felt cathartic to name wounds left undressed for so long. We talked, of course, about much more than my queerness: a whole childhood.

Next day in the car, on the way back to the airport, I told Mum the story about Bill.

'That's got nothing to do with me,' she said.

I didn't reply. Shame welled inside. Mum only wanted to show me the last of the wildflowers, and I'd made things so hard. We returned to the city in silence. We were running early, but I told her just to drop me at the airport.

I made my way through security, scrubbing my eyes. A middle-aged woman with a brunette bob and sun-weathered skin watched as I waited for my bag to roll under the scanner. Walking through the security archway I pulled it together. I grabbed my akubra, mustered a weak smile.

'Are you okay, honey?' asked the woman when my bag reappeared.

'I'm sorry,' I said. 'But my mother is dead.'

I just wanted to be left alone, in silence.

*

Adjusting my skirt, I wave goodbye to a friend at Konjo Cafe and rush for the bus. Hot skin clasps the skirt's heavy fabric. I'm late, but happy. A small Melbourne publisher has just emailed to say they'll take me on as an intern. After my interview a few days earlier, I'd stood at the top of a flight of stairs outside the State Library, looking – my friend told me – like a young, camp Bon Jovi. 'Whatever,' I'd said. 'I'm a zany publisher now.' Cocking my head, I wafted my wine glass over the city and made a retaliatory threat to my friend's future career.

Back in Footscray, I read the publisher's offer another two times. Do a little dance at the bus stop in front of Sunny's. The 216 must almost be here. There's a bunch of people about. It's a nice day and I'm feeling cute, despite the coffee stain on my white skivvy.

I hear muttering before spotting the guy. His red face is henpecked, grey hoodie mottled with some darker lint. He shuffles along. Bit rough, maybe wired; getting louder. A few metres off now, he's shooting me spasmodic glances. I keep one eye on him, sly peeps so as not to provoke. It's fine. He passes. Then, ten metres or so up the street, he halts and hurls back over his shoulder: 'Fuck you up the arse with a baseball bat, cunt!'

I laugh, loudly, for others to hear, and then affect an extravagant curtsy. Looking around at those waiting with me, nobody seems able to meet my eyes.

When Worlds Collide, Words Fail

Thinesh Thillainadarajah
தினேஷ் தில்லைநடராஜா

On a September morning three years ago, Appa called me, crying on the phone.

Two weeks earlier, I had dropped off a letter at the mailbox around the corner, unsure of when it would reach Appa's tender hands on the other side of the world. Hands that swiped the metro card at four in the morning, wading through Canadian avalanches to make ends meet. Hands that had hung a canvas print of Mufasa and Simba on the wall above the bed he and I used to share, symbolic of just a morsel of the love that only children of immigrant parents know. The same hands that used to hold me on Saturday mornings as I split open chocolate eggs to reveal the plastic magic contained inside, magic that Appa revelled in as much as I.

When I saw 'Appa calling' on the screen of my phone, my heart sank, anticipating the disappointment of my parents, the breaking of a chain that stretched across the globe, holding them and me together. My white boyfriend, our relationship just shy of three years, stood in the doorway to our bedroom speaking to his own parents, as he had for years, in a kind honesty and openness I had never known.

Appa sobbed. He asked why I was choosing this. Through his wails, he asked why I had not told him earlier, said that he would have had another child to be my keeper. I wanted to comfort him, but in that moment I failed to do so, unable to articulate my thoughts the way my letter had, the way six months of writing and rewriting had allowed me to do. I never hated myself more – for speaking Tamil, if you can even call it that, with a childish cadence

127

and a Western intonation, unable to bridge a canyon's worth of vocabulary between us. I wanted Appa to hear past my inarticulate sentences. I wanted my words to convey precision and conviction. I was desperately grasping at all the Tamil I could, but I could only muster up '*alavendaam*' ('do not cry'), removed from the poetic world of Surya and Jyothika – reminiscent of a lilt you'd hear in children's programming.

I choked on the silence and pain, unsure of where to take the conversation. No amount of YouTube videos and queer think pieces prepared me for this moment. But I was not naive enough to think they would. It does not get better. It just gets lost in communication.

Amma interjected. She said that someone she knew had got married – and had separated shortly after. In coded language, she insinuated that she was familiar with my secrets. She asked if I was okay – I was. She asked if I needed to speak to someone – I did not. She thanked me for sharing this part of myself and said I needn't worry. She dismissed Appa's sobs and wails, and said that he would get over it.

I felt a sense of calm take over. As I looked out the window of my apartment, the Australian sun's morning rays seemed to shine brighter with the glimmer of a salvageable relationship. Of course Amma, level-headed Amma, would know how to handle this. Amma, who would run to catch the bus in her $20 wedges to get to her factory job miles away, would again know what to do so we could make it through.

'Do not tell anyone about this,' Amma then said.

And just like that, my heart sank to the floor.

There was silence, and in that silence it became clear that private tolerance – even private acceptance – was still public shame.

Amma and Appa now knew my deepest truths, and we were at the brink of a relationship we had never had before that morning. But the fear of stigmatisation, exclusion and gossip fodder would follow Amma and Appa, snapping at their heels like a pack of hungry wolves. That fear would drive them to keep up appearances for *Sithappa* and *Sithi* overseas, *Oor* gatherings, and *Kōyil* folks, enabling them to continue living their lives in relative peace. I was stupid to think that my parents' love could not withstand who

I loved. It was not them not loving me or accepting me that would keep my love for him a secret. Rather, it was their fear of sharp tongues spitting venom and spreading lies about them, isolating them from their community and shredding their souls, and consequently shredding mine.

My queer identity took me away from not only my family, but also my Tamilness. I had split open the Red Sea, and torn myself away from the world that my parents had built for me stone by stone, and moved to Australia – a land that rejects my Tamilness – trading it in desperation to feed my queer soul. In the blood-orange desert, my queer identity was a battle I could fight alone, wrestling with myself in isolation, saving Amma and Appa from an unnecessary struggle with Tamil society. They'd spent their entire lives fighting for everything else that they had. Who was I to deprive them of the only community they connect with? The only space they have allowed themselves to have so I could grow up free from trauma and with the privilege of choosing to leave?

Now, as I sit in chrome birds suspended in the night sky, memorising the layouts of yellow flickering cities below me, I think about how the person I loved made the same journey across the world to understand where I came from, knowing it was unlikely he would be welcomed with open arms. I think about how he stayed in my old room, felt the *manjal* between his fingertips, dunked the *vadai* into the *sambar* at my best friend's wedding in a *Kurtha* – as just my 'friend'.

I wanted him to experience a fraction of Tamilness the way I had and get to the fulcrum of my straddling identities, to sit through problematic *Rajinikanth* films with Appa, fall in love with the melodic richness of *Anjali*, eat *roast paan* and *sambal* on my family's cloth-covered couch with Amma, with the Tamil radio humming in the kitchen and Sun TV simultaneously blaring from the TV.

But even then I could see the wolves nipping at my parents' door.

When the wheels hit the tarmac, I wonder whether my queer existence will ever be reconciled with the duties of being an only child in the Tamil community. I want to care for my parents into old age, ensuring they feel a sense of belonging, despite having embraced their queer son. How much longer will I betray myself into small silences? Will I ever be able to rejoin Tamil society, having fleshed out my queerness on my own terms, while raising a queer family of my own? Or will I be ground into dust, waiting for someone else to speak?

I dream of creating space and having a queer presence within the Tamil community. I am tired of waiting to be represented. There are queer Tamil activists doing amazing and much-needed work in white spaces. However, I want to weave together my Tamil life and my queer one, because there are undoubtedly many others like me: Tamil society is complex and should be represented as such. As Audre Lorde says, if I don't define myself for myself, I will be crunched into other people's fantasies for me and eaten alive.

However, I am nervous. To fully embrace my Tamil and queer identities, I need to make myself visible. I need to be visibly Tamil in queer spaces, and dare to be visibly queer in Tamil spaces. I don't want other people to have authority over my Tamilness or my queerness. I know this community has not been made for me.

But I am not going to apologise for being here. I am not going to apologise for existing.

Radelaide/Sadelaide

Gemma Killen

You are born in 1987, on the fourteenth of June. Your 10 pm arrival makes you a Gemini sun with an Aquarius rising. Basically, you are prone to both vacuous chatter and long bouts of staring pensively out windows, certain that the whole world is about to collapse. This could be because of a perfect spewing of planets across the sky at the exact time of your birth, or it could be because the world is large and your nervous tongue is small but ambitious.

The Queen Elizabeth Hospital is just over the back fence of your parents' house and Mum waddles over when she goes into labour. You are delivered into the world a full month earlier than expected – impatience is another key feature of your Gemini–Aquarius complexion – so you spend your first days in a box, carefully monitored, gently regulated. When it is all done, Mum waddles home again, a nurse carrying you all the way to the front door. Dad buys a bottle of Gordon's Dry Gin to celebrate. Mum rolls her eyes.

Depending on who you ask, Adelaide is known as the city of churches or the murder capital of the world. There are certainly a lot of churches – more than five hundred built from stone and sand, and countless more unseen, sacella born of lounge-room piety and furtive glances across classrooms. You are never sure exactly how the city got its murderous reputation, but the halfway point between home and school is marked by the house where a man killed his lover, chopped him to pieces and put him in the freezer for safe-keeping. This, too, feels like a kind of prayer.

Mum wants you to go to Sunday school. You make a face.

Geminis are fickle and the Aquarian influence makes you susceptible to rebellion.

When the powers that be first designed Adelaide, they argued over the exact location of the city in relation to its main harbour. Colonel William Light chose a site fourteen kilometres south-east of the port, and planned to run a canal between the two points. It would be the aorta of South Australian trade. However, the route was uphill, and the water refused to flow in the right direction.

In 2001 you decide to become a Goth. This is, in part, a response to your parents' divorce, which is at once messy and completely silent. One day Dad is there and the next he's not, banished to the other side of the world. It feels as though the scripture is beginning to reveal itself as nothing more than desperate scrawling. In part, it is because of Izzy.

Adelaide was designed with morality in mind. Good men, definitely white, definitely not convicts, would be sold tiny boxes of land and they would live sensible, straightforward lives with sensible, straightforward wives. The South Australian Colonisation Commissioners drew up plans and bickered about how best to strike lines in the dirt so that the men who walked them would be on the right side of virtue. Never mind what came before, as long as they could control what came after.

You buy a black dress with lace sleeves from the old Brickworks markets, borrow your sister's battered Doc Martens, strap an upturned cross to your neck and smother your eyes with so much cheap eyeliner you immediately begin to cry. Which helps, because tear-stained is just the kind of dramatic look you're going for.

Izzy's legs are hairy and she is so pale you swear you can see the messy knot of blood beneath her skin, thudding in time with your own heart. On days when you feel the teetering of the Earth and the pull of the Moon too strongly, she strokes your back and lets you wear her favourite cat necklace.

Your sister warns you about how obsessive lesbians can be, and you burn with silence in the back of the car. The lights of the western suburbs flash past the window, blinking in code.

The streets of Adelaide are lined with steel-wrapped concrete poles that commune with the edges of the sky. They were designed by James Cyril Stobie from the Adelaide Electric Supply Company when the city was faced with a dwindling timber supply that twisted and crumbled between the teeth of termites. Now, primary schools are given licence to mural their local poles, and some neighbourly folk coat the ones outside their houses with chalkboard paint, inviting passers-by to see the resplendent contents of their minds and the occasional drawing of a penis. These indestructible alien forms were not part of the plan for the city, yet there they now stand, sacred towers adorned with art and dicks.

Izzy holds your hand when you go to see *Bridget Jones's Diary* and afterwards, over pancakes, she asks you to be her girlfriend via a tiny note, haphazardly torn from her maths exercise book. You turn the piece of paper over and write *yes*, push the paper back into her hand. She is an Aquarius, her birthday two days before Valentine's Day. She jokes that she was born already resisting heteronormative romance narratives. This makes you exceptionally compatible. She is eight hundred and fifty-two days older and three centimetres taller than you. The taste of her lips cannot be quantified, but you learn that it can be drawn out, made to linger in the chasm of your mouth.

The school calls your mum and tells her about your inappropriate relationship with another female student.

For all its plans and well-drawn lines of rectitude, Adelaide's main exports are AFL players and wine. It also leads the country in number of sex shops per capita. The idea was a forgetful utopia, so drunk on middle-class propriety that it could ignore its violent beginnings. The reality is something else.

After you swallow handfuls of pills, Izzy comes to visit you in the hospital, climbs into the bed next to you and puts her head on your shoulder. She brings food too, eager to keep you safe from hospital meals. You can barely eat, having turned yourself inside out in search of God's plan. She is kind, but her kisses feel like rough penance.

At home, Mum comes into your room and tells you the stories of the babies she lost before you arrived. She outlines the plan she had for each of them, for you: a husband (white, of course), a baby, a house in a suburb just like this one. She gently tucks your hair behind your ear. Sometimes, she says, the best part happens after you lose faith in the design.

Sometimes the planets dance, the rivers run the wrong way and the timber curls. Sometimes, you turn out gay.

LGBTI-Q&A:

William Yang

Australia's leading social photographer

Benjamin Law: Tell me about where you were born and grew up.
William Yang: I was born in 1943, in Mareeba in north Queensland, and I grew up in the town of Dimbulah, where my father had a tobacco farm.

Before we talk about you being gay, tell me more about 'discovering' you were Chinese.
When I was about six years old, one of the kids at school called me 'Ching Chong Chinaman, born in a jar, christened in a teapot, ha ha ha'. I had no idea what he was talking about. But I knew he was being horrible to me. So I went home to my mother and said to her, 'Mum, I'm not Chinese, am I?' And my mother looked at me very sternly and she said, 'Yes. You. Are.' Her tone was hard and it shocked me. And I knew in that moment that being Chinese was like some terrible curse, and I could not rely on my mother for help. Or my brother, who was four years older than me, very much more experienced in the world. He chimed in: 'And you'd better get used to it.'

Was it similarly confronting discovering your sexuality?
Well, I knew from a very early age that I was attracted to men, although because I was so young, I didn't really realise it was sexual. We had workers on the farm, and I was always attracted to the good-looking ones.

You're really painting a scene there. Handsome farm workers picking tobacco. Very cinematic.
It could be a fantasy, yes.

Do you still remember your first crush?
Yes, it was a person in high school. It was kind of painful in a way; it never went anywhere. Around that time, I was at high school in Cairns, maybe about sixteen. I was reading the afternoon newspaper, and I came across an article on homosexuality. It named three famous ones in history. The shock of recognition hit me like a thunderbolt. I thought, 'Oh god, there's a name for it.'

Was that reassuring or terrifying?
It wasn't reassuring, but there was a certain recognition of self. But now I thought there were four homosexuals in the world: Oscar Wilde, Michelangelo, Leonardo da Vinci and me. It wasn't until many years later that I came out, in Sydney, after university in Brisbane. I was swept out in the gay liberation movement in the early '70s in Sydney.

Was it only after arriving in Sydney that you met another openly gay person?
No, no. When I was in Brisbane I was extremely friendly with another person. We kind of knew that each other was gay, although it was never physical. There was a friendship.

Was it a friendship where you were able to have frank conversations about your sexuality?
No, no, no. That was never mentioned. Or it was hinted at, rather than never mentioned. He'd tell me … he'd sometimes go down to Sydney and have a wild, debauched weekend. I was very unconfident, but as it was, I took his photograph. That was the substitute for having sex: taking his photograph. With the camera between us, I felt I had certain liberties. I could say 'take off your shirt' or 'lie on the bed' and these commands didn't seem as threatening as they would have without the camera between us. So that was how I kind of got my substitute. I found that intensely exciting: taking photographs of handsome men. It was a ritual very much like

having sex with a person, only we didn't have sex, we acted out – or at least I was acting out – a kind of fantasy.

Do you have a coming-out story, per se?
When I came to Sydney, this friend of mine was living in a gay situation, with drag queens. They all just assumed I was gay, so I didn't really have to come out. So that was easy, although only those people recognised I was gay. But during gay liberation in the early '70s in Sydney, there were more and more people coming out as being gay. We, the early gay people, really had a lot of trouble recognising other gay people. There were always conversations: 'Is he gay or isn't he?' And, 'Should I put the hard word on him?' Those kinds of situations. One of the things that developed in gay culture in those early days was a dress code: moustaches, butch clothing, like construction workers.

What about now? What are the things central to gay culture nowadays that you couldn't have anticipated when you were growing up gay?
There's been an evolution in how to find people. You can be very specific on Grindr, and find people who have specific tastes. I'm fairly old in terms of the gay – what would you say? – scale of desirability. Yet there are people who like older men.

Expand on that for me. What do you mean low on the 'scale of desirability'?
Well, most people don't like older gay people. There's age discrimination. You become less desirable. But there are people who like older men. You would never find this out at a bar, but you can with the internet. It's just a more sophisticated way of hooking up with people.

How do you feel about where we are politically and socially with our attitudes towards the queer community? What do you think of the progress that's been made in your lifetime?
Oh, a huge amount of progress has been made. In fact, the history of the gay community in Australia shows that there can be social change within forty years, or fifty years. From the attitudes I grew

up with in Queensland – totally suppressive – to attitudes now where the majority of people approve of gay people and give them permission to marry, that's a huge change. Even I feel emboldened by that. I feel more confident in telling the gay story of my life.

Say you could go back in time and speak to the young version of William Yang: the teenage version of you crushing on boys; the twenty-something version of you in Sydney. What advice would you give them?
Well, there was one thing: I always thought I was extremely unattractive. I would tell my younger self that I had something that I didn't realise that I had: I had youth. I was young. That's something you never realise until you've lost it. So I'd say to my younger self to be more confident. I didn't feel confident about the way I looked, and that's a racial thing. There's still lots of people who say, 'No Asians.' But Asians have got a much higher profile now in Australia than they had in the '70s.

And what advice would you have for people growing up queer today?
You're okay. You have a right to be on this earth as much as any other person. There are a lot of people still that tell you that your sexuality is wrong, or sick. That isn't true. You're valid as a human. You've just got every right to be here as the next person.

LGBTI-Q&A:

Georgie Stone
Actor and transgender rights advocate

Benjamin Law: Your immediate family includes a mum, a dad, a son – your twin brother, Harry – and you, a daughter. When did your parents discover they had a son and a daughter?
Georgie Stone: It was different times for both of them. I first told Mum that I was a girl when I was two and a half years old – very young.

That's so young. Do you even remember telling her?
It's sort of my earliest memory. I just remember having watched the movie *Cinderella* – the Disney animation – I turned to Mum and was like, 'I'm a girl, just like Cinderella.' I was so young, she would've thought, 'Oh, it's a phase; experimenting and exploring.' But it was about the age of four or five, when I was in kindergarten, I really wanted to dress up in the dresses. But I was conscious people would find that weird, and I was getting quite distressed about it. I kept telling my parents, 'I'm a girl, I'm a girl.' That's when Mum thought, 'Oh, this is more than what we thought it would be,' but Dad was like, 'No, just don't think about it; it's alright.' Apparently, both of them were praying to God that I would end up gay, not trans.

Oh, that's interesting. Why?
When Mum was twenty, she was going to rallies – she's from Tasmania – for being gay to be decriminalised. But in terms of trans people, she didn't know much, and there was no representation of trans kids. She thought that if I was trans, I'd have a very

bleak life. It was when I was around five when Mum thought I was actually female. For Dad, it was seven or eight, because I started to become quite suicidal. He realised that the best way to support me wasn't to stop me [from being a girl], but to listen to me and accept me for who I am.

To be suicidal at eight is really serious. What happened?
It was really in school. I was made to use the male toilets, wear the male uniform, have short hair. I felt very, very restricted. It was getting to the point, when I was seven, when I thought enough is enough, I can't keep doing this. What helped me out of that dark period was Mum. She was looking on the internet for help and, after a long time searching, she finally found Dr Campbell Paul at the Royal Children's Hospital – the only person she could find who was working with trans kids. That was in 2007. I ended up being the third trans kid he met with.

It's one thing to be trans. It's another thing to publicly advocate for trans rights and issues. You've appeared on TV a lot: *Four Corners*, *Australian Story* and *The Project*. Why was it important to you – even as you were still growing up – to tell your story publicly?
It definitely wasn't something I wanted to do all my life. For a long time I just thought, 'Okay, I'm a girl, but I'm just not going to talk about it. No one needs to know.' I liked the feeling of being taken at face value. Then when I was fourteen, I came out to my friends and they were so accepting of me. I started to see that the world was different to what I thought it was; that there was more acceptance than I thought there was. So then I thought, 'Okay, I don't care who knows.' I felt like I had an obligation: there are so many young trans people who are so isolated, and feel so alone, and in that really bleak space, who can't do anything or feel they can't speak up. I'm supported by my family, I have the resources, I have – I suppose – the privilege to do it. I experience privilege as a white person, as an able-bodied person. So I thought, 'I'm in this position where I actually can make a difference.' And I felt like I should. We need that positive representation.

When you share your story publicly, what are the reactions that you get from people? What reactions have surprised you?
What's surprising is that the people you think would be supportive are often not – or are a bit ignorant. For example, I've never met her before, but J.K. Rowling is someone I looked up to my whole life, and it turns out she's a bit transphobic. She's very progressive – and she's supportive of the gay community to an extent – but in terms of trans people, not so much. It disappointed me because I was such a massive *Harry Potter* fan. And then, some people have called in on talkback radio from outback Australia who've been very supportive. So, support can come from very unexpected places. I've found that the majority of the time, there has been support, or at least people have been willing to have an open mind and listen. That said, I get attacked sometimes on Twitter. After I won Victorian Young Australian of the Year, there was so much hatred, and that was actually a bit hard to watch. Usually I've been able to brush stuff off, but they'd organised themselves, so there were heaps of people who were really up in arms about it.

Are there also other ways in which transphobia can manifest, rather than the ways that are probably more obvious to people?
Two weeks ago – on my first day of uni – I was in a lecture and the lecturer went off on a tangent about how there was a push in Japan against the restrictive traditional way people dress, especially when going for jobs. Then she said, 'Women want to wear pants and men want to wear dresses, so there's a push for transgender people.' I was thinking, 'That's a bit stupid,' because trans people aren't men in dresses. I'm not a man in a dress; I'm a woman. She wasn't against trans people, it was just ignorant. Another one is people saying, 'I don't see gender' – which, firstly, I think is bullshit, because it comes from someone who isn't non-binary. And it disregards the trauma a lot of trans and gender-diverse people feel. If you say you don't see gender, you're also refusing to look at the transphobia that we face, and you're refusing to acknowledge our gender identity as well.

What are the things you'd be happy never to talk about again when it comes to transgender issues?

One thing I do get asked about way too much – and it is actually quite disrespectful – is my genitalia. For some reason, complete strangers feel like it's appropriate to ask a trans person whether they have a penis or not. I got that at a function when I was sixteen, by this old, white person, and I felt really uncomfortable.

It's like: in what other situation would a grown adult ask a sixteen-year-old about their genitals? Or anyone?

I was almost tempted to ask, 'Well, what do *you* have?' I didn't, obviously, but it was really yuck. And it happens a lot. People feel like they have the right to ask trans people that.

Do you have a strategy for when you get that question? Especially for young trans people, have you found a best practice for responding?

I'm a bit of a people pleaser. If someone asks me that I'll try and go, 'Oh no, it's alright. You didn't know. It's okay.' But honestly, don't feel like you have to make them feel right. Don't feel like you have to answer that. Don't apologise. Don't feel like you have to explain yourself. You absolutely have the right to say, 'No, I don't want to answer that. That is disrespectful.' You can educate them by doing that. So I'm perfectly happy to not answer that question ever again, and for people to not ask that.

What conversations should we be having more about and with transgender people?

How to be a good ally.

What constitutes being a good ally of trans people, for you?

Learn the pronouns. It's good to ask questions about this; don't feel embarrassed. Like: 'What pronouns do you want me to use?' and 'What do you feel comfortable with?' Then listen. Really just listen to what they have to say.

LGBTI-Q&A:

Tony Ayres
Screenwriter, showrunner and director

Benjamin Law: Where and when were you born and where did you grow up?
Tony Ayres: I was born in Macau in 1961; we came to Australia in 1964. I kind of grew up in Melbourne, then when I was eleven I went to Perth with my sister and mother. That's probably where I first realised I was gay and where I came out.

Do you remember your first crush?
The very first clear crush I had was in high school. I would have been about fourteen. It was a boy I was just madly in love with.

Describe him for me.
His name was Michael. He was a basketballer and I was a nerdy, academic chess-player – the cliché of the Asian student.

Whereas he was the classic hot jock?
Yeah, but he had this other part of him which was a little bit unknowable and he was a bit of a loner. He actually became my best friend. But I knew I was in love with him because whenever it was recess or lunchtime, I would look from the classroom into the rectangle to see whether he was there or not. [*Laughs*] I basically stalked him.

Were you equipped with the vocabulary for what you were feeling?
Well, I was reading a lot of D.H. Lawrence then, so I did have a vocabulary, but it was all very tortured and kind of Freudian. I was

also listening to a lot of Joni Mitchell, so I had another sort of vocabulary – also very tortured.

[*Laughs*] You were such a sensitive boy.
In my first year at university, I went away to Canberra. Just before I left, I wrote him a letter saying what I felt for him. I basically told him I was in love with him. He never responded.

Oh. Was that devastating?
I guess it was. But you know, I'd also discovered beats and saunas then, so I had lots of distractions.

You soothed yourself with the ancient remedy of cock.
[*Laughs*] The weird irony is that the year after, when I was seventeen and at university, I met the next man I fell in love with, whose name was also Michael.

[*Laughs*] You've got a Michael complex. When you were first becoming cogniscent of your sexuality, what was the social conversation around you at the time when it came to homosexuality?
Homosexuality was never discussed. I went to high school in Western Australia. My best friend was an Indian guy called Bobby and my other great friend was a guy called Steven, who used to star in all the school musicals. In subsequent years, I discovered both of them were gay, but we never talked about anything even remotely gay.

But you were on the same frequency.
Somehow we were attracted to each other, but it was never raised. I'm not conscious of anything overtly homophobic from those years. It was just an invisible topic. And maybe we avoided it because it was too close to the bone … too closer to the boner.

Tell me about your coming out.
I became an orphan young, so I wasn't dealing with family expectations – which, I think, particularly for a lot of people from Asian backgrounds, is such a big thing. Whereas I had no one to come out to.

So your letter to Michael was your first coming out?
No, my first coming-out experience was to my history teacher.

How old were you?
I was sixteen. It was my final year at high school. I was living with him and his wife and two kids at that stage, because I was an orphan, and he took me under his wing. I just very nervously said to him one night, 'Oh, I'm gay.' He was a sort of progressive straight guy who was trying to show me that it was all okay. He said, 'Oh, okay. Well, let's celebrate,' and took me to an illegal casino and we gambled. Because I was coming out to him as something illegal, he was showing me his world.

Showing you something illicit too.
It was just a strange night, but he accepted me and I told his wife. Then I told my sister. She and I went on this driving tour through New Zealand. The first thing she did was get up, burst into tears and run away down a track. She came back about ten minutes later and said, 'I don't know how to respond.' Then after that, it was just kind of fine.

Have you ever had hostile experiences when it's come to your sexuality?
I guess when you're walking along the street and you're holding hands with someone at Mardi Gras, someone will shout out of a car. But it means nothing to me.

I guess you've built yourself on that bedrock of having everyone okay with it.
The most difficult thing that I had to face, in terms of my sexuality, was that it was my first real experience of racism. That was the headfuck for me. Originally I thought, 'No one around me is upset about it, so I'll just walk into this gay world where I'll be accepted by all these other men and have a friendship circle.' I kind of went bang into this brick wall where suddenly I wasn't a gay man; I was a Chinese gay man.

You come into this other minority world and encounter – how would you describe it? Exclusion?

Racism only hurts when you actually want to be a part of something. I remember going to this gay bar in Canberra and being really nervous and excited and cycling there. I sat down in the bar, bought myself a beer and looked around. Over two hours, no one would look at me, no one would talk to me. The only people who ended up being nice to me were the drag queens. Who were hilarious! But I just felt that I was not a part of something.

Which makes you question your worth and attractiveness; all of that stuff.

At a time when you're trying to come to terms with who you are and your own sense of who you are within the world, you're constantly second-guessing. 'Oh, did that person not like me because of who I am, or did that person just categorically not like me?' All of those questions were very undermining. Coming out was both coming out as being gay and coming out as being gay and Chinese. Those two things can't be separated. They cannot be untangled from my experience of the gay world. It's a complicated issue because nothing triggers gay men more than the accusation that they're racist.

Yes. 'How dare you! I'm homosexual, I'm already oppressed, I can't oppress others!'

And also: 'You can't tell me who I should and shouldn't be attracted to! I've fought my whole life for the right to be attracted to who I want.' You can't be critical of that. And of course, you're not going to force people to sleep with you if they don't want to sleep with you.

But if you're saying someone is unattractive solely on the basis of their race – in a sexual context or otherwise – that has to be fundamentally racist.

I agree with that. But I sort of feel like in a way we need to reframe the argument. Desire is racialised for some men. Not for all men but for some men. And there are cultural institutions that reinforce those things. And the more that we can try to break down those things – like even representations of what is attractive – then maybe the rigid barriers we put around race and desire will also start to become more porous. When I was growing up, even I had that feeling: 'I don't find other Asian men attractive.' But that changed when I went on this long trip to China and found myself surrounded by other Asian men. They stopped being Asian men and they started just being men.

Same thing happened for me. I told myself I didn't find Asian men attractive. Then I spent months in Japan. And of course you're just surrounded by attractive Asian men, and new images of beauty.
It makes you realise we are all affected by culture. For me, the questions about sexuality and coming out are deeply entangled with racial questions.

If you could go back in time to those mid-teen years and give young Tony a pep talk or advice, what would you say?
I would just say, 'You're going to get through this.' Now I feel completely blessed. Michael and I are having our fortieth anniversary this year and we've been together all this time. We've had ups and downs – and ins and outs [*Laughs*] – but we're at the point in our lives where we are both so deeply grateful to still have each other. To still feel for each other the way that we do, I feel like I'm blessed.

LGBTI-Q&A:

Sally Rugg
Executive director at Change.org Australia

Benjamin Law: When did you first think you were different to the heterosexual kids around you?
Sally Rugg: When I realised I was gay, I was about nineteen. It was honestly like this penny-drop moment, where all of a sudden everything made sense. All this information about myself – all these memories and feelings – suddenly crystallised. Retrospectively, it's like, 'Oh my god, of course.' But I didn't know. I was having sex with women and didn't ...

Put two and two together?!
No!

You were already having sex with women, so why hadn't it already crystallised in your mind?
Partly denial. And everybody was doing it. My friends at school – I went to an all-girls school – were all making out with each other at parties in front of boys, which was my favourite thing to do.

But the others were doing it in a more performative way?
Definitely. But also I can imagine they were exploring their sexualities as well.

But you were going all the way.
But always with their boyfriends, never just one-on-one. So that also felt risqué.

What changed at nineteen?

I had a crush on a girl in a way that was different to anything before. I couldn't get this person out of my head. I would go to sleep thinking about this girl. I remember driving down Stirling Highway in Perth and it clicked in my head, this sudden realisation. I had an autonomic response to this realisation. And it felt like realising I had cancer.

Gee. How so?

I was driving and crying, because all of a sudden there was a thing inside me. I didn't choose it, I couldn't get rid of it, I couldn't control it.

Where do you think you got that negativity from, in terms of how you saw gayness and queerness?

I remember feeling the world was going to be hostile towards me. I'd always been really ambitious and wanted to do big things. All of a sudden, I was realising it was going to be much harder for me if I came out, because the world is hostile to gay people. I didn't know any gay people growing up. The first time I heard about gayness was when I learnt it as a slur, and that slur was used against me in high school. All my friends in high school suspected I was gay. [*Laughs*] They called it. I got called 'Rugg-muncher' in high school.

You don't want to be the thing people tease you about.

Exactly. One of the other things I was scared of was that friends of mine would say, 'I told you so.' The shame that other people knew this thing about me before I knew it. I hated that.

Is that what ended up happening? That friends told you 'I told you so'?

No. They were just supportive. And uninterested. [*Laughs*]

A lot of people know you mostly for the work you do advocating for LGBTIQA+ rights. When did you get into activism?

Well, the roots of my activism largely come from the fact I've always really cared about children and young people. When I left school, I did a lot of volunteer work with kids and young people who came from disadvantaged – or 'under pressure' – backgrounds; kids who had behavioural issues or hard family lives. I got a job at GetUp while doing my masters, because they were focusing on mental health campaigning and refugee rights. Then the national director of GetUp was like, 'Great, you're gay. You can also take care of our marriage equality campaign.' And I was like, 'Absolutely not.' [*Laughs*]

Why did you have that reaction?
Because I thought marriage equality was a sham. [*Laughs*] I obviously don't believe that anymore, but I thought it was not a priority for the community. I thought, 'I never want to get married.' And I thought marriage was …

A distraction from other important LGBTIQA+ issues?
Exactly. And I kind of thought the institution itself was gross and weird. And I took umbrage with the fact I was given the campaign: 'Well, it's just 'cause I'm gay!' Whereas now I look back on it, and I'm like, 'That's good. We should have people from affected communities involved and leading.'

What swung you around to the fight?
At the end of 2013, the ACT accidentally legalised same-sex marriage for six days; it was a bureaucratic fuck-up. I went to Canberra in my capacity as a same-sex marriage campaigner, and attended a bunch of weddings as a guest, making videos and lobbying – stuff like that. And I went to the wedding of Ivan and Chris Hinton-Teoh. It was the first time I'd been to a wedding where I didn't think it was gross and weird. I felt like I belonged there. When I looked around, there were my people.

Suddenly it was a queer space.
Yeah. Watching Chris and Ivan get married, seeing this demonstrated to me, I realised marriage belongs to us as well. It's not a heterosexual thing that's being extended to us. We're just as entitled to it. From that moment on, I became completely obsessed with it. I remembered being nineteen, discovering I was gay and feeling like

I had cancer. And I didn't want other young people – when they're discovering who they are – to feel like that. That was the other part of my obsession with marriage equality. My belief was – and remains – that if kids grow up knowing it's okay to be gay, they're going to have the same opportunities and the same acceptance.

In what ways do you feel you're still growing up as a queer person in Australia?
I grew up a lot over the five years I worked on the marriage equality campaign. For better and for worse, I developed a hardened shell to withstand that much criticism – from opponents and community alike – to withstand the torrents of anonymous abuse and attacks in the right-wing media, and to withstand the constant setbacks on the campaign.

It's a trade-off, isn't it? On the one hand, emotional vulnerability is a really important asset to have, but it can be a liability.
Totally. And the nature of the marriage equality campaign – but also the nature of all LGBTIQA+ reform – is built on the back of people telling their personal stories. As queer people, we open up the most intimate parts of ourselves and our lives and our families, in order to appeal to the majority.

For them to recognise our basic human dignity.
In the desperate hope they'll see their humanity reflected in ours.

And that's taxing.
Yeah. So I think in the wake of opening up myself repeatedly, again and again, once my book is out I'll close myself up for a little bit.

You mentioned attacks from enemies: that's expected. But attacks from within the community might be less expected for some people.
Attacks is probably too strong a word. But when I first started receiving hard criticism from the LGBTIQA+ community, it hurt so much more.

You can never please everyone, even if ostensibly you're on the same side.
Absolutely. But at the end of the postal survey, I understand that being an almost self-appointed spokesperson for our community's issues and having a public profile means I might get reported in the media as a spokesperson for a community. So it's not only fair but right that I'm criticised and held accountable.

That's a healthy way of looking at it. For a lot of people, it's really challenging to get any criticism. Our immediate reaction is defensiveness.
Especially when it's criticism about work that's taken so long, and required your blood, sweat and tears. It's hard. But if I'm not getting criticism, I'm not progressing the conversation around our rights and the legislative reform we need.

Say you could go back in time and go back to little Sally Rugg and give her advice about her burgeoning queerness, what would you tell her?
I'd tell her to stop having sex with men to try to figure out who she is. I'm surprised I didn't get pregnant! And I'd tell her to try to find her community. Had I found a queer community sooner, I would've known I had the belonging and unconditional love of the community as chosen family.

LGBTI-Q&A:

Kate McCartney
Writer/director and actor

Benjamin Law: Where did you grow up, Kate?
Kate McCartney: I was born in Perth, but I left Perth when I was three, moved to Sydney until I was nine or ten, then moved to Melbourne after that. Now I'm thirty-eight, so I've been here for a long time.

Tell me about the first crushes you remember having.
I had a cartoon crush on Aladdin. But when I was a bit older, I certainly had a crush on Atreyu from *The Neverending Story*.

So there's a theme going on of smooth-chested boys with open vests.
With no body hair! I still feel that way, to be honest. There was also the princess in *The Neverending Story*.

The Childlike Empress.
Yeah, I think for a long time when it came to women, there was always that sort of confusion there, about whether I wanted to *be* them or *lusted* after them. Ultimately it was possibly a hybrid of the two. I feel that way about Sarah Paulson now.

Did you have an understanding of your capacity to have crushes on the Childlike Empress and Atreyu?
I don't think I had any language around my queerness or bisexuality, which is how I identify. I understood it in relation to other

153

people, but I didn't really understand it in relation to myself, until my early twenties, I think. I was quite comfortable when I realised I was queer and going, 'Oh, I think I'm bisexual; I don't think it means I'm a lesbian.' But then there was tension around that for other people within the LGBTIQA+ community, as well as straight people. People are a little bit more comfortable with binaries.

I feel bisexual people occupy such a unique space within the queer community because—
Well, we're vampires.

[*Laughs*] —you're the ones that are looked at with suspicion by both straight people and queer people simultaneously. How have you felt that personally?
Less so from non-binary people, or anyone who operates on a spectrum of non-binary identity. I've never felt like that from them.

They understand that there aren't any binaries for gender, so they understand there aren't any binaries for sexuality either.
Yeah, there's just a little bit more lived experience that's similar there.

For straight people, with bisexuality they're often like, 'Oh, they're confused.' For queer people, it's often, 'Oh, they're gay and in denial.'
Or they're 'experimenting'. I spent the majority of my twenties in relationships with women. But the next person I happened to go out with after a long-term girlfriend was a man.

How was that news greeted by people?
For my straight friends and my family – not all my family, though – it's like my queerness never happened. It's very easy to get wrapped up in the heteronormative world. It was a bit of a struggle. In terms of the queer community, it's hard to say if I lost friends. A lot of change happened during that time and it was just a time of fluctuation, but I'd also have people tell me that my membership to the queer community had been revoked.

Oh god, as a joke or seriously?
Sort of as a joke but also, like ... *not*. There was a bit of acid to it.
There's a sting there.

You've mentioned your bisexuality in *The Katering Show* and *Get Krack!n*. What were the viewer responses to that?
People at an executive level asked if I was comfortable talking about it. Like: 'Just to let you know, you've accidentally just said that you were bisexual, just flagging it.'

A bit of pastoral care! What were they afraid was going to happen, exactly?
I don't know, but obviously that spoke more to their discomfort than it did mine. 'Like, yeah, I'm aware.' I also have a very fierce and protective watchdog in Kate McLennan, so I basically wouldn't respond, and McLennan would go for them. From the community itself, and from other – particularly, young – bisexual kids, it has been really beautiful. Just saying, you know, 'Thanks for saying out loud that you're bisexual.'

Did you have anything or anyone like that growing up? Bisexual characters, bisexual representations or discussions of it, as a kid and as a teenager?
No, just vampires in films. [*Laughs*] Maybe in my twenties, but certainly not in my teens. As a teenager, absolutely not.

Right, so prior to your twenties it was exclusively Anne Rice.
Exactly. [*Laughs*] And I was a Goth, so you know all the signs were there. In my twenties, there was *Buffy*.

Willow and Tara.
I don't know if I was reading that necessarily as being bisexual or being gay. I think I was just sort of like, 'Ah! Lady love.' *The L Word* happened at about that time, but that's not a great representation of bisexuality, because Alice – the bisexual lady in that – got one boyfriend who left the picture pretty quickly. After that, there was zero mention of her identity.

Bi-erasure!
That was her bi-erasure, yeah.

Did you ever have a moment where you had to come out as bisexual and reveal yourself for the first time?
It was actually pretty easy for me. My mum basically called it. She just was like 'That's your girlfriend.' And I went, 'True, that is my girlfriend.'

Wow. How old were you?
I think I was twenty-three.

And beyond that, what was her reaction once you'd confirmed it?
I mean, she said some slightly silly things. But the big, guiding, base-level kind of message was love. My dad came to that realisation as well, eventually.

So you've had a pretty good run with your family. Do you still find yourself repeatedly coming out, though?
Yeah, I came out the other day, on radio. But usually if I'm in a situation with someone who is from the queer community, who is also in the media, they're aware.

We've all passed that information around to each other.
It's gone through the newsletter ... which you edit, right?

And distribute. Final question. Go back in time and talk to the teenage bisexual Kate McCartney. What advice are you gonna give her?
Just, you know, have another Sub Zero and be more honest with yourself.

It's only a very specific generation that gets that reference. I feel honoured to be part of it.
Also: you probably don't just want to *look* like that person; you probably want to make out with them. AND YOU SHOULD! Go right ahead!

This is something I still struggle with as a 36-year-old! Do I just wanna look like them or fuck them?
Honestly, I will say this: across the board, I've never felt like I fit in to one place, ever. That includes my bisexual identity. Socially, community-wise, work-wise, identity-wise. Now I'm realising that the grey space I operate in is my greatest strength. I'm not a director, I'm not a writer, I'm not an actor. I think that my ability to exist in my own space is actually probably my biggest strength.

You're all of those things! You're not just bisexual in your life but also bisexual …
[*Laughs*] In my work!

LGBTI-Q&A:

Christos Tsiolkas
Award-winning novelist

Benjamin Law: Where and when did you grow up?
Christos Tsiolkas: I was born in 1965 and grew up in Richmond in Melbourne. At that time it felt completely migrant, largely Greek, Italian, Slav and Turkish. Now it's probably one of the biggest Vietnamese communities in Melbourne. I didn't speak English until I started primary school and was shocked to find that English was the language of this country. In Year 8 we moved out and that was a strange period too, because at that point I was also aware I was gay. I had a sense of that from really young.

What attitudes about gay people did you grow up with?
In Greek culture, there's two derogatory terms they use all the time. One is *malaka*, which means 'wanker'. One is *poufti*, which means 'poofter'. But it's almost like I didn't, as a child, make the connection between those words and sexuality.

So, it was more about being effeminate and therefore not desirable?
Yeah, it wasn't as much about knowing you were gay or queer; it was about whether you were conforming to really strict ideas of gender. You can be quiet and silent about it as long as you don't make it common knowledge.

Did people pick up on this about you?
It was much more an internal struggle for me. I was much more

conscious of being the wog at high school than I was of being the poofter.

Do you remember having a crush on anyone in particular?
There was a boy who was in my class – I must have been in Grade 5 – and I had a mad crush on him. We were really physical together. One of my teachers – god, I hated her – in the middle of class said, 'Take your hands off each other, that's really disgusting.' That really changed our friendship.

Also, I started masturbating really young, towards the end of primary school. With those first tremors of sexual awaking, fantasy life suddenly became more and more prominent, and I realised that my sexuality was not normal. I didn't have the words for it, but I knew it wasn't something I could talk about. Two things were pivotal for me and, in a way, saved me. One was literature. I started reading really young. My parents – who, as migrants, hadn't had the opportunity for education because of the rural-class world they came from in Greece – were so proud of the fact that I was a reader. I was reading books that these days I would probably be told I shouldn't be reading. There was a Harold Robbins that got me called *Dreams Die First*. I devoured it.

Tell me about that book. I'm not familiar with it.
The reason it was really important was the main character was bisexual. It was the first intimation that maybe I could be both a good Greek boy and also have another type of life. And there was this Australian TV series. Do you know *Number 96*?

It wasn't of my generation, but the show was really saucy and explicit, right?
It was. Again, I am so fucking grateful I didn't have censoring parents. My mum and dad loved *Number 96*. They didn't have a fear of sex, and because their English wasn't very good, they would watch it with my brother and me so we could interpret for them. There was a gay character in *Number 96*, and there was no demonising of him at all. That was crucial and something we should be proud of: out of this culture came one of the first positive representations of a gay man on Western screens. And so I loved the

show. I'd also go to the library and read up on what were considered the world's great films. There was an Italian film called *The Conformist* by Bernardo Bertolucci and there's a scene of gay sex in that movie that formed – still forms – part of my sexual fantasising.

Isn't it so interesting how that stuff imprints?
Exactly. I'm really thankful that I had that, and I think that's why I'm a writer. I think I perceived that if I was going to make my way through the world, that it was those kinds of films, those kinds of books, that were going to provide me with a map.

Did you start writing because there was a subconscious drive to provide others with a map?
It was more a way of making sense to myself. I grew up in a world where – according to my parents and their peers – there were only four jobs available to you. One was to be a doctor; one was to be a lawyer; one was to be an accountant; one was to be a factory worker. Those were the choices. But in that constellation of opportunity, I realised that there was another thing you could be, and that was an artist.

Did you have a coming out as a gay person?
I was one of the very few wogs at that school; it was such an Anglo environment back then. I became, for two years, quite religious. We're talking the late '70s, early '80s. I think for me it was a desperate attempt to deny my sexuality. My background was Greek Orthodox, but I became involved in a really evangelical Protestant sect. I would pray to God all the time to not be homosexual, then at night I would wank and think of all the boys and men I wanted to fuck. After I would cum, I'd start scratching myself, like I was possessed by a devil. When I look back at that young kid, I just want to go to him and say, 'You'll be alright. You don't have to do this. There's another way. Even if you're interested in God, that's not the God you need to worship.' Then I was about fifteen and in a Bible-reading group, and I remember – clear as day – just going, 'I don't believe in this anymore.' I just shut the Bible and walked out of that church room. It was like a little assembly room. And I remember thinking, 'Okay, if there's no God, then everything I've

been told is up for grabs. I can start thinking for myself.' And at the end of that year, I started having sex for the first time.

What happened next?
I did tell my best friend, then I told another friend, then I told my cousin, who is like a sister to me. The hardest one was my parents. My parents came from such a different world to the one I grew up in. I knew before coming out to Mum and Dad that I couldn't live at home, so I moved out at eighteen. It seems absurd now, but they were absolutely mortified by that, absolutely heartbroken. But I also knew that if I was staying at home, I would just kill myself. So I moved out of home and that was actually the beginning of taking on a gay identity.

Who else did you tell?
Actually, the first Greek adult I told was my friend Lisa's mum. God bless her, she had such an amazing soul. Hard drinker, hard smoker. I was over one night and she really wanted Lisa and me to get together. I kind of said to her, 'No, Sofia, I'm gay.' We were drinking whisky and she put down the glass and said to me, 'Look, Christos, all men love sex. My brothers have fucked men. I'm sure my father did.' I can't believe I said this to her, but I said, 'Sofia, I don't only fuck, I also get fucked.' [*Laughs*] She put down the whisky glass and just said, 'Okay, that's different.'

And your parents?
I told my mum first. I must have been nineteen. She was so stricken by it, and really angry. Mum initially didn't want me to tell Dad, but I did tell him and, unlike her, he wasn't angry. He was really sad.

Did their attitude change over time?
Of course it did, because they loved me, and because my brother was supportive, and my cousins were supportive. In that kind of world, that's very important. Also, I met Wayne really young. I was nineteen. We were living together first as friends, and Mum really loved Wayne. That helped as well.

What do you think the younger version of you would think of this adult, openly gay, queer version of yourself?

There were so many things that I beat myself up on to do with my body and with sex. That damage of fearing sex was something that took me a long time to really come to terms with. So, I would say to that boy, 'This is your body. Just treat people respectfully but don't be scared of pleasure.' It was so frightening when HIV and AIDS came into the world. I remember going for that first test, sure that I would be positive. Even though I was terrified, those books I'd read, those films I'd seen, those people I had met who'd steered me towards another way of understanding the world stood me in great stead. I could've run back into the closet, but I didn't. I actually got angry. I thought, 'That could have been me.' It convinced me that to be a good person in the world, you had to treat people with AIDS with the utmost dignity. I think you just have to treat everybody with dignity. That's the gift you get from being the outsider.

Coming In

Joo-Inn Chew

Michelle stares at me like I'm an alien. 'If you don't say, you can't play,' she insists, and pouts her strawberry-glossed lips.

Kylie and Debbie nod, ponytails bobbing in agreement.

It is dim in the cubby and it smells of Vegemite sandwich. There's not enough room, so the baby's cot is on top of the fridge, and I'm sitting on the stove. Through a gap in the stick wall there's a glimpse of blue sky and scraggly gum trees.

I sigh down at my dirty toes poking out of my uncool sandals. I scratch my short hair. For some reason a flash of Lisa Kennedy from Grade 5 acing elastics arcs through my mind.

'I don't have one,' I say.

Michelle frowns. 'Everyone has one. You have to have one for Mothers and Fathers. Otherwise who are you going to marry?'

'Yeah,' says Debbie, 'but you can't have Greg, he's mine. We're going to have twins.'

I pick at the scab on my knee and wish I was in the library, reading a book. Should I say Alan? He seems less germy than the others. Or Jason – but he likes to squash ants. They're all so gross. Mothers and Fathers sucks. It was better when we liked horses.

'I don't really want to get married,' I blurt out, horrifying myself. The girls all glare in disbelief. Already lips are curling, hair is tossing, mean words are fizzing on tongues. I stand up and they draw back and closer together, like I'm a bomb. The baby's cot wobbles and I don't even bother to catch it this time. It hits the dirt and the doll tumbles out onto its face, one blue plastic eye staring sideways accusingly. Probably dead. The cubby's gone blurry and I stumble over the cot with its tangle of blankets, out the low door.

I hate that I am crying. 'I don't care, I don't want to play your stupid game anyway!'

Outside it's cold and fresh. I run down the hill away from the shrieks and the dead baby and my future husband and triplets, run into the open, jumping anthills and logs, looking for a tree to climb, scaring the magpies into flight.

*

'Brad's *so* cute, but he got with Nadine at the Blue Light and my life is *ruined.*'

'She's such a slut anyway.'

'Jason said hi before Woodwork, but was that hi or *hi*?'

'You should totally ask him out, Nic. He's such a spunk.'

I hitch my short uniform up even further to let the sun bite into my thighs. Eight tanned legs lie parallel along the concrete, like long shiny coconut-scented rolls. Forty painted toenails loll at ease. Four mouths gossip or mmm-hmm, while trying not to eat too much fattening food. Four sweaty backs with trainer bra straps lean against the warm bricks of the canteen wall. Distant shouts and the crack of ball against bat float up from the oval. The air is heavy with wattle and sun-tanning lotion, and the drowsy droning of flies.

Shar strides across the netball court with her friends, and suddenly I'm wide awake. She burns across my retina like a comet. My skin is prickling and shivers ripple down to my toes. Electricity dances all over me. It's hard to sit still, hard not to run. Hard to act cool as she walks towards us. Sun is in her hair and sliding off her arms, spilling down her long legs, teasing out a sinuous shadow behind her. She stops to say something to her friend, so close I can see freckles on the side of her neck. Her voice tickles my ears. I can't look at her lips, her green eyes, the way she's laughing, or I might explode or give myself away. I stare at a wad of gum flattened into a whitish splot on the concrete by my left ankle, run my eyes round and round its rough edges, until at last she moves away and I can breathe again. My heart is skittering and blazing, faint and fierce all at once. I let myself watch her as she walks away, the way her hair slides across her shoulder and one strand lifts in the breeze. When she disappears round the corner she takes light and colour with her. The afternoon is empty and dull, a stage after a show.

Around me the others are still chatting, they haven't noticed, or maybe they're used to my silent weirdness. Now they're talking about which boy has the best bum. I make myself nod and mmm. I concentrate on acting normal. I file Shar away with the others in my secret Quite-A-Few-Crushes-But-I'm-Not-A-Lesbian-It's-Just-A-Phase file. Lots of girls love Madonna and Jodie Foster. Lots of girls aren't into boys yet. Lots of girls are too busy reading books and getting As – okay, well, not that many, but if there were more with glasses and Chinese fathers like me then there *would* be lots. I'm just a late bloomer. And Shar is just distractingly beautiful. It's not like I love her or want to kiss her or anything. I'm not a perv or a lemon. Those Grim Reaper ads are nothing to do with me. When I imagine rescuing her from a fire in assembly, or saving her from hypothermia in the snow when we miss the last bus, it's not like I … oh god – think about something else.

I can do this. Only ten minutes till the bell goes. I focus really hard on what I can add to the group analysis of Derek's personality and Wayne's shorts. And I keep my dangerous and delicious secret hidden under my uniform, right over my heart.

*

I wipe the steel kitchen bench again and again, even though it's shiny clean. The last elderly resident has shuffled out of the dining room, and Carol hurries in with an armful of trays. I open my dry mouth then close it again. I watch her stack porridge bowls into the dishwasher and feel my heart doing a tap dance of terror. Come on, you coward. Don't pike now. It's 1992, you can do this.

'Guess what?' I squeak.

'What?' she asks. She has kind, dark eyes and a gold nose-ring, and she is an Indian dental student.

'I'm … I'm bisexual,'* I blurt out. And start sorting trays like a maniac, feeling my cheeks heat up the room.

---

* This is true at the time. I do have a boyfriend (I have to give blokes a try, and he's a good one) but I'm in love with my best friend, and I'm about to break my boyfriend's heart in a long, messy, self-absorbed twenty-year-old way to go out with her … and never look back.

'You're kidding me,' she says.

'No, really.'

The longest silence in human history ticks by. I fight an urge to hide under my apron. Instead, I wipe the pink-and-purple floral placemats, the true hideousness of which I've never taken in before. Mrs White's radio blares golden oldies from Room 9.

'Wow ... well, that's okay,' she says.

I drag my eyes up to her face and see she means it. Something in me collapses, a breaking wave of relief that washes warm tingles to my toes and salt water to my eyes.

'Course it is,' I say gruffly. I line up the water jugs. Their painted daisies and teddy bears seem about to gambol off the glass. Just seeing them frolic beside the stack of attractive floral place-mats is making me grin absurdly.

Carol is staring at me.

'Um, thanks,' I say.

'No problem.'

Who knew dental students could be so cool? I skip away at the end of my shift, leaving my old skin a tattered remnant on the mopped kitchen tiles. Outside, my new skin fizzes in the sunlight, alive to the breeze, smelling much more like me.

*

The line snakes down the block outside the Builders Arms, into the warm Fitzroy night alive with glittery grunge. Thursday is Queer and Alternative night at the pub, and it feels like everyone radical and fabulous is queuing to get in. Dreadlocked ferals and tripping ravers suck lollipops next to my lesbian separatist house-mates, next to gay boys with sparkling pecs, and a sprinkling of Asian queers. Hot dykes in dog collars, radical feminists, drag kings and queens – they all let eachother be tonight. There's even a sheepishly excited handful of medical and engineering students, and a couple of fellow formerly closeted survivors from high school, freed at last. Doc Martens and goddess tattoos abound.

There's lust and revolution in the air. Last week was Melbourne's first pride parade, thousands striding defiantly through the St Kilda streets – where some of us had been gay-bashed – holding hands and kissing, strangely buoyed by the cheering voyeurism of the hetero crowds. Heads high: we're here, we're queer, and we're not going shopping. We don't belong in your 'straight suburban breeders' world; we're roaming in wilder terrain outside the map, making new tribes and families, seeing more clearly from the margins.

Our love is in the spotlight in the early '90s, zigzagging between wicked and chic. k.d. lang is on the cover of *Vanity Fair* in a suit, lathered up for a buxom Cindy Crawford teetering in stilettos to shave. There are gay flicks in the cinema, and Queer Studies at uni. We go to AIDS rallies, Reclaim the Night marches and Queer Kiss-Ins. We come out to family and some of us are thrown out of home, or told to pray away the gay.

I am lucky; my parents and siblings accept my sexuality. Perhaps softened up by the long teenage years of tortured girl crushes, they are more surprised by my two-year heterosexual detour than by my eventual coming out. They see how happy I am with my girlfriends, and welcome them into the family. Still, we keep the secret from elderly and religious relatives, here and in Malaysia, not wanting to identify a devil incarnate in their midst and be fending off prayers and condemnation for eternity.

My father comes to the launch of a book I have contributed to, a collection of coming-out stories. He stands awkwardly in his hand-knit jumper and cargo pants, a lone Chinese dad in a crowd of people he once would have called fairies and poofters, just to be proud of me. He used to jeer at Mardi Gras on TV; now he drops me off at Pride March and warns me to be careful. But when I try to stay over at my lover's house, her father shoves a twenty-dollar note under the bedroom door. 'Get *that woman* out of my house,' he snarls. And we flee into the night, and I never go back.

But for now we are gorgeous radicals, uncloseted and in love, ordinary and extraordinary. Dance anthems throb from the pub doorway and my girlfriend grins at me in the streetlight, setting me aglow. A passing ute-driver rolls down his window to yell, 'Fucken homos!' The drag queens in the line blow him a kiss. The lesbian separatists muscle towards him and he drives off fast, silenced. 'Dickhead!' chorus the engineering students. And we laugh and growl and shimmy, because tonight we own the night.

*

A rainbow balloon slips loose and disappears into the wide blue sky. My daughter frowns and clutches hers more tightly. My son leans against my leg in his black hoodie and pink socks, reading *Harry Potter*. He's bored with rallies now and has only come to get his ice-cream bribe afterwards. Next to him, my partner holds a banner with the kids' donor dad. Around us, the feisty crowd listen as gay dads, lesbian union organisers, politicians and religious leaders speak with passion and honesty. A wave of cheers echoes off the buildings and the march is away.

What do we want? Marriage equality!
When do we want it? Now!

We surge down the Canberra streets alive with rainbow flags and banners. The kids skip and chant, glad to be on the move, hopeful of getting on TV and being famous at last. At the edge of the crowd, a handful of men shake placards scrawled with Bible verses and shout that we'll burn in hell. My son glances at them in confusion and I hurry him on. Another thing to explain over dinner tonight. There are too many things that are too hard to explain. Why the whole country is 'voting' on whether their two mums are allowed to get married, even after seventeen years together. Why everyone at school is talking about it. Why we keep muting the news as another politician spouts bile about the slippery slope to bestiality, or how we are not fit parents. Why their mums have been edgy for months. The stress of wondering how everyone we know, how our whole country, is going to 'vote' takes its toll. We discover things we wished we hadn't known about workmates and family, things that can't be forgotten. As a doctor, finding out my valued nursing colleagues are voting 'No' stings.

One, two, three, four, stop this homophobic law!
Five, six, seven, eight, how do you know your kids are straight?

*

It's the week after the plebiscite. The resounding 'Yes' vote has brought wave after wave of emotion. First: relief. Then, surprise, gratitude, a melting wonder. I realise I had been dreading a kick in the guts from the entire nation. Despite the confident lesbian life I am living now – rainbow family, queer community, LGBTIQA+ health work – I was still carrying around an '80s-kid view of Australia.

Believing that outside my little protective bubble the great masses disapproved, thought I was abnormal, lesser, sinful, wrong. A perv and a lemon. I hadn't dared hope that my country had moved on from homophobia to affirmation.

Now I walk around the shops, the schoolyard, the waiting room, knowing I am welcome in my real skin. I came out decades ago, but it has taken this long to truly *come in*. Married or unmarried, our family of 'Mothers and Mothers' has a place in the cubby too. Our love has come in from the fringes, into the muddle of humanity in the middle. Bringing its own radical gifts.

And somewhere inside me, an eight-year-old girl up a tree shakes out her short hair, then breaks into the most beautiful smile.

Androphobia

Heather Joan Day

As far as I know, I am the only girl at my high school. I wake up every day with an ache in my stomach like something growing inside me is desperately trying to claw its way out. The more I wish it wasn't there, the more it feels as though it's going to burst out of a cavity in my chest, spraying blood all over the breakfast table and my family. Pregnancy doesn't cross my mind because I don't have a uterus.

My mother, the owner of a physiotherapy practice, tells me my biggest problem is my bad posture. She drops me off at the bus stop on her way to work. She hopes I have a nice day at school. There is a convenience store by the bus stop, run by an old married couple. I go in to buy a coffee and the wife surveils me, as she does all teenagers. At the register she counts my coins carefully while the husband watches a kennel-sized TV behind the counter. An ad is playing for a show called *There's Something About Miriam*. It's a British *Bachelorette*-style dating show where the 'gimmick' is that the titular Miriam has a big secret, to be revealed to the contestants during the final episode of the series.

'SHE ...' the ad teases, 'is a HE!'

Miriam holds her index finger to her lips and winks right at me.

After they finished making the show, the male contestants sued its producers for 'emotional and psychological damages'. Miriam Rivera eventually moved to Spain, rich from TV appearances and high-end sex work.

The husband chuckles, and I stare longingly at the cigarette boxes on the wall, golden packaging with royal-looking insignias that will be illegal in a few years' time.

On the bus, I find a seat so I don't spill my coffee, and I put in my iPod headphones. It's not even 8 am and the bus is already stinking hot. Queensland summer makes the air thick and sticky. I play a song called 'Pray for Plagues'. At the next stop a school of fish (cis) girls my age board the bus, rummaging through their purses for their paper tickets. I stare enviously at their uniforms. Mine is awful: a waiting-room blue button-down shirt with gravel-grey pants. Their ocean-blue pleated skirts and billowy summer-cloud blouses look breezy and cool. One of the fish sits in the row in front of me and reties her ponytail. Her long red hair spills over her shoulders in slow motion like a cartoon mermaid. At my school our hair has to be short at the back and sides and over the ears. My head of year, who after I graduate will be convicted of paedophilia, has threatened me with detention several times for having my hair too long or wearing my fringe over my eyes.

I arrive at school and buy my third coffee for the day from the tuckshop on the way to my locker. I didn't really sleep much last night because I stayed up chatting with L.

My locker stinks of old tuna cans from whomever was using it last year, so I have to hold my breath when I open it. I grab my books for periods one and two. As I turn, W shoulders me into my open locker. My elbow bangs hard into the rusty edge of the locker door. Puberty has hit W hard since last semester and he has tripled is size and greasiness. He tells me to watch where I'm going and then 'books' me. 'Booking' is a school-wide phenomenon where a victim's books are swatted out of their arms as hard as possible. Precautionary measures such as holding your books across your chest with your arms folded tightly only makes you a more highly sought-after target. Anyone who displays signs of fragility or femininity is attacked. Those are the rules.

'Fuck off!' I say as I bend over to pick up my books.

W snorts and pushes me over like I'm made of paper.

'What's wrong, Daisy? Got your period or something?'

I don't say anything. He's laughing.

'Look! You're bleeding! See, Daisy's on her rags!'

Blood drips down my leg and onto my books. The stinky old locker must have cut my elbow. I feel sick.

I'm late to class because the closest toilet block is back by the tuckshop, and I walk into first period clutching toilet paper to my elbow to stop the bleeding. F waves me over to sit with him in the back row. During rollcall he tells me about his plans to fuck S with the big tits at this party on the weekend, without asking me about my arm or inviting me. I often find myself befriending boys like this: tall, strong, rebel types who want someone to be protective of. F is a boarder, but unlike most of the others his parents don't live in the country or overseas; they're just too busy earning money to be bothered dealing with him during the week, I guess. He is a spoilt drunk and a compulsive liar, but he is nice to me. Years later he will run into me on the street outside a bar in the Valley, shirt torn open, prematurely balding, coked up and sweaty, and he will hug me fondly. Now he tells me about a gang fight he saw in a park that he's probably making up. I wonder if I'll ever have big tits like S, but it seems unlikely.

*

Art is the only class where I feel respected at all. Even the too-cool jocks will stop by my easel on their way to wash their brushes to compliment my paintings. This is the only class I like besides English and Ancient History. The teacher lets us play our own music while we work and A, who often sits at my table, always tries to play emo music to piss off the TCs. Today I'm painting a portrait of an actor I'm currently obsessed with. A TC comes up behind me.

'She's hot. Is that your girlfriend?'

I tell him she's an actor.

'Dope,' he says.

I don't tell him how much I wish I looked like her. After graduating I will go to art school for two years, where I will have my first major manic episode.

During lunch I sit with T, the only out gay kid in my year. He wears Doc Martens to school. The TCs call him 'Nazi fag' with no sense of irony. I ask him if he hates it here as much as I do, and he tells me it's a lot better than his last school. I don't normally sit with anyone in particular. F usually spends lunchtimes playing video games in the boarding house. Sometimes I go to the art block.

Other times I just walk around, listening to music. T asks me if I'm going to eat anything and I tell him I feel sick. Even though we don't really know each other, we will catch up in a few years, when he is performing cabaret and experimental theatre and I'm studying creative writing. I open my lunch box and take a bite of a sour apple.

After school I have basketball practice, but first I meet some of the boys from the team at Subway to gulp energy drinks and smoke cigarettes in the car park. I'm feeling a bit faint by now, so I buy a triple choc chip cookie. G gives me one of his cigarettes and then offers me his Lynx to cover up the smell before practice.

I'm the shortest person on the team and my lungs sting as I sprint up and down the court.

'Alright, ladies!' the coach yells when a few of the boys start to lag.

'Come on, Daisy!'

In the change room I feel like throwing up. Everyone on the team is white except me. G says I'm cool though, because I'm mixed, 'not full Asian'. I'm the only 'ranga Asian' he knows, he tells me. There are only communal showers, so I just wash my face in the sink.

My dad is waiting in his car to pick me up. We don't talk much on the drive home, but we haven't talked much for a while. Ever since he walked in on me losing my virginity, things have been a bit weird. In the '80s, he worked in an AIDS ward and I won't realise for a long time that his love of rules – making and following them – stems from anxiety. I'll waste a lot of time being angry with him. He asks me if I have much homework and I tell him I'm going to see C after dinner. He tells me I have to be home early because I have school tomorrow.

*

I met C online. She lives a few suburbs out from mine and her mum drives us to Blockbuster to rent some movies and buy snacks. C is tall, thin and white, and has big blue eyes. I never know if I'm dying to kiss her or to be her. I just know there's something painful about being around her. We did kiss once, but we were really drunk at the house party of a boy she was sleeping with. We never talk about it, but we have been hanging out ever since.

In her room we lie on the mattress with a floor fan pointed at our faces and eat sour gummy worms. We watch *Ace Ventura: Pet Detective*, a movie co-written by and starring Jim Carrey, which culminates in the reveal that the villain is trans. Jim tears off her clothes in front of a group of cops and they're all disgusted because they believe they've all been kissing 'a man pretending to be a woman'.

After the movie C and I walk around the park talking about music. She's shy but a good listener. We will soon drift apart when things get complicated with her boyfriend. In ten years' time she will message me to say that she's proud of me.

When I return home, I get into bed with my laptop to find I have a bunch of missed messages from L.

hey girl where u been?

I take off my jeans and shirt and change into a singlet and some nicer undies.

hi ;)

He wants to video chat so I throw a thin scarf over my bedside lamp for mood lighting and tousle my hair so that it covers my forehead. I turn on my webcam.

u look sxc as heck tonight!

I smile. *yeah?*

fuck yeh

I pose for him, twisting my body carefully.

what do you feel like doing, baby? I want to fuck ur sweet arse so bad!!!

I laugh. He asks if I'm laughing at him, he tells me he missed me. He doesn't want any foreplay tonight. I do what he tells me to do, watching myself in the grainy little chat window. For a moment I think about taking some screenshots but decide against it. I look good in this light. I could be a real girl.

When he's done he sends me a photo of himself and tells me his fish girlfriend doesn't make him cum like that. He says he wants to meet in person but that he can't. He thinks it's safer here. I tell him I'm tired; I have to be up for school in a few hours. Later that year I'll run into him on the bus and he'll ignore me.

I close my computer and go wash my hands, tiptoeing down the hall so as not to wake my parents or siblings. The bathroom light always flickers a few times before coming on, like in a horror movie. In the mirror I see a boy. He looks sad.

Back in bed, I wish that I'll wake up and be an entirely different person. I finger the self-harm scars on my body, imagining them opening and closing like gills. Blood pours from them, emptying from the shell that I live in.

*

Things will get a lot worse before they get better. It will be ten years before I come out and begin hormone replacement therapy. I will visit my parents and they will be trying their best. My mum will be sad about my name but say sorry for sending me to a boys' school, and I will tell her it doesn't matter now. My dad will ask me about my medications and whether I've been exercising enough, which I will know means he worries about me and loves me. My fiancée will squeeze my thigh when I'm being too sensitive or defensive. Mum will tell them how she made me a fairy costume when I was three out of a coathanger and a pair of hot-pink tights, how she got me a Barbie because I asked for one, and how I was always very quiet and observant and questioning.

'You haven't changed at all,' she will say.

Living in a Fridge

Michael Farrell

When I think about the idea of growing up, it makes me wonder if the conditions of queer adulthood are possible – or even desirable. The notion of adulthood seems so enmeshed with heterosexuality. It also makes me think of Paul McCartney's 'Coming Up': 'like a flower', to bloom, to be plucked, or mowed. Mightn't it be better to remain a bud, full of potential, a seedling?

Ways of being queer are ways of being human, but being human can feel limited sometimes. Poetry helps me think metaphorically of how I was trained, like a vine, to grow and flower in certain directions. A human child is closed off from the adult world in many ways, and as much as I might have wanted to join it, I thought more about joining the animal world. The cattle-farming world, the bush world. I still have a residue of this, a deeper sense, in fact, of relation to Melbourne birds; to kangaroos, in statue or poem; I look out for them in a roadside mob.

*

After my first attempt at writing this, I realised I hadn't mentioned that staple of gay memoir: religion, growing up (predictably) Catholic. But I don't think of the rituals, hymns or altar-boy smocks, or of naked Christ on the cross; the only abuse I suffered was from a priest's knuckle to the head once, and from the nuns' 'dark sarcasm / in the classroom' (Pink Floyd). What I think of is truth. The rite of confession did, I think, influence me strongly. I haven't always been a completely honest person; I confess that the truth doesn't always seem personally honest – or kind – but I find social lies and performance difficult. And growing up queer means, for me anyway, growing up secretive. I am structured like a nut, in the hard-to-get-at-the-seed sense.

*

It's a slow process, finding out how other people live, when you've grown up in a small country town. I think that observing animal life broadened that perception, however – and reading books. In an unlikely sense, Henry VIII, whose life I stumbled on in the school library, was a liberating example: he wasn't constrained by marriage or the Catholic Church. Just like the Protestant side of my own family (no beheadings, however).

*

As the concept of queer, and attitudes towards gender, gets more diverse, the way we understand and tell our growing-up stories gets more diverse. Ten years ago, I would probably have written this as a fairly standard growing-up-gay-in-the-country story. This is not so different, perhaps, but back then the emphases would have been identified in a more positive way, the non-normative aspects would have been presented as badges of being gay. As if I was struggling towards something recognisable, rather than being something that was in itself interesting.

*

I like how vague 'non-normative' sounds; it's like a category of ambient music. Growing up non-normative ... it sounds like it would be hard to be abused in those terms. But back then, the word 'abnormal' had a fair amount of derogatory power. (Still does in some playgrounds, no doubt.) Growing up how I was meant a lot of hiding and a lot of insults (how much is a lot?) and a lot of hating (inside me). It meant not wanting to have a body at all. Which meant never wanting to play football or do PE, and never using the boys' toilets in six years of high school. I put all my energy into being invisible. Which probably made it harder for me to perform visibility later on.

*

What do I wish I'd known then? That there were other gay boys at school, even in my small class. But perhaps they didn't know what they were going to be either. Hill towns before the internet were like living in a fridge with the door closed but the light on.

*

'Does Your Mother Know?' (ABBA). I remember my brother being appalled that I liked the '80s singer Marilyn. I still like that type: fey but tough, skinny and pretty. I was probably more attracted to Andy Gibb, but I was too young then to feel much about it. I recently saw the documentary *Paris Is Burning*, about queer Harlem ball competitions: a world to desire (the romantic highlights of the movie, the competitions, not the everyday reality of the performers' lives). One thing that interested me was the judging of the competitors on their 'realness': not acting or copying, but realness. I perform poetry. But I've never been much of a performer of straightness, or perhaps I should say of gender. Except by default. I can grow a beard; I have a deep voice.

*

Pop music was like an oxygen tank, aural ice-cream. But now I'm trying to think, what were the queer songs? Something like Helen Reddy's 'Angie Baby' rather than Marilyn's 'Calling Your Name'. 'Walking on Thin Ice' and 'O Superman' were pretty queer too, but that was later. I'd almost survived by then (like there was only one round). I had no concept of art yet, let alone the avant-garde. Australians must have changed (surely?) in the '70s while 'Bohemian Rhapsody' was number one. Imagine Gough singing 'Bohemian Rhapsody' in the shower. Imagine the governor-general. I sang 'Somebody to Love' under the noise of the lawnmower, but I imagine straight boys did this also. I really just want to keep naming songs. They're signs of happiness (and loneliness). Songs and the bush.

*

Growing up non-heteronormative means growing up double. Growing up as what you're not, as well as what you are. That sounds a bit essentialist, I know. Every secretive act of the past becomes an analogy for sexuality. I would make up what I might now call 'image families'. I was no Brontë, with a shared secret world; I couldn't imagine sharing my secret worlds with my brothers and sisters. I thought constantly of the cows on the farm, of the chooks at my grandparents'. I had my own plastic animals to play with. But I still needed to create more families: with grass (from seed heads), broken pegs (wooden ones, grouped into two different types: those with and those without a head), buttons and plastic counters. These were found families. I don't think the worlds I created were very elaborate. I can't remember if I even made up dialogue. I think the structures, and to some extent the naming, were what interested me. I was curious about family trees and the possibilities of instability (and change and complication) when it came to marrying. Something I couldn't imagine myself doing.

*

I had a vague sense of masochism from dreams of barbed wire, and stories of wounded princes (which I would dress up as). I thought having a harem, or what I later learnt was called promiscuity, was the ideal: learnt from the animals on our farm. I could identify with bulls more than with men. I could imagine sex with cows, although I didn't imagine it as a literal act (despite having seen it between cows many times). I imagined that cows were my girlfriends, and innocently told someone at school. Shamed again. I demonstrated for my cousin a very perfunctory servicing, perhaps with a pillow, which my grandmother walked in on. She knew instantly it was something we shouldn't be doing, although we were probably ten at the most, and not naked or touching each other. I suspect such fantasies are not so abnormal for farm boys. Generally, I felt I could do what I liked, I think, whether it was French knitting or having my own flower garden, but even these were to some extent secret activities. (We were not a very social family.) I could do them, but I couldn't, ultimately, do them and be considered normal. In small towns, there's a lot of pressure and anxiety around being normal, but on farms no one cares about their neighbours most of the time. Or maybe that was just us.

*

I can't separate growing up queer from growing up as a poet. I could see correspondences with my own life in the biographies of John Ashbery and Les Murray. Not only the farm experience, but the sense of having access to a present that is considered history to other people. That sense is partly due to growing up in a pre-internet rural environment, but also due to having young grandparents. I spent a lot of time with my grandparents when I was growing up; their stories were of the past, and we drove through the places of that past, where they used to live, where the people they used to know used to live and sometimes still did, miles from town life, in the bush.

*

As long as I had a hat and a waddy to fend off snakes, I could wander wherever I liked: into the bush, or to the river, or on parts of the cleared land of the farm. I had vague fantasies, as I grew older, of meeting a man, maybe a naked man, in the bush. There were naked children nearby – we saw them on the side of the road: the 'hippy' kids. This was kind of titillating, but not erotic for me.

*

'What is the point of being a little boy if you grow up to be a man?' (Gertrude Stein). I never saw the point of gender division at school, just as I never saw the point of being 'Master' or, later, 'Mister'. Boys who didn't want to play with boys got shamed by the girls, even if the other boys didn't care. By high school they did care, though. Friendship with a girl meant her boyfriend threatening to beat me up. I had crushes on a couple of the boys in my year, and I hadn't completely left masochism behind either, but there was not a lot of affection going around.

*

If your body is different to other people's, then by some weird logic they own it. They get the right to speak about it. I started school as a fat boy and that didn't change. But in any other context than school, this would probably seem ridiculous. I look at photos of myself from high school and I don't look fat at all. Just not athletic. I was obsessed with calories, and my weight, and eventually took up jogging. But I had to literally cake my emotions and anxiety with eating. I had my appendix removed in Year 10, but I don't think I had appendicitis. I remember the week in hospital as a happy one, however, of running around the grounds in short pyjamas.

*

If I could live in a song, it wouldn't be 'Angie Baby', which is kind of scary, or the cool, hard songs of the '80s, but maybe the even more before-my-time Mary Wells' 'My Guy' or Dusty Springfield's 'Son of a Preacher Man'. (And if there's one lyric I'd like to unpack, it's Nina Simone's reference to 'Liberace's smile' in 'My Baby Just Cares for Me'.) It's 1983, the year of Eurythmics' 'Love Is a Stranger'. I'm eighteen, and the straight rites of passage mean nothing to me. I haven't been to a nightclub; I haven't read Barthes, or Stein, or Frank O'Hara; I haven't kissed a boy.

Wanting

Fiona Wright

Even now, I sometimes think that I don't know my own desire. I always close my eyes, I do not look, even as I feel my body held in another's gaze. I read once somewhere that a woman's desire is less visual, less dependent on what she looks at or sees, but I don't trust the fact to be true.

What I do know is that I have three stories I tell myself about wanting, about desire: three of those strange beliefs we all have embedded in our brains that we're often not aware of until something rubs against them. The first is this: you will not get what you want, so do not bother wanting. The second, closely related: if you want something too badly, you will not get it. The third: wanting is always better than having.

How is someone who believes these things ever going to allow herself an appetite?

*

As a child, I was always crushing on my school friends. I knew from a very young age that my desires weren't usual. Perhaps both of these things are true of queer girls everywhere; perhaps we all have varying degrees of knowingness of what is happening. I didn't have the words but I knew.

In Year 3 I held hands in the classroom with a long-limbed girl with long red hair; I kissed her hand, chastely, as we sat side by side on the dusty, carpeted floor. The teacher told me to stop. 'I know we all love our friends,' he said, 'but still.' I was chastised, and felt it keenly.

In Year 4 I, the smart kid, was asked to help the new girl with her reading, and we sat together in a light-filled room adjacent to our classroom, poring over large-format books aimed at children half our age. Eventually, we had a sleepover at her house, three cul-de-sacs away from mine. We shared a bath, and I was fascinated by her pubic hair, mousy brown despite the white-blonde hair on her head. We lay on air mattresses and wondered, with our voices and our jigsaw bodies, exactly how it was that lesbians had sex. She was cruel to me on a school excursion the next day, and I didn't know what to do with the hurt and confusion.

In Year 5, a new school, and one of my classmates already had breasts. Beautiful, big breasts that I couldn't help but look at. She caught me, rolled her eyes. She was eleven years old and already used to people staring. I was ten, and so ashamed.

In high school, there were three women: Lara, with her dark brown eyes and tangle of auburn curls; Sandra, with her long, slim limbs and boyish manner, her glossy black hair almost reaching her waist; and Katherine, crooked-grinned and effortlessly cool, who loved real lingerie and expensive make-up, who once made me promise I would tell her if I was ever crushing on her. I promised, even though I already was.

This was in our final year of high school, and Katherine and I swore that we'd stay friends, whatever happened, as we moved out into the world; we swore because we couldn't bear – I mean this literally, it was physically painful – the thought that we might fall out of each other's lives. Perhaps all teenage friendships are this intense, but I suspected mine were coloured differently than my friends', and I had no way to act on this. Perhaps all teenagers feel this hurt and frustration, trying to find their place in a world they have not yet had the chance to shape or change. Perhaps they all want to be different. I was awful to all my friends' boyfriends because the very fact of their existence always felt like a betrayal. I cut my hair short for my Year 12 formal, even though it didn't suit me. I was trying to tell my parents something important. We all wanted to be different, but I still felt my difference keenly.

*

But even then, I knew this wasn't everything. I knew this vaguely, as an unsettlement, but I never turned it over in my mind. In Year 10,

I walked into a room of actors during my work-experience week in the costume department of a theatre school, where one of the actors, a man – I can't remember anything about how he moved or looked – was standing in the doorway, and as I passed I caught the smell of him, baritone and musky, and I felt my body sharpen. I tried to explain this to my friend later that evening, but her dad was in the car and I felt exposed. This wasn't the narrative I had of who I was, this wasn't the person I, or any of my friends, expected me to be. I knew, but I didn't have the words, and I pushed it from my mind.

*

It wasn't long after I left school that I fell ill, and a different type of want, more insistent, more essential, began to dominate my days. I told a friend who I had a thing for at the time – rakish, exuberant and strawberry-blonde – that eating had been making me vomit lately, and she asked why, in that case, I was currently eating my lunch. It was lunchtime. Eventually, I stopped trying to eat at all.

When I think of this period, though, I don't remember wanting. I don't remember feeling hungry, just feeling time slow, feeling distracted, feeling spacey in the brain. I remember small aches in my body, but I mostly remember feeling fine – and my dogged insistence that everything was fine. The languor, the swooning pull of my body as it fatigued. I didn't need desire to make my body feel alive. When I think of this time, I still catch myself, sometimes, thinking of it as a kind of innocence. I didn't know how, precisely, I was sick. Sometimes I catch myself still wanting this, instead.

*

The first woman I slept with had green eyes and brown skin and had decided that she wanted me and was going to get what she desired. She said this, afterwards: 'I always get what I want.' She was one of those people who wear their sexuality like a cocktail dress, shimmying inside of it and letting the straps fall down the shoulder. Afterwards I fell asleep, and woke wondering if I had been transfigured (I hadn't).

The second wouldn't let me touch her in return.

The third took me back to her apartment on election night, at the end of the Howard era, when all of Newtown seemed to be on

184

the street and dancing, and she gave me a pill and made me shower and kept asking, 'How did I get you here?' I walked to work at 5 am and everyone was buzzing, everyone seemed electric along their skin. Everyone had desired change, it seemed. Everyone had wanted this, and the relief, although short-lived, was wonderful.

The first time I slept with a man, it was also my first time overseas, and I kept thinking, before I flew there: no one will know me and I can be anyone and any way, without the weight of expectations, even my own.

I arrived after midnight, and fell straight into my guesthouse bed, and it felt like I woke in a brand-new world, the light dusty and gold, the soil red. This man showed me his city, kissed me on a beach one night, just out of reach of the lights of a bar with tables that sprawled out onto the sand, and I was surprised, until hindsight made it all make sense. He said, 'Sometimes I don't think I understand you,' and I felt the shock of that, its risk, so quickly and so profoundly that I deflected, saying, 'Sometimes I don't think I understand myself,' and so whatever else he was going to say was lost, is lost, forever. We drove around the city at night, parking on abandoned sports ovals or at the edges of farmland or jungle. The gearstick bruised my thigh. I pretended that I knew what I was doing, that none of this was startling, none of it new. I was so afraid. I was being anyone and any way, and I felt borderless. I buried myself deeper, hiding to keep safe.

*

I always knew, but I didn't have the words. Years later, a boyfriend would say, 'Wait, you moved to Newtown and *then* figured out you like dick?' And I laughed but didn't say that it wasn't ever that simple. (He also said, in the same conversation, 'But you're not gay now because you're with me.') I didn't say I had always doubted my absoluteness, the exclusive direction of my desire, but didn't want to admit to this complexity, in case it diluted my difference, that one clear characteristic that I'd always felt able to claim. Usually, by then, I'd say, 'I spent years trying to figure all of this out and it caused me a whole world of pain, so now I just say: "Whatever goes."'

Because when I was growing up, queer was not included in the acronym. It had not yet been reclaimed by the people against whom it had, for years, been levelled as an insult. I don't remember when and how I first came across it, only how well the word seemed to fit: it was, and is, a word without expectations, with undiluted difference, a word that can be everything and every way.

A word can be a wonderful thing. It can be a container. A mirror. It can click everything into place.

*

But wanting, wanting is still hard for me to bear. I still try to push it aside or power through it. I still catch myself, sometimes, equating it with weakness – because a person who wants nothing cannot be disappointed, cannot be harmed. It's difficult instead to claim a thing that's so long been denied. I keep messing things up as I muddle through, but at least I know now that wanting isn't uncomplicated for anyone. I'm learning, however slowly and belatedly. And it helps, in no small part, to have the word.

Coming Out, Coming Home

Adolfo Aranjuez

You know how they say travel changes people? How being thrust into a foreign context inevitably forces you to reconsider what you find 'right' or 'good', and which parts of yourself you are comfortable with? Well, naff as it may sound, it's true – at least in my experience. (Totally authoritative, relying on a significant sample size of one, but as they say: *write what you know*.)

I'm not talking about my trip to Japan in September 2016 – solo, after I'd broken up with a boyfriend who, shall we say, I had deemed lacking (but whose birthday present for me, in the form of a plane ticket, I decided to stay in a relationship with). Nor the incredibly portentous, but in the end rather pleasant, trip I made back to the Philippines, the motherland, over Christmas that same year (conservative Catholic family learns to embrace initially threatening queer boy with weird hair and tatts). Nor the fancy-as trip to Thailand in July 2018, all expenses forked out by the kingdom itself because I'm an impressive queer whose queer expertise is extensive enough to merit my presence at an LGBT+ conference (y'know, as the token Q in a sea of alabaster Gs).

No, I'm talking about the protracted, life-changing trip I made in 2003: to Australia as an international student. You could say being an international student is the ultimate form of travel. You're visiting, but also kind of staying. You're not just shedding the trappings of your usual life for several months tops; you're changing core elements of your personality to adapt to an entirely new environment.

My parents wanted to ship me off, at fifteen, to a Western country because, as they put it, 'There's no future for someone *so brilliant* in the Philippines.' To accomplish their goal, which we'll call 'The Plan', they paraded me through various American cities – San Francisco, LA, Reno, Vegas; then to the east: New York, Richmond, DC, Jersey – in the hope that I'd fall for of one of those potential future homes. But I was (and remain) a picky bitch.

The Philippines-based Australian consul general (a tennis friend of my parents' – which betrays my disgustingly privileged upbringing) tipped them off that international students in Australia could apply for permanent residence after two years in the country. This was true at that time, before immigration laws changed, so they swapped the Land of the Free for the Land Down Under. Sydney was in their sights – it was big, it was booming – but I got there and … no. Melbourne wasn't even in their purview, which was weird because my Ate (older sister) was already there, completing her master's. But life has a penchant for throwing curveballs: we detoured there to attend her wedding and, golly, was I bewitched by the place. Like most romances, it's difficult to explain – something about the wide streets and leafy trees; the grey-white light of mid-morning; the temperamental rain and the smell of wet grass recalling Manila after a monsoon.

This is a sprawling origin story, I know. But the backdrop for the seismic disruption that was to occur in my life is important: the dislocation wasn't only geographical – it was also about affect, culture, intent.

Back home, my life was pretty set-up. You may have guessed by now that I'm a huge overachiever, and that overachievement was in full flight by the time I migrated. I was on track to become the school paper's editor-in-chief and graduate top of my class, while also kicking butt in choir, mathletics, cheerleading, the school council, and so on. Admittedly, I had no real friends, and my sense of self was entirely grounded in accomplishment. Plus, I felt my parents' love was conditional on me bringing home another award or performing in another talent show, or two, or five. But this *was* my life. While I really did fall for Melbourne, my parents' decision to extract me from my stable, streamlined Manila life, without my consent, was pretty fucked: I had to discard everything I'd built up to that point and start all over again.

*

My relationship with my birthplace is much the same as my relationship with my family: rocky, and replete with both affection and avoidance. I was my parents' golden child – a trophy they could wave around at family reunions. Lots of passive-aggression and guilt-tripping were deployed to make me play piano or sing for relatives, even when I was shit-scared. And the compliments were often backhanded: but how come I 'only' got second prize in that last school competition? Until early adolescence, I was obedient and hardly spoke up at all – the consummate child for the traditional Asian family, for whom kids should be seen, not heard.

I loved school, though. There, I felt an immense sense of mastery over my life; I did what I wanted, worked hard and got results. I suppose this engendered a fabricated sense of belonging or purpose, compared to my stifled silence at home; it was at school that I could be myself.

High school is infamous for being a pressure cooker of hormones and emotions and existential crises: *Who am I? What do I want to be when I grow up? Why does this pimple keep reappearing on my chin?* But being booted off to another country by *your own parents*, who have the gall to *not move there with you* (Ate took on de facto parenting duties, bless her – apparently she felt responsible for me because it was by her request that I was conceived in the first place) certainly intensified things for me. And it really was tough: the increased independence, coupled with Australia's secularism, led me to question and soon abandon my faith. My mental-health issues also made themselves felt around this time – I developed anorexia and did some self-harming, with the first blushes of yet-to-be-diagnosed bipolar and anxiety soon to follow. Geographical distance catalysed an increasing emotional rift between me and my parents, and the more I came of age, the more the chasm between us – which had always been there, seething beneath the surface of ceremony and courtesy and my striving to be the perfect child – solidified.

You could say my parents really messed up by sending me to live in a liberal Western country: in Australia, their silent, servile child couldn't stay silent or servile for long. Then again, they'd messed up earlier than that by sending me to a cosmopolitan,

English-speaking, super-prestigious inner-city private school whose corridors have been graced by the offspring of celebrities, diplomats, media figures, artists, sportspeople and expats. In both cases, I know my parents were doing the best they could. It's said that we inevitably regurgitate the parenting styles we're exposed to, and the world was very, very different in their youths – though Mom grew up rich and Dad working-class, both were similarly expected to be deferential and defined by their achievements. Perhaps they just miscalculated, with my rigorous education breeding in me a rebellious philosopher instead of a hyper-qualified follower.

Thankfully, school in Melbourne offered sanctuary once again. By the end of Term 1, I'd re-established my overachiever status: four school bands, the school play, school council, yearbook editor, debating team, accelerated-learning program, A+ average. On top of that, I'd achieved something I never had before: I actually made friends. Within six months I'd even come out to the whole school and, two months later, I had a boyfriend (who, seven months later, would cheat on me on a school trip to Paris – but that is an essay for another time, likely a confessional one on anxious-attached dating styles).

Another naff trope we all know and love (to hate) is the 'bumpy coming-out' episode, and mine, shamefully, matched this trope to a T. Everyone in my family always sort of knew, but it was at the six-months-in-Melbourne mark that I made it official: first to my sister, then my mother and, finally, my father. Dad reportedly didn't eat properly for a month afterwards, and I discovered later that he'd grovelled to Ate's then-husband, begging him to teach me to 'be a man'. I thought my mother was on side, but Ate soon clued me in to Mom's secret whispers of longing that I would one day 'just find a wife' so that I could 'give her grandkids and not be lonely'.

I'd anticipated this antipathy. Identity in the Philippine context is heavily premised on communalism: anything said about you is said about your family. So there's a lot of pressure to blend in, to be 'respectable', to do things 'right'. While the Philippines is broadly accepting of queerness, thanks in part to pre-colonial conceptions of gender that transcend the binary (*bakla*, an expansive term that lacks a true English counterpart, for instance, tends to be translated to 'gay' even if it spans a range of identities across the Western gender and orientation spectrums), this acceptance is complicated by class and status. In my case, bourgeois Manila society would have frowned upon me identifying as, not to mention performing the identity of, a *bakla*. Homonormativity – that desire to 'pass' as a member of the majority, to appear straight-adjacent and conservative-approximate – permeates everyday life, so queerness is reined in through play-acting what a 'normal' cis-gender, heteronormative person would deem palatable. And this isn't even to broach the still deeply-rooted influence of the Catholic Church, which literally demonises queerness.

*

One of the first things I learnt in Australia was the phrase 'She'll be right.' It wasn't clear to me who the mysterious 'she' was, but the sentiment quickly piqued my curiosity and captured my imagination. More than just a stock saying, 'She'll be right' is a philosophy for life, a mode of being in the world. This optimistic phrase encapsulates Australia's predominant laidback ethos – informed, arguably, by centuries of serendipitous luck (what country just *strikes gold?*), isolation and relative safety from invaders (the irony!), and vast expanses of land and resources. It embodies a stoic attitude towards hardship as well – one that conflicted with my over-achieving life, which had always been about pushing against, pushing away, pushing and pushing until everything was 'fixed' and my body and brain had reached their limit.

The prevailing migrant narrative is one of always doing more than expected, to the point of effacing yourself. And this is heritable: speaking anecdotally, I've found that second- and third-generation migrant folks exemplify this in their often-stereotyped, but nevertheless observable, work ethic, their frugality, their success. Privilege aside, self-effacement was key to my own upbringing. Growing up in the context that I did, I consciously amassed tools with which to dodge unpleasant situations, suck it up, shut up and put on the best face. Why *wasn't* I like all the other boys? Why *couldn't* I just do what Tita (aunty) asked one more time? Why *didn't* I have a girlfriend? Little did I know that, in Australia, this crafty resilience would serve me well – as a queer person.

Coming out, like moving countries, is a journey: you've got a target destination, even if the direction you take to get there isn't all that clear. At the same time that you labour, pushing feet against pavement, you also have to let the road take you where it leads. You both know and don't know what you're doing, so you have to settle in – and surrender – to the movement. I took heart in the Aussie brand of Zen. Divorced from familial expectations and the familiar context of Philippine Catholic conservatism, I had to not only grow up pretty damn quickly, but also learn to embrace my distinctive tribulations. The completely unnatural upheaval that coincided with puberty forced me to really think about who I wanted to be and what I wanted to do with the rest of my life: not just to keep kicking butt at school, at work and in relationships, but also, ultimately, to be happy.

There are things you can fix and things you file away or feel your way through because they 'become right' in their own time. In two years, I'd finished high school (graduating dux, of course), applied for another student visa, finished uni (with a high distinction average), applied for temporary residence, almost got deported but managed to secure permanent residence. Ten years after first immigrating to Melbourne, I finally got my citizenship (at the ceremony, I was given a certificate and a native grass; the latter died within a week because this impressive queer has no clue how plants work). I've sped through this part of the narrative not because it's irrelevant – it amounted to a decade of living, waiting, wondering whether The Plan and my happiness would ever eventuate – but because, when it comes down to it, it isn't special. All migrants go through a bumpy path to citizenship, and despite the dark place I went to when faced with the prospect of deportation, my experiences were nothing compared to the devastating difficulties that asylum seekers, less fortunate migrants and Australia's First Nations peoples go through.

Still, there's something compelling about the specific, intertwining experiences of queerness and migration. Much like how I managed to eke out for myself a place in this land I now call home, a 'new normal' has emerged in my family dynamic – not a fully-fledged embrace of my *bakla* 'tendencies' per se, but a respect for my assuredness in owning who I am and my ardent advocacy for others to be able to do the same. In my overachiever life, too, I've broken new ground in terms of meshing my values with my accomplishments, and understanding that the person I am is so much more than the next accolade or sought-after byline. Most significantly, my queerness is now manifest to its maximal degree – and at no other point in my life have I loved myself sick.

This descriptor, *queer*, can't help but remind me of the critical framework of 'queering': going against the grain of a text or artwork, or prying deeper to uncover alternative, sometimes unintended, readings. Because identity *is* eternally in-process. Ideological constructions such as 'gay', 'Filipino' and 'Australian' are so fallible, and frequently fail to embody the shifting, ever-evolving notions that we're trying to pin down. I'm a natural*ised* Australian, the processual suffix highlighting that I'm forever locked in a struggle of reaffirming that I belong. Never just *natural*, I'll keep getting asked, 'Where are you really from?' In much the same way, my queer identity is processual because I'm constantly changing. The word itself – signifying 'weird', 'odd', 'left of centre', 'going against the grain' – encapsulates what I'm about, encompassing sexual attraction, gender performance, even overall lifestyle. It's an acknowledgement that fixity is fallible, that perhaps it is always an illusion. The journey – to find home, to embrace myself – continues.

The Wall of Shame

Natalie Macken

On the bus home at 3.30 pm, it's still hot. Every time a girl gets up to get off, her thighs make a sound like they've been velcroed to her seat. At my stop – me, some other kid, and three boys who shoot Girl Guides with cap guns get off.

I have to walk home with the other kid, who's having a piano lesson with Mum. It's the longest eleven minutes of my life. After two blocks of silence, my neck and throat are smarting with awkwardness, so I do what I can.

'Do you reckon some people can see their eyebrows?' I ask.

He looks at me like I've just licked a street sign. 'No,' he says.

I wait for more, but that's it.

Whatever comes next has to last two streets, so I go mainstream. 'Are you doing three-unit music next year?' I say.

'Probably not,' he replies, mercilessly.

Like a demigod, my neighbour, Mrs Lalor, appears in her driveway and waves to me. She's wearing three different types of denim.

I walk through our front door and head straight up to my room, bypassing the kitchen and an unsupervised Milo-straight-from-the-tin opportunity.

I have drum lessons on Wednesdays while Mum's students play melodies that make the piano sound like it has dementia. I'm debuting my new padded drum-kit stool, hiding behind my hair, nailing a paradiddle rudiment on the snare. A cheap and desperate pine-scented deodorant overrides the smell of limp lettuce coming from my schoolbag. My almost-a-man drum teacher seems impressed with my progress, and I prepare myself for a compliment. Instead, he asks, 'What's wrong with you?'

'Why?' I ask.

He's staring at the far wall of my bedroom. 'All other girls your age have posters of boys on their wall,' he says.

I feel my whole body fill with white-hot shame. I barely blink, swallow my bile, slow my breathing and, with the nerve of a sniper, say, 'I took them down when we painted the walls.'

After he leaves my room, I wait for him and his pine-accented armpits to get paid for being only a bit better than me at drums. I stay still and hold my breath until the don't-get-found-out snake has slithered over my feet and back into its box. Then I open my bedroom door and come out into the space the rest of me takes up. I close the door on my boy-bare wall.

With beats on repeat in my head, I decide to walk up the road to buy a copy of *Smash Hits* magazine. Mostly because that's where Heather Brewer got her folder cover of Christian Slater.

'Yeah, it's hard to look at all day – NOT,' she'd said. I think he permanently looks like he's mildly surprised while squinting into direct sunlight. I don't get it but ... whatever.

With my shoes keeping a solid four-four, I lock into the tempo until I pass Eddie's petrol station with its huge new 'Shell' sign out the front. I press play on my Discman and Tracy Chapman's 'Fast Car' comes on. I keep walking the four.

Deep in the rhythm – that's when I know it's not going anywhere, the gay.

I know it's not what other people are, so I decide to paint my puberty by numbers, copying the moves Heather Brewer makes because she makes the right ones. That's when Tracy got in her Fast Car, and I went along for the ride.

Jeff at the newsagency has an unspoken ten-minute rule for flipping through magazines. After that, he'll say, 'Better buy it to see what happens next.' I always let him get that one out, but I try to pay before he plays the 'I'm not a library' card. I make a detour around *Cosmo* and *Dolly*, and pick up a copy of *Smash Hits*. But, instead of reading it, I open it on a random page to play 'Six Degrees of Kevin Bacon'. Who knew that only six or less steps along a *Footloose* path were what separated the whole world?

Julia Roberts. Too easy. She was in *Flatliners* with Kevin Bacon. Her Bacon number is one.

I don't really want *Smash Hits*. It's very Corey-heavy. There's also a healthy side of Vanilla Ice, Jason Priestley, Emilio Estevez, Charlie Sheen and Rick Astley. In between all the testosterone, there's Julia Roberts, like some weird uber-smiling mistake. The thing is, everyone's got it wrong: I don't want to be her, I want to be *with* her. And I know there's a difference, on a cellular level, on the level where it's about your skin and your blood and not just about your mind.

'I'm not a library, you know,' says Jeff.

I buy the shitty magazine, and Jeff counts out my change on the counter, including two two-cent coins and one one-cent coin.

'Don't exist anymore,' he says, holding up one of the copper coins.

Yes I do, I think, but out loud I say, 'Yeah, they're supposed to start disappearing.'

*

That night, I wait for the lull after *Home and Away* and dinner, when everyone's doing their own thing. My brother's annoyed with me because I got the same stereo as his, and I'm annoyed with him because he eats too slowly. He's playing the Chili Peppers in his room while I pull out posters of shiny, improbable-looking boys from a centrefold of teenage sexuality. It feels alien and abrasive. I feel like I'm betraying myself.

I Blu Tack a panorama of perky-pecced boys onto my wall so I can use them as human shields; my hunky disguise, my boyband safeguard. All I can hear is gay static. There are no discernable gay sounds anywhere on my radar. No gay people in my orbit, no gay news, no gay dogs even.

It's dark, and everything and everyone has shut up except for the Wonga pigeon that's taken over my four-four. All the Coreys have combined, and they're pushing down on my chest. I can't sleep because I feel like my wall is too loud.

*

In the morning, before I get up, I decide I want Julia up there too. I reason that twenty-two boys cancel out one woman. I put her on the second-last row from the bottom, using the same logic you'd use to answer a multiple-choice test without knowing the answers.

Meinmasha

Atul Joshi

'*Meinmasha, meinmasha,*' my mother giggles, wagging her finger at me.

'Hee, hee, hee,' my white-saried grandmother hoots through gapped teeth. My aunt, in demure *htamein* and blouse, holds her hand over mouth, eyes squeezed shut, and shakes in her chair.

Lapping it up, I twirl faster, hands extending and folding, head cocking side to side. The three women applaud as I take a final bow.

Meinmasha. Never sure what it meant – compliment, endearment or judgement? That Burmese word has haunted me throughout my life.

*

They say the process of coming out is unique for every individual. At one extreme, it's a dramatic outburst at the dinner table, the whole family gathered around, torch song optional. At the other, it's quiet and sequential: you tell your best friend, then your next best, and so on; a kind of LGBTIQA+ musical round. Sudden life-changing flash, or tentatively drawn out over time – and dozens of other variations. No one way is right; and let's face it, every time we meet someone new it's another moment of coming out.

For me, I went the slow, hesitant route. I assumed it was finally done when I came out to my mother at the age of thirty-eight.

Lately, I've come to realise that it's the same with growing up. At what point do you stop? It's not just admitting your same-sex attraction, but numerous other aspects that fall within the universe of being queer. Some of this doesn't happen until well into adulthood.

*

'Oi, mate, get outta the pool.' In Australia, a school swimming carnival is an almost clichéd place to realise you are different. 'Are you a Paki?'

By midsummer, when the solar noon had done its work and turned me almost black, that question would turn into a statement. 'We don't want bloody Abos here.'

It was then, in that moment that I first felt – was made to feel – different. And it was in the same moment that pale male flesh became erotically charged for me.

Difference: first, of colour. The colour of my skin. The light spectrum interpreted by our brains. Why do we trust our eyes given that sense's evident deficiencies and illusions? Clearly those Aussie kids at the pool couldn't recognise a Burmese Indian when they saw one. Why is sight a basis for both prejudice and attraction?

*

'What're you looking at, ya poofta?' The name-calling changed as I entered my teens.

Here was a second type of difference. No longer just the colour of my skin, now also the feelings it contained marked me out.

I discovered it while loitering a little too long in the changing rooms, excited by the first sight of a pink penis framed by golden pubic hair. I'd joined the school orchestra, and I got lucky at music camp with a bunk right in front of the open shower room. I'd delay getting up so as to watch two gods of my wanking heaven bathing, exposing shockingly large appendages while my hand did its furtive work under the blanket. Not wanting to be a perpetual voyeur, I found the courage to do something about it.

'Do you, um ...' I started asking my strawberry-blond clarinet-playing friend, 'masturbate?'

'What's that?' he asked, and got me to spell it out for him so that he could look it up. Pressed up next to him on my bed as he flicked through the dictionary, I placed my shaking hand on his thigh.

'I'm not a homo,' he said, but didn't push my hand away. The son of a pastor, he added, 'It's a sin,' before lying back to give me better access.

Thereafter ensued a period of sleepovers where we'd invariably end up in the same bed. While I instinctively knew what to do, he seemed at a loss, particularly when it came to my foreskin-covered penis.

'It's like you have a crown sitting on yours,' he observed, comparing his shiny circumcised head to mine. 'It's smaller too.' Having only seen cocks like his, I began to wonder if I was deformed.

*

Around that time, my family made a pilgrimage to reunite the family dispersed across the Burmese diaspora. After marriages, wars and coups had scattered sisters, brothers, mothers and fathers to Australia, Canada and England, most had settled in India, and that's where we went to meet aunties and uncles and cousins I'd never seen before. The word 'gay' wasn't common in India and no one spoke about homosexuality. There were the *hijras*, men who'd chosen to live as women, either with or without surgical procedures. They were a caste of their own, feted at weddings and celebrated for their theatrics, but ostracised in society more widely. I was scared of being labelled one of them and shaming my family.

Riding pillion with my cousin through the streets of Bombay on his two-stroke Bajaj scooter, I pressed into his body and inhaled its musky smell. I kept my hands to myself.

'You're a handsome boy,' one uncle said. 'You should go into movies, forget the music stuff. More money there.'

'Have you found a girl for him?' an aunt asked. 'I can find a nice one who wants to be a doctor or lawyer. She can earn the money for them both.'

This refrain continued when I visited again after high school. 'Guests' were invited to my aunt's place so they could introduce their daughters. My aunt would report the details to my mum back at home. I had no idea how to react to these set-ups. I couldn't exactly blurt out that the servant boys bringing out the snacks were far more appealing. I smiled, feigned shyness with the girls and ate the *pakoras*, vowing never to visit again.

*

Things went rapidly downhill with the pastor's son as our sins grew worse.

We'd go to symphony concerts together, where I'd touch him in the dark. With the music of the Romantics swirling in my head, I booked the next season for us.

'Can't come now,' he said, when I showed him the tickets. I began to sense avoidance and the beginning of an expulsion. Pimples and bushy facial hair signalled the emergence of raging hormones that were now drawing him to the opposite sex. I was hurt, then jealous.

With no one to take to the performances, I put a notice up on the school board. Someone, I assume him, scribbled on it, 'Only faggots need apply'. I was scalded by both the aggression and the rejection; humiliation burned through me.

*

For the remainder of high school, I hid in music-making and the arty crowd. Music began to obsess me, especially operas with their larger-than-life love affairs, which started to intrude into my reality. Wagner turned me into someone seeking my own love-death, waiting for the one who would understand me, love me and deliver me. Mahler made me want to quit the world. Music was a type of closet, but it was also a refuge. It offered a relief never matched in real life.

Inside I was feeling shame: colour shame, sexual shame and body shame. I felt like a bad son, not living up to family expectations. It would take me years to get over this and find the courage to seek out another guy.

*

I met him at uni. We were in the same course. We listened to albums together and talked about art and books. I gave him a *Tristan und Isolde* box set for his twenty-first birthday. *Brideshead Revisited* was on TV and, after each week's episode, we would meet up and have our Sebastian and Charles moment. As well as a natural accompaniment to our courtship – a soundtrack – music became a language of emotional intimacy between us, a gateway to and then a foundation for an intense friendship. I came out to my uni friends and, believing I was falling in love, I told my sister (in the safest possible way – a long letter sent while she was studying in the United States).

Our first and only sexual encounter happened in my bedroom after a night dancing at Patches. It was the evening before my departure for music studies in Europe.

'I can let you out, or park the car and come in,' he said on the drive home.

'Park the car. We need to be quiet, though.'

In my bed, we kissed. 'I've never done it before,' he said.

I sensed his nervousness. When it came to penetration and anal sex, I too was worried. It had never featured in my fantasies as a boy. I thought how great it would be to be a hermaphrodite. Or to have superpowers that allowed me to change physical sex at will – so that I could turn female when it came to *the act*. Growing up, I fantasised about being Honey Ryder to Sean Connery's 007. Looking back now, all those expectations I placed on myself – that get placed on us, seem to be just noise that gets in the way of connection. No amount of transformation, real or imagined, would have made that first encounter less awkward or challenging.

We settled for oral sex, and I swallowed when he came, thinking we were now bonded. I loved caressing his hairy chest.

We parted agreeing that international estrangement wasn't the time to call each other 'boyfriend'. I still have a photo of him and my best friend seeing me off at the airport. It's a memory that means so much.

I should have heeded the warning signs when we first met and he told me he attended church on Sundays. While I was in Europe, he sent a letter saying that he'd found his calling: he was enrolling in theological college to become a missionary and was leaving his 'gay past' behind. I wondered what kind of god these white boys prayed to. I wept tears of anger and betrayal. It wounded me most that he was rejecting all of my 'kind'. He's now married, a husband and a father. Sometimes we meet by chance at concerts and have a surreptitious cigarette together; I give him gum so his wife doesn't find out.

A pattern was set and all through my twenties and into my thirties I chased men who were wrong for me. There were people, friends, I behaved badly with. After a particularly self-destructive break-up, I gave up on finding someone. I realised that music had become a crutch that had accompanied many years of sadness and frustration, but that couldn't offer me the life I wanted to live. I gave it up as well. It seems to me that we create habits and masks for ourselves, hiding our personal traumas behind work, routine, obsessions, afraid to come to terms with our own identity. The cost is heavy – so much time missed on fully engaging with others and with the joy of living. (The creative urge never disappears, though, and I turned to words later in life.)

*

Coming out of the musical closet, I found my gay family and became more comfortable in my skin, my difference, my queerness. As the end of my thirties approached, a friend and I got drunk and agreed we both needed to shake things up before we hit our forties as single men. He introduced me to the world of online dating and hook ups.

After a decade of celibacy, I became a slut. I figured there was wisdom in numbers. And there was: those years showed me that we're all different colours, sizes, shapes, as many with as without foreskins. It was a revelation I enthusiastically embraced, and much of my shame melted away.

And through online chatting I found someone to love me back. We met in a room in the Undernet (there was no Grindr or Scruff then). He lived in Norway and loved dogs and Indian food. After a series of trips, both of us crisscrossing the planet, he became my husband and lives here with me now.

On one of his first visits, I took him to meet my mother. I was thirty-eight and figured it was time to come out to her; having someone by my side helped. Without saying anything about being gay, I explained that I wanted her to meet the person I wanted to spend my life with. In our family home, we sat either side on a sofa of her. She held both our hands and blessed us.

*

I recall being older, but my sister assures me I was two. On the days my grandmother and aunt visited, I'd dress up in my mother's Burmese *htamein*, a brightly patterned silk sarong, slip on one of her matching blouses, and apply her *thanaka* paste across my cheeks, her lipstick to my lips and a spray of her perfume. Picking up a fan, I'd dance for them, imitating the *minthamee* Burmese dancers we saw at the all-night *zat pwe* festivals.

'*Meinmasha, meinmasha …*'

I decided to once and for all find out what it meant. It turns out the word means a man imitating or destined to be a woman. When I read this I was stunned. My mother had called me this? It didn't matter if she was judging or complimenting me. The word was a gift of understanding, a little clue my mother had left for me, planted in my brain to sprout at the right time. Did I really need to wait so long to come out to her? It wasn't just as a teen that I'd been different – I'd been different since birth and she'd gently applauded that difference.

I'd never considered myself caught in the wrong gender, but it dawned on me that the roots of that difference could be tracked back to a lifelong desire to express a feminine side of myself, a queer part of me that didn't conform to either the 'oi mate' or the 'find him a suitable girl' masculinity norms. It came out in those James Bond moments, those teenage desires to magically transform my body's sex. More recently it has emerged in stories I write with transgender leads and androids with the ability to change gender at will. *Meinmasha*. I started to make sense.

*

My sister and I've talked recently about visiting our ageing relatives in India, before they pass on. 'It's okay, they know,' she'd said a few years back, after taking a trip there. 'They'll be fine. They ask about the both of you all the time. They want you to be happy.'

India no longer feels like the place of arranged marriages, and there's a visible LGBTIQA+ community there now. I plan to go with her and my niece next year. My husband can't come, but I'll tell my aunts about him, show them pictures, explain what we're up to. My sister thinks they'll be content to see me loved, and loving someone in return. And, I hope, in a completely matter-of-fact way, this will be another coming out.

Kissing Brad Davis

Scott McKinnon

In the well-to-do Sydney suburb where I grew up in the 1970s and '80s, there was a single-screen movie theatre where my film-loving mother and I would often spend our Saturdays. Inside was a grand staircase, swirling up from the box office on the ground floor to the theatre doors. The cinema was usually dotted with grey-haired old ladies from the nearby retirement village, sitting there with me and my lovely mum taking in an afternoon matinee. I was a shy, anxious kid, but when the lights went down and the curtains parted, nothing mattered except the movie.

Apart from at a cinema, the only other way to see movies was on television, and I'd scan the newspaper TV guide religiously each Monday to plan my film schedule for the week. When I was in my early teens, we bought our first VCR and I would go to the local video store as often as I could, gathering a pile of weekly rentals to work my way through. When a film was good, I would often rewind it immediately and start over, or just track back to a favourite sequence, holding the rewind button down and then running the scenes through, again and again.

I watched countless movies and TV shows. Dramas and comedies, mysteries and musicals. Saturday-morning cartoons and Sunday-night movies of the week. Event miniseries and blockbuster debuts.

Thousands, maybe tens of thousands of lives lived on the screen, and all of them straight. At best they contained a hint of something shadowy that couldn't quite be brought into focus. Every kiss I saw, every romance, every single scene of love and intimacy and passion was between a man and a woman. The kind of relationship that I would eventually have was entirely absent. It was so absent that for a long time I didn't even know I missed it or that I might search for it. An enormous amount of effort went into making sure that queers would never be visible to children.

Images of gay love existed somewhere, certainly but, like a town that has been left off the map, they played no role in how I imagined the world to be. When I was born, in the 1970s, lesbian and gay liberation movements were in full swing, and newly relaxed censorship laws allowed queer movies like *Sunday Bloody Sunday*, *A Very Natural Thing* and the previously banned *The Boys in the Band* to appear in Australian cinemas. The risqué soap opera *Number 96* cheerfully shocked television audiences with the first openly gay and transgender characters on Australian TV. Gay male pornography was even making quasi-legal appearances in disreputable inner-city screening rooms. There were plenty of images of gay male sexuality emerging ... somewhere.

But all of these screen entertainments were strictly for adults only. Even the simplest of kisses between men was considered so shocking, even pornographic, that it could never be permitted to appear in a movie accessible to kids.

The 'won't someone think of the children' brigade will claim that I was being carefully prevented from becoming 'prematurely sexualised'. Protecting children from adult sexual images may be a worthy goal, but I certainly wasn't safeguarded from seeing all forms of sexual desire. Children's entertainment was a hotbed of heterosexuality. The central romance in *Lady and the Tramp* ensured that I had seen a loving kiss between two animated dogs before I witnessed one between two human males. *Herbie Goes to Monte Carlo* saw the heroic little Volkswagen fall for a sexy powder-blue Lancia named Giselle, revealing that even cars had heterosexual desire in kids' films. Of course, a core component of Disney fairytales like *Cinderella* and *Snow White* is Prince Charming on the hunt for a kissable heroine. And Miss Piggy's feelings for a somewhat startled Kermit were nothing short of barefaced, voracious lust.

What I was prevented from seeing was anything between people (or cars, or animals) of the same gender. The sequestering – that is, the censoring – of even relatively chaste queer images as the province of the 'adult' and the 'sexual' meant that heterosexuality was the only imagery available to kids like me. Queer youngsters had to make do with lives as subtext in a world keen to pretend we didn't exist at all.

My budding sexuality positioned me as a subtext, yes, but the colour of my skin placed me unquestioningly at the centre of almost every movie I watched. As a white kid in Australia at that time, I don't think it ever occurred to me that someone else might be missing from the screen; for queer kids of colour, the whiteness of both Hollywood and Australian cinema added further layers of absence.

From the movies I voraciously consumed as a child and as a teen, certain moments linger in my memory as landmarks in my halting sexual and romantic education. Those small, intriguing scenes and images, the likes of which many a queer person will be able to call up as a recollected marker point, caught my attention and suggested, ever so briefly but with vital consequence, that there was something I wasn't being told.

Watching the early-'80s Australian movie musical *Starstruck* on VHS, I remember the single moment that caught my eleven-year-old attention: in one short scene, two male characters float on a li-lo in a rooftop swimming pool, wearing nothing but matching blue Speedos and with their legs casually touching. To adult viewers, the moment was intended to very plainly indicate the homosexuality of these characters, and we see the disappointment register on the face of the female lead, the rising rock star played by Jo Kennedy, who had been hoping to attract the romantic interest of one of them. To me, sitting on my beanbag in our family living room, none of that was clear and my lasting memory is only of those two legs touching.

I had, to that point, watched men punch, shoot, stab and otherwise harm one another in any number of imaginatively violent ways, but this was the first time I had seen affection between two men expressed as an indication of sexual or romantic desire. Those two legs touching was a form of male physical intimacy that I had never seen before and it was fascinating. Instead of wanting to harm one another, these men were enjoying a shared moment of easy, sensual touch.

My own desires were gradually, confusingly, disconcertingly taking shape: a crush on a student teacher who all-too-briefly taught at my primary school; a post-match visit to a rugby league locker room that was far more interesting to me than the game itself; the smiling male underwear models who, compared to their seductively posing female counterparts, seemed slightly shame-faced standing in only their jocks in the pages of department store catalogues. Beyond these occurrences, it was TV and movies that provided opportunities to look unguardedly at men. In *Lethal Weapon*, Mel Gibson climbed out of bed and walked across a room naked and it was just ... bloody ... great (rewind, watch again, rewind, watch again, rewind, watch again). Rob Lowe in *About Last Night*, Christopher Atkins in *The Blue Lagoon* and Patrick Swayze in *Dirty Dancing* all provided thrilling, if undefinable and puzzling, moments for me. But even in those moments, some-thing wasn't right: these men were sexy, sure – sometimes shirtless and yes, occasionally even naked. But they were just glimpses. The blokes never lay languidly in their underwear or slowly undressed while the camera traced their flesh and the soundtrack piped sexy '80s saxophone. The hero always had to be somewhere in time to kill someone. I was a feminist film critic on training wheels, wondering why the camera only ever offered women as objects of desire.

I'm not sure when I first saw two men kiss onscreen, but it may well have been *Midnight Express*. I was twelve or thirteen and, while my parents were on holiday, my aunty Wendy and her boy-friend Phil came down from Tamworth. *Midnight Express*, the harrowing, and somewhat controversial, late-'70s prison drama is most definitely not a kids' film, but Wendy grabbed it from the video store and allowed me to watch. Adapted for the screen by Oliver Stone, the film tells the true story of a young American student imprisoned in Turkey for attempting to export hashish. The film's star, Brad Davis, beautiful and, more than once, naked, intrigued me. In a steamy prison shower scene, Davis is kissed by a fellow inmate. I was quietly awestruck, while Phil expressed his discomfort: 'I think he's turning a bit weird, Scott.'

Phil was a good guy, and his 'bit weird' was fairly mild, but there were few straight Aussie blokes at the time who could let such a moment pass without some kind of comment – a cautionary notice. The film itself echoed that particular lesson: Davis pulls away from the kiss and gently but firmly shakes his head; no, the all-American hero will not participate further in such activities. Never mind that the memoir upon which the film was based details a loving romantic and sexual affair between Davis' character and that fellow prisoner. Never mind that Davis himself was bisexual.

The movie obsessions of my childhood and teen years reveal an unwitting – if, retrospectively, all too clear – fascination with sub-textual queerness. I loved the 1987 horror comedy *The Lost Boys*, in which teen idol Corey Haim (with a Rob Lowe poster on his bedroom wall, no less) tries to defend his hunky big brother, played by Jason Patric, from being recruited to a gang of equally hunky, leather-wearing vampires. Patric is given a female love interest, played by Jami Gertz, but the film is far more interested in the calls from the alluring bad-boy bloodsuckers for him to 'join us'. I didn't *consciously* recognise the movie's now bleedingly obvious queerness at the time; I just knew that I loved it and watched it so often I could recite much of its dialogue.

The Lost Boys also features Dianne Wiest, one of my many actress obsessions, those who played the strong female characters who I always wanted the story to be about, but who were generally relegated to love interests or subplots. Sure, Harrison Ford was incredibly handsome, but why couldn't *Raiders of the Lost Ark* have been about Marion Ravenwood, the fierce, brawl-starting, drinking competition–winning Karen Allen character? She was a woman running a dive bar in Nepal, for goodness sake. And how could anyone want to see more Roger Moore in *A View to a Kill* with Grace Jones in the same film? I was never much interested in religious education at my Catholic school, because my holy trinity already comprised Bette Midler in *The Rose*, Barbra Streisand in *Funny Girl* and Liza Minnelli in *Cabaret*. Amen. I prayed at their church long before I had the slightest clue of their ordained central place in gay culture – before I had the slightest clue that there even was such a thing as gay culture.

I don't know when exactly that snippets of information accumulated into certainty that there were people called 'gay' who loved and desired people of their own gender and existed outside the shower room of Turkish prisons. By the time that uncertain flicker burst into a radiant glow, I was determined to remain forever in the dark. In my school playground, being gay was the worst thing you could possibly be. I didn't really buy into that idea – I had no problem with *other people* being gay – but I was a well-behaved kid who rarely pushed even the tiniest boundary of what was considered good behaviour. How, then, could I ever step into a world that seemed to only lurk on the fringes? Surely I, like Davis, would shake my head, no? Surely I was still Herbie looking for my Giselle, a Tramp in search of his Lady, a charming prince looking for a girl in a coma protected by dwarves?

You can raise an entire nation of children on nothing but heterosexual imagery, and the result will still be a bunch of queer kids in there among that hetero-majority. We've given censorship a red-hot go as a means of preventing homosexuality and yet, even with all that straight kissing up there on the screen, there are still boys who want to kiss other boys, girls who want to kiss other girls, along with all those kids who suspect that the label 'boy' or 'girl' doesn't quite fit them like it seemingly does everyone else. By keeping these children in the dark we don't protect them – we just keep them in the dark.

When, somewhat belatedly in my early twenties, I finally admitted what my feelings for *Dirty Dancing*–era Patrick Swayze had clearly been indicating for some time, my first step as a newly minted gay man was to search out *every queer movie I could find*. This was the era of New Queer Cinema and I saw *Paris Is Burning*, *Swoon* and *The Living End* at arthouses like the Academy Twin in Paddington and the Valhalla in Glebe. At the legendary Video-drama video store on Oxford Street, I found *Maurice*, *Making Love* and the ridiculously beautiful Joe Dallesandro in *Flesh* and *Trash*. I devoured Vito Russo's book *The Celluloid Closet* and searched out Hays Era classics like *Cat on a Hot Tin Roof*, *Rope* and *Rebel Without a Cause*.

I still hungered for a great gay rom-com or a queer action hero. And so, I remade movies in my mind, retelling the story to myself as I watched, imagining the happy queer romance or heroic victory that the story could have included in a different world.

That's part of the work that so many of us have to do. We make leaps, restructure and remake so that the world onscreen begins to look a little more like our lives, or the lives we imagine for ourselves. At its worst, such work makes us feel excluded, pushed to the margins or out of the picture completely. But it can be powerful. It expands the possibilities of our world, revealing the porousness of otherwise impermeable-seeming borders. Watching *The Matrix*, I was never Keanu Reeves but always Carrie-Anne Moss, revelling in this incredible, powerful, leather-clad female hero; sometimes making her the centre of the story and giving her a female love interest; sometimes making her character male. Gender becomes malleable, a performance, something we can shift around and play with; sexuality becomes fluid.

In recent years the onscreen possibilities for queer childhoods have expanded. In 2012, *ParaNorman* was reportedly the first animated children's film to include an openly gay character. Not the main character, sure, but visible in the text nonetheless. Teen-friendly soap operas from *Glee* to *Riverdale* feature queer characters with active romantic and sexual lives. Ruby Rose is set to star as Batwoman, the first openly queer television superhero (the character has openly been a lesbian since she first appeared in the comic books, in 2006). And the recent *Love, Simon* is the gay romantic comedy I would have killed for as a teen. I'll admit to shedding a few tears at the end of that totally charming movie, partly out of happiness for Simon, and partly out of sadness for the queer kids like me for whom it came too late.

Despite all this positive change in representation, the moral panic around the Safe Schools program in 2016 demonstrated a continued unease in Australia over the very idea that some kids might be queer. Queerness is something that children must be protected from, so the story goes, not something they should be allowed to accept as a potential part of themselves. This notion infuriates me. It turns childhood into a period of limbo that queer people have to get through before the world will finally, grudgingly admit we aren't going to be straight or cisgender.

As a kid, I was invisible to myself because of adults who would rather I was worried and confused than gay. A world of adults more troubled by the idea of Bert and Ernie coming out than by the number of queer kids who take their own lives. Movies have brought me much happiness over the years, but I still wonder about the damage done by all of that silence. I think about the anxious kid I used to be and feel enormous anger on his behalf. If I could go back and give him anything it would be a pile of movies in which the teen hunk has a crush on another boy, where the action hero saves her girlfriend, where two muppets are in love and their gender is nobody's business. He could stare into that screen and be made visible. Not opaque or shadowy or uncertain, but vibrantly, joyously and unmistakably queer.

Something Special

Rebecca Shaw

This is going to come as a shock to most people who know me, who (I imagine) assume I am perfect in every way, but I sometimes have trouble expressing my feelings. As I am now in my mid-thirties, which is approximately six hundred in Queer Years, I've been reflecting on how my past has informed who I am now, and asking, 'Why am I like this?' Not to get too crying-drunk-girl-in-the-club-toilet-at-2-am about this, but one of my main issues is that I struggle with being honest and open about what I am feeling, or what I need. From advising romantic partners what would please me to simply asking a good friend to support me in some way, being honest about my desires in any situation makes me feel extremely vulnerable, and terrified of rejection. Instead, I simply lay a series of traps using passive-aggressive language in order to have the person solve a puzzle and do what I want, without me having to actually ask them. (Thank you for asking, yes, it's *extremely* healthy, and not frustrating for anyone; psychiatry academics clearly want to use me as an example of how to do things right.)

It may not be healthy, but at least I have partially figured out why I am like this. In an M. Night Shyamalan twist for the ages, I think it's because of my experience growing up queer in small-town Queensland. Shock!

It may be hard for younger readers to imagine, but for a long time I didn't have easy access to the internet. I couldn't find information (what do lesbians DO) online, or secretly contact communities of like-minded people to discover I wasn't alone in the world. So, from the age of ten, when I started to realise I felt differently to my friends, to seventeen, when I was able to connect to the rest of the world, I felt alone. Excruciatingly, desperately alone. Partly this was because, when I was nine, my family moved from the regional city of Toowoomba to a small locality outside the city, called Charlton. To set the scene a bit, according to the 2016 census, Charlton had a population of 120 people. The school I went to had thirty kids in it. So, my world was tiny when puberty hit and I discovered my queerness.

This would end up consuming me. As a teenager, I thought I was the only person on earth who felt the way I did. As well as not having the internet, I didn't meet an openly queer person until I was in my twenties (unlike now, when I refuse to meet straight people), and I didn't see a queer person on TV until I was sixteen (hello, I love you, Tara, and no, I still haven't forgiven Joss Whedon). The only time I even heard about the *concept* of being gay in real life was when I started commuting to high school in Toowoomba. Toowoomba has a population of 150,000, but is not exactly a thriving metropolis. It is still country, it is conservative, and I actually felt even more isolated there. That's because I did finally hear about gay people there, but exclusively as slurs, or in a negative context. I went from not knowing what queer was, or that anyone else in the world was queer, to understanding that some people *are* queer but it's bad and everyone will fucking hate you for it.

I spent almost every waking moment thinking about how I was queer, how it was bad, and how I could change it. Or, if I couldn't change it, how I could make sure nobody ever found out my terrible secret. This didn't only mean not telling people I thought I was attracted to girls. It meant figuring out what I was 'supposed' to be like, and mimicking that. Making sure that nothing I did would raise suspicion.

When I think back now to that girl, I feel heartbroken for her. Not only because she felt she had to hide who she was, but because those years were so full of secrets: faking emotions and actions, and having to self-monitor constantly. The loneliness and fear she felt is tragic, but so is the exhaustion of living a lie. Just about every memory I have of those seven years, even those unrelated to my secret, evokes the immense weight I felt on my shoulders, the pit in my stomach. It was always there, humming under the surface.

I couldn't express what I was feeling. I was worried that if I told the truth about what I desired for myself, I would be rejected, ostracised, or worse. My world would end. Even when, in my late teens, I was able to see a world beyond mine and consider that maybe I could be honest and happy one day, still I couldn't face it. The first time I decided to come out to someone, an aunt and uncle I loved and thought would be okay with it, I heard someone at their house say 'faggot'. I didn't try to come out to anyone else for two years. Even then, in a late-night conversation in the freezing cold in Toowoomba, drunk with a friend from university who I knew was queer and would therefore be okay with who I was, I struggled to bring myself to say it. I twisted and turned and deflected until she asked me point-blank if was attracted to women. When I came out to my mother, it was after a long conversation in which I manipulated her into asking me directly. It was still almost impossible for me to say the truth.

That brings us back to me in 2019, struggling to be upfront with those I love. I think you can see what I'm getting at. What I went through then has obviously informed who I am now. It has been hard to overcome how the world taught me to be. But many years have passed, and I've become more openly and powerfully queer with each moment. I have evolved from that place of fear to one where I truly and absolutely cherish being queer, and I believe it is a gift. Now, I get to process my problems, my limitations, with people who understand where they spring from and who aren't judgemental; with people who can empathise fully, based on their own experiences. I can be completely honest with them. They know why I am like this, and they love me for who I am. Nothing feels better than that.

Of course, I hope that all the queer kids of Australia today are having an easier time of it than I had, but if they aren't I need them to know something: your world might seem small now, but your people are out there waiting. The classic saying goes: 'It gets better.' That's a nice message. But I believe it doesn't just get better, it gets *the best*. It is a privilege to be in this position. If I had the choice, I would go through all those hard years again if it meant I would end up where I am now, in the beautiful, diverse community I get to call family. So do what I am still learning to do: be honest about what you want. Be open to loving and to being loved. You're part of something special; get here as quick as you can.

Floored

Nic Holas

This is a story about being on the edges.

*

In the mid-1990s, my family lived on the edge of a golf course on the Gold Coast. Large swathes of the town had been transformed into golf courses, in an attempt to cash in on the Japanese tourist market. Sliced into the curved perimeter of the golfing green were residential fence posts, easy enough to jump over but rarely did I dare to do so. The threat of being killed by an errant golf ball from some Gold Coast real estate agent trying to impress 'Mr Takahashi-san', or similar, was too great a risk. Anyway, I was not a risk-taking kid.

I was on the edge of adolescence, a slip of a boy, not quite twelve. I had just kissed my first girl, and I knew I was different but hadn't yet named what that difference was. I lacked something other boys had. The deficiency was anxiety-inducing. A year later, I would know that I desired men, but for now I was deeply suspicious of boys my age, especially since I didn't know how to interact with Australians.

My family was on the edge of one era, moving into another. After several years living in Malaysia, and having recently left my stepfather, my mother had brought my brother and me back to Australia so I could start high school here. To be close to family and friends, she chose to settle us on the Gold Coast. It was quite the culture shock.

Living abroad in Kuala Lumpur, where my mother worked in fashion and my stepfather was a pilot, had afforded me a relatively cosmopolitan upbringing. My mother's job had exposed us to a network of designers, fashion buyers and local homosexuals. To my young eyes, they seemed like an exciting underground: part Parisian bohemia, part Chicago gangster. Given homosexuality was outlawed in Malaysia, I wasn't entirely off the mark.

My white skin made me a valuable commodity as a child model, so Mum would often make my brother and me pose for the catalogues and walk the runway shows. My latently homosexual ten-year-old self took to this with gusto and aplomb. But weirdly, my new Australian classmates were not impressed by my portfolio or tales of stomping the runway.

In KL, I went to an international school in the heart of the embassy district; my classmates were the children of diplomats. Our classroom looked like a United Colors of Benetton ad had fucked the 'It's a Small World' ride at Disneyland. It was so diverse, Peter Dutton would have accused it of making Melbournians afraid to go out for dinner.

When apartheid ended, our white South African teacher cried in front of us and then suddenly disappeared, never to return. I'm not sure if she was crying tears of joy or sorrow, but it stuck with me. Growing up white in a former British colony in South-East Asia affords you a degree of privilege that is different from growing up on the unceded land of what we now call Australia. Different, but not better or worse. In KL, we were 'expats', with all the terrible trappings that identity allows.

Back in Australia, nothing could prepare me for the shock of starting school on the Gold Coast. The shock was not just from seeing only white faces in my classroom, but also at the way the school seemed geared to appease freckled little Australian boys, with its endless sports activities beneath an unforgiving Queensland sun, sports that as a boy I was supposed to be familiar with. The choice given to me was rugby league or soccer, and for some ungodly reason I chose rugby league.

The only memory I have of my school football career is of the coach yelling at me to go play some sort of on-field position. I had no idea what he was talking about, but I was too intimidated to ask, because all the other boys knew how to play. So I ran into the middle of the pack and pretended that this was exactly where I was meant to be – while he screamed at me, over and over.

They say masculinity is a prison, but mine was more like Nicole Kidman in *Bangkok Hilton*: a foreigner, overly proud and weirdly up myself, while simultaneously incredibly anxious.

So, come 1994, my family and I were literally and metaphorically on edge. Adding to this sense, for me, was my strong loyalty to my mother and my belief that I needed to protect her. There had been a time, before she married my stepfather, when it was just her and me: a bonding time as a little boy, made more intense by my latent queerness.

In my mind, my mother's decision to leave my stepfather was irrevocable. I never dreamt of a *Parent Trap*–style plan to reunite them. I had been too young to experience my own parents' divorce, and this meant that I believed that when Mum left someone, that was it. Marriages end; you move on.

My stepfather, however, was not of the same mind. Mum leaving him wounded him deeply, and he did not cope well with the separation. This was his third failed marriage, made all the harder by distance. He remained in Malaysia. When the boxes filled with our stuff followed us home, they arrived covered in handwritten notes to my mother, begging to be taken back.

He eventually turned up on the Gold Coast, hot on the heels of those same boxes. It wasn't a surprise. As with my father, her first husband, Mum was determined that a divorce would not prevent her son from seeing his dad. Maybe it was school holidays, maybe not.

One afternoon during his visit, my stepfather sent my younger brother and me out of the house. According to him, he and my mother needed to chat. By the time we got back to the house from wherever we'd wandered, Mum was gone for the evening, and he was looking after us.

Hanging thick in the air was something that made me feel uneasy, a child sensing the desperation of a grown man. I knew nothing of the complicated nature of marital heartbreak, but I knew Mum had left him and that her mind was made up. This was an edge that had to be leapt off. Divorce meant never turning back.

So there we were, my little brother, my stepfather and me. Apparently, Mum was over at her friend's house, and would come home eventually. So I decided to stay up as late as I could to ensure

I was still awake when she returned. A little moral guardian, like some sort of anthropomorphic Disney creature, there to cheerfully ruin my stepfather's chances of a romantic reunion.

I'm not certain what prompted it, but when I was eventually ordered to bed I detoured to Mum's room and declared that I would be sleeping in her bed that night. I was not a toddler. Here I was, on the edge of puberty, already kissing girls at blue-light discos, instinctively climbing into my mother's bed in a ham-fisted attempt to protect her from my stepfather's charms. Or her own choices.

Suddenly, the space between my stepfather and me moved from Disney comedic relief to full-blown Oedipal tragedy. He told me to go sleep in my room. I told him I wanted to stay there. When pressed for the reason I, a boy of my age, needed to sleep in my mother's room, I had nothing. I had no words to describe the feeling in the pit of my stomach, the feeling that came out of my belly button via an emotional umbilical cord that was still connected to her, all gristle and blood wrapped up with the metaphorical apron strings we are told must be cut.

I will only state what I recall happening, what it felt like then, and how it feels now.

I recall his rage, volcanic and apoplectic. Breaking without warning, out of nowhere and directed entirely at me.

I recall his big hands on my bony shoulders.

I recall the feeling of being shaken, the sensation of being pinned to the mattress. It only lasted a moment, but during moments of trauma, time becomes heavy; black matter.

I recall him barking at me to return to my room.

I recall his desperate anger, a ploy designed to hurt and shock me out of her bed.

'Your mother likes it on the floor anyway.'

That's all I can recall.

I can't recall who won the battle that night: I don't know if I returned to my own bed or managed to stay in hers. I suspect I gave in to his commands, and I have no memory of Mum coming home that night, so in all likelihood I fell asleep at the post. A failed attempt at being her little moral guardian. Regardless, there was no place for him in that bed, with or without me in it. Eventually, I won the war: the divorce was indeed final. He moved on and remarried, and in time so did my mother. They are both still with these partners, and are happy.

That night was at the edge of many things, but more than the golf course or puberty or another divorce, the events of that evening kept me at the edge of ever feeling entirely safe around heterosexual men, from then until now.

It is possible to despise and fear the thing you pity. It is possible to understand that what my stepfather said and did to me as a child came from a place of utter weakness. I see it now as a pathetic move by a desperate man, so wounded from being rejected by his wife that he struck out at a child, her child. I think I saw it that way then too, but growing up queer is questioning how you see the world – because we are repeatedly shown it is their world, not ours.

We are expected to permit, forgive and make room for the behaviour of heterosexual, cisgendered Australian men. We are expected to understand that they aren't to blame for how they are. We just rent space in the edges where they permit us to dwell, and when we try to stand up for ourselves, or others, we are just bony shoulders for them to shake.

But as my little bony shoulders grew broader, I learnt the value of standing with – and up for – others. For women, like my mother and my sisters. For my queer siblings. For my HIV+ siblings. For those whose tribe I am not a part of and whose shoulders have borne much greater burdens than mine. That little boy on the edge of the golf course grew up to dedicate his life to fighting with those tribes.

With every victory, every legislative win, every man who is shown he cannot get away with acting like his fathers and forefathers, our many bony shoulders knit into something stronger than all of them. And on those shoulders will one day stand younger queers, who will look upon that impotent, white, male, cis, heterosexual rage and do what I wish I could have done that night: laugh.

Not Special

Tim McGuire

Before I was diagnosed with HIV, I thought that I probably would be. Not just on the day I went to the doctor for my test result, though I thought it then, too. Just before I left the house, I changed out of my favourite San Francisco Giants hoodie into a less special one, because I didn't want the jumper to be associated with what I imagined would be a memory best repressed. I would want the hoodie later, I figured – something comforting to change into after my world was changed as well.

I'm good with dates (the ones in the calendar, not the other kind), and I knew this one was auspicious already. It was 22 September: the first time I went overseas, my sister's first book launch, the day Oceanic Flight 815 crash-landed on *Lost*.

No, I suspected it much earlier. In high school, I read *Holding the Man* by Timothy Conigrave, Australia's best-known gay love story and AIDS tragedy, which charts Tim's struggle with the disease until his death in 1995, shortly before the memoir was published. I bought the book in secret after my high school cancelled our Year 12 drama excursion to see *Holding the Man* on stage. I was indignant but unsurprised; this was the same all-boys college whose entire sex education curriculum across the eight years of my schooling there comprised a single lesson taught to just one of four Year 7 classes, chosen seemingly at random, and involving only a VHS screening on the reproductive behaviour of dingoes. I never saw it, but the plot was retold on the handball courts in reverential whispers, and it was evidently powerful enough to trigger the onset of puberty in all thirty boys by the rolling of the end credits – just in time for our Year 7 camp. Strange for a Catholic college, I've realised since, to choose, of all the sexual positions to introduce us to, doggy style. That said, nobody in my graduating class got anyone pregnant.

And so I learnt more about sex, its mechanics and its consequences from Timothy Conigrave than I did in a classroom. I wept while I read his book, afraid for myself and grieving for this man I didn't know and with whom I shared a name.

After high school, I continued to learn about sex – often when I had the house to myself, a strong wi-fi connection and a spare twelve minutes – from the internet, and in doing so discovered a gay porn studio that primarily produces movies in which the actors have sex without condoms. The relatively notorious studio – sex without condoms, or barebacking, is a divisive topic in the gay community – is called Treasure Island Media, or TIM. The same acronym was later adopted by the Australian grassroots collective for people living with HIV, The Institute of Many – *also* TIM. It's not that I'm particularly superstitious (my boyhood careers as a Charmed One and a Vampire Slayer notwithstanding), but I took these coincidences as portends, evidence even, that I would someday contract HIV.

Tim, the universe seemed to be saying. *Tim, Tim, Tim.*

Even after I was diagnosed, the coincidences continued. The clinical trial through which I currently receive my lifesaving antiretroviral medication is called the GEMINI study. Can you guess what my zodiac sign is? It's not Virgo the Virgin.

*

A year before I read *Holding the Man*, I fractured my left wrist for the third time. This latest fracture was my brother's doing. Nan's birthday party, a backyard scuffle. After the celebrations were cut short (sorry, Nan), I was fitted with a cast that my mates at school jostled to sign. On it, near my thumb-now-claw, my friend Carleigh wrote, 'AIDS. LOL.'

The joke worked, I guess, because AIDS felt very far away – geographically and historically – from Brisbane's South Bank cinema, outside which Carleigh wrote her double acronym in the practised penmanship of a Year 11 student during exam block. There was something fantastical about AIDS; it was a disease that happened to other people in other places or times, like The Plague or scurvy. In developed countries, the AIDS crisis reached its peak before we were born. It was 2007 now, we were sixteen, and the worst tragedy we'd known was a thrice-fractured wrist.

Still, I didn't laugh. I don't think I laughed at HIV/AIDS jokes until after I was diagnosed, when it seemed suddenly necessary to find humour in them, to wrest back control of what was happening to me. Though it made me anxious for reasons I couldn't yet properly articulate, I thanked Carleigh for her contribution to my cast; it would have been rude not to, given she was my fourth-top friend on Myspace at the time. As the weeks went by, my cast got grimier, the well wishes and the biro band names rubbed away, but the AIDS message endured, imperishable, written in a black marker whose ink was permanent.

*

I asked my secret top friend, Rosie – secret because she didn't have Myspace, and so there was no public way to rank her – to come with me to my first sexual health test, at the Metro North Sexual Health and HIV Service on Roma Street. We were in our first year of university, and I had been sexually active for a while. All the way back in Year 2, my parents received concerned phone calls from my teachers after I was discovered leading girls behind an old demountable building to make them kiss me. Word got around. Mum's friends started calling me 'Casanova'; Dad's friends, 'The Chick Magnet'. None of them was concerned. What did trouble my parents was my friendship with these girls, not my ability to lure them into witness-less spaces to touch them against their wishes. Too many female friends, they thought, and I'd end up a sissy. They sent me to my all-boys college at the earliest opportunity, Year 5, but my libido continued to run high in a school full of guys, one of whom I eventually started having terrible, muted sex with. Terrible because we were both racked with guilt, muted because we were doing it in the school toilets, next to the classroom where he'd witnessed the dingo documentary years earlier. It was actually him who prompted me to get tested at the clinic for the first time.

I was tested for everything, not just HIV. In the examination room, I lay on my side, knees hugged to my chest as instructed, the white hillock of my bottom exposed to the nurse's gloved finger, which he inserted into me with as much notice as you would provide a pot plant before dipping your finger into its soil to check for moisture. I stared at the wall, memorising the building's evacuation route from a poster there. Afterwards, he tickled the back of my throat with a swab and I gagged dramatically.

Giving blood makes me feel faint and so, after I failed to stand properly upright, a different nurse had to fetch a biscuit jar from the clinic tearoom. There was one biscuit left, an Orange Slice, the worst of the Arnott's Assorted Creams, but I munched it gratefully, wondering whether it was left over from an assorted pack or not, and feeling a flare of sympathy for the clinic staff if it wasn't.

The clinic rang with my results a week later. Negative. But, even still, my fear marched on, as thrumming and resilient as a pride parade. I got tested for HIV many times after that, even when I had no reason to, and though I always tested negative until I didn't, I only ever felt like I'd dodged a positive result for now, not forever.

*

Because I was afraid of HIV, I saw it everywhere, and engaged with it nowhere. Every day seemed to be World AIDS Day. Under a pink sky breaking across the morning, and wearing last night's clothes, I walked from the house of a stranger to a cab rank in Fortitude Valley, up Ann Street, where giant red ribbons hung like Christmas bunting.

I avoided films about HIV, articles, books and news reports. In doing so, I learnt nothing about it, and in my ignorance I became complicit in its stigma. To my friends, I pretended to have seen *Dallas Buyers Club* and the screen adaptation of *Holding the Man*, because they were in the gay canon. A canon, I realised later, that had impressed on me, as if by osmosis, the idea that I would likely become HIV positive, or that my life would be tragic in some way. Not because my name was Tim, but because I was gay.

Fear, though, can be a terrific motivator. I wish that mine had been sufficient, or that education had been enough to keep me from making an error of judgement, a quick misplacement of faith, that I will regret, probably, forever.

*

The best thing about being diagnosed with HIV is that you never have to take another HIV test. When I was twenty-five, an anxiety I'd harboured since I was sixteen was finally realised, and then it was done. I was HIV-positive now, and the world, though it felt perilous at times, didn't stop spinning.

Because I am lucky. I am so miraculously, circumstantially fortunate to have been diagnosed with HIV in 2016, in Australia. HIV has always been a lifelong illness but, until recently, its prognosis has never been long life. Forty years ago, the world didn't know HIV. It was a disease without a name, much less a treatment plan, but still it was coming, a gathering storm on the horizon. Now, HIV is permanent but treatable, serious but survivable. And because I live in Australia, I have free access to the medication that enables it to be so. Other people living with HIV are not so lucky.

So, now what?

*

A few hours after I was diagnosed, I watched the season one finale of *Stranger Things* with my sister, who had attended the doctor's appointment with me. At the end of the episode, one of the boys vomits up a little alien slug into the bathroom sink and stares, horrified, as it slithers away. I scrunched up my face in distaste, and my sister turned to look at me and said, 'And you think *you've* got problems.'

She was right; I didn't really. I started thinking a lot about amputees who go on to run marathons and win gold medals at the Olympics, blind people who become celebrated musical or even visual artists. Cancer patients who tick off bucket-list dreams in an impossible time frame. We love these stories because they inspire us, they remind us that life's challenges are in fact surmountable. *Look what they did*, we think, *and they did it with one leg*. It's the kind of tale of human perseverance we make movies about, the kind of triumph over adversity that might also win you a book deal. As a writer, and an opportunist, it did make me wonder: *How do people living with HIV get in on that*? What equivalent, aspirational, against-all-odds goal should we be setting ourselves? To have sex with as many people as possible? I'd been working towards that goal, with varying degrees of success, since I was teenager. I needed something new, something special.

'You're *not* special,' my sister reminded me, 'just because you have HIV. It's an *epidemic*.'

She's right. I'm not special. Just lucky.

Jack and Jill and Me

Stephanie Convery

*I am not outside the language that structures me, but neither am
I determined by the language that makes this 'I' possible.*

Judith Butler, *Gender Trouble*

I met Jack when I was in high school. Only he wasn't Jack then, he
was Jill.

Jill had a tattoo on the nape of her neck, dyed black hair and a
face full of piercings. She had a bright barking laugh that cut
through the tension in any room. She wore low-slung jeans and
boots, played the saxophone and studied visual art and design. We
were introduced by a mutual friend who dragged four of us to
Melbourne's Alexandra Gardens one lush spring day because he
wanted us to start a band.

The band never eventuated, but a network of friendships did.
Jill lived on the opposite side of the city – my first proper friend
from the west side. We caught up on and off over the next few
years, mostly chatting online, but occasionally trekking over to
each other's neighbourhood. She drove a restored but temperamental Ford Fairlane; I caught endless trains and buses. Sometimes
we'd convince a mutual friend to drive to each other's parties.
When I moved away from the sharp, dry heat of Australia to spend
months in a midwinter depression in the snow-swept mountains
of Eastern Europe, she wrote me letters filled with the intimate
trivialities of her day-to-day life: something about cheese; fixing
her car; a copy of her receipt from the milk bar; an instruction to
listen to 'Doughnut Song' by Tori Amos because it would make

me feel better about the things I'd left behind. I listened to it one snowstorm-dark morning, watching tiny snowflakes spiral softly onto the windowsill, thinking it was possibly perfect.

Ours was a friendship that would flare into life unexpectedly and fall dormant just as quickly, and it continued in its uneven way after my return from Europe and throughout my undergraduate degree. Then, late one October, a dozen of us took a weekend trip to the country. We drank, listened to music and drove too fast along the highway. Friday night lasted until Saturday morning. Hangovers abounded. We piled plates with eggs and bacon, and washed it down with mugs of coffee. As the evening closed in, beer cans cracked open again; fuzzy-headed, raucous conversations on the porch dissolved into relaxed murmurs when a joint was passed around, and somewhere along the way, Jill and I sank into cushions on the floor of the living room, curled up together under a sleeping bag, talking, touching, sleeping.

Our romance quickly became formal. I started my honours year and moved into a flat so close to hers we practically lived together. We shared a car, house keys, kitchen utensils, clothes, our bodies, and a friendship that had given way to something much deeper. For almost a year we existed like this, until I finished my degree and, in a reckless, cathartic moment post thesis submission, got drunk in the city with an old friend and ended up in bed with him. I owned up to it the following day, but it fractured the fragile ecosystem we'd created.

The relationship disintegrated rapidly after that; a cold and sullen silence sat between us. I moved out. We both moved on. With patience, we managed to salvage the acquaintance, and then, after a while, our friendship. It wasn't long until the person I had known began to change in ways that were far more significant.

*

I resented the idea of coming out. It wasn't that I was introverted, or that I felt like my romances were shameful (I talked blithely about the intimate details of my affairs whenever the fancy took me, possibly to my detriment), but that I loathed the idea of being pigeonholed. The social narratives around homosexuality had always left me with the impression that coming out was more than a courtesy. It was an expectation: like taking a ticket to join a queue or picking up litter; it was the responsibility of every good citizen to keep things neat and tidy.

Not only that, the idea that my relationships or my identity required formal sanction by others frustrated me. Even in my hetero relationships, that sense of obligation weighed on me: was he my 'boyfriend'? Was it serious or not? I never knew how to answer those questions in a way that felt honest or comfortable. How long did you need to be fucking before you became 'more than' friends? How was this the business of anyone and everyone with whom I had little more than a passing acquaintance? The whole interrogation seemed grounded in ideas about property, women, marriage and family that I believed had no right to dictate my life.

But I had also never thought of myself as gay. I had identified as bisexual since my late teens, but only because it was the least-categorical category I knew. At the time, I'd never heard of *queer* – the term I would more likely use now – or *pansexual*, or any of the other words people use to characterise a non-exclusive, non-traditional sexuality. I just knew that I was attracted to women as much as I was to men, but that being into men made my interest in my own gender a lot easier to hide, even if I found it hard to ignore. But being bi had its drawbacks, too.

When I was growing up, there was a lot of smack talk about bisexuality, both from within the queer community and without: about how bisexual people are just being greedy, how they don't really know what they want, how they should 'pick a side'. Like most discrimination, its roots are both cultural and political; some recent contributions have been the conflation of sexual politics with sexual identity that characterised the lesbian feminist movements of the '80s, or the misplaced blame on bisexual men for the HIV/AIDS crisis.

To some gay people, being bi seems easy. We have the supposed luxury of being chameleons, the freedom to sit on both sides of the fence, the privilege of choosing from the entire buffet rather than being confined to a corner table, as if sex were simply a smorgasbord and falling in love a matter of calculated odds. Perhaps when you look at it from that point of view, the surprisingly sharp economic disadvantages of bisexual identification look less like structural disadvantage and more like privileged whining (one Californian study found that while gay men and lesbians earned 2 to 3 per cent less than straight men, bisexual women earned 11 per cent less and bisexual men ten to 15 per cent less).

The truth is, being bisexual means being invisible, especially if you are in a monogamous relationship, whether you paint yourself like a rainbow or a white picket fence. This is something I still struggle with in my thirties, though there is marginally less social presumption in some circles now; at the age of twenty, it seemed like a no-win situation. As a young bisexual woman I was presumed to be performing for an audience (of men) – 'bi for the guys' – experimenting, or else excluded from the conversation altogether. I found this alienating and difficult. To the queer community, I wasn't serious enough, but in the hetero world I was just fodder for pornography. There was, it appeared, no room for those who quietly straddled categories or defied them altogether. So I washed my hands of it and hung around instead with the freaks and geeks, Goths and punks and pixies and nerds, because with them I felt more often than not that my sexuality was just another dimension of me: not a flag I had to fly, or an aberration I had to justify, or something I had to think about all the time. We called ourselves 'alternative' – a word all the more appropriate in retrospect. We were not the opposite of the mainstream, but simply 'other'. We were all a bit NQR in our own way, and there was a kind of solidarity in that.

When my friendship with Jill turned sexual, I was in the process of ending three years with a guy I'll call Paul. It had begun as a long-term affair under the nose of his girlfriend. After a six-month break, which I spent in Europe, it developed into apparent exclusivity. We knew all the same people, went to the same parties, listened to the same bands. It had all the appearance of conventionality, but that façade belied the rottenness at its core.

Romance is a narrative of power. The 'falling' part of 'falling in love' gives only the barest clue to the absolute abandonment of sense, control and responsibility that characterises these experiences. Falling in love with Paul meant that what I wanted (him, his attention, his affection) subsumed my own needs (agency, independence, self-determination) so completely that I allowed a relationship to develop with the power differential skewed entirely in his favour. The result was passive-aggressiveness and manipulation on his part, near total emotional dependence on mine. A balloon of insecurity billowed up around me, expanding and contracting on his whim, distorting every experience and feeling, and I did not know how I would ever escape it.

I eventually escaped it because other women punctured it. First there was Cara: an affair at a party he had refused to attend – rain, oranges, cold air and warm breath, rushes of heat; and something solidified inside me, a kernel, a core that was mine and mine alone. Then there was Dana, a covert fix up by a gay friend – a drunken night on the town, an airbed in a spare room on the other side of the city, a mortifying 6 am taxi-ride home – and I stepped across some invisible threshold.

And then there was Jill.

*

I was not prepared for the amount of attention our relationship would attract. If I had expected anything, I suppose it was that having a girlfriend would be much the same as having a boyfriend, only that men would understand you were neither available nor interested (they would assume you were a lesbian – bi-erasure at work) and that they would accept that, even if they didn't exactly respect it. On the contrary, the objectification became worse.

Much of the attention was lascivious: men expressed leering disappointment at 'another hot chick off the market, such a shame' (the egotistic presumptions underpinning such a statement astonish me still). Propositions were made to us as a couple by friends and strangers alike, with no encouragement on our part. (*Why do they assume our relationship is less serious than theirs?* I used to wonder.) Some of it was just plain nasty, like the man at the bar who came up to me while Jill was in the bathroom and said, 'Do me a favour, don't order the ox tongue' (it took me a few minutes to register that he wasn't talking about the bar menu). To some, it seemed like our relationship made us cooler; to others, it simply made us objects of scrutiny.

At the same time, I was buried in books about gender and narrative, sexual politics and the politics of love as part of my studies. I viewed my relationship with Paul, retrospectively, through the prism of Simone de Beauvoir's *The Second Sex*: 'Every woman in love recognises herself in Hans Andersen's little mermaid who exchanged her fishtail for feminine legs through love and then found herself walking on needles and live coals.' I began to understand romance as a narrative of male power and female obliteration. I found solidarity with women writers in a way I never had before, and those books were helping me to politicise my own identity as a woman. Simultaneously, I began to reject the idea of essential maleness or femaleness; we were gendered and oppressed not by our intrinsic nature, but by society and culture. I found this galvanising, but my actual experience of it was contradictory: I saw the expectations that came from gender categories as damaging and destructive, yet I still invested a lot in marking myself as feminine in many ways; although my relationship with Jill was founded on a mutual desire for intimacy, not politics, I couldn't help but begin to see the politics of it, too.

Jill didn't share my feminist political compulsion, although she listened and nodded along when I talked about it. The work I was doing might have been academic but it was also intensely personal, and the deeper I went into it, the more imperative it felt to interrogate all the disparate pieces of myself on political terms. What role was this relationship playing in my life? How had the past informed my sense of identity? What collateral damage had I sustained? And how, crucially, could I fix it?

None of these questions helped with the fact that despite being in a relationship with a woman, the roles prescribed for lesbians felt uncomfortable to me, like I was wearing clothes that were slightly too small. I started to understand why other queer folk became so strident about performing their sexuality in a particular way, why they embraced the structure and certainty provided by the stereotype, even as they were restricted by it. Because I felt like I was failing somehow. I knew what I wanted, but I didn't know how to perform it. I didn't know how to perform *myself*. I felt like I was learning how to fuck all over again. I felt clumsy in my body, like a fifteen-year-old virgin, uncomfortable with my own experiences, and unsure of what progress meant in a relationship that felt so unthreatening. A lifetime of hetero conditioning had set me up for relationships based almost entirely on conflict, yet this was pleasant, comfortable, easy, *nice*. I didn't know what to do. It was a completely unfamiliar power dynamic, and I didn't know how to move within it.

Perhaps by the time I finished my thesis, I'd given up trying. Perhaps I was too tired, too bruised, too emotionally drained to do anything but fall back, for a while anyway, into the at least familiar head-fuck of hetero sex. Perhaps I was just twenty-two and care-less. Or perhaps Jill wasn't getting much out of the relationship anymore either, and it was falling to pieces even before I stuffed it full of dynamite and lit a match.

*

When Jill emailed a couple of years later to explain that actually she felt more male than female, that *he* was a better pronoun to use, and he had chosen to change his name to Jack, it was unex-pected, but not wholly surprising. We had been broken up for a few years by that point, and our friendship had slid back into its old sporadic patterns. Still, my relationship with the person I had known as Jill had been so important to me, so formative, precisely because I had understood that person to be a woman. Jack was at once the same person and not the same, and the revelation created a dissonance between memory and knowledge that could up-end the way I had understood our relationship, even the way I under-stood myself.

Many trans people do not want to be associated with the gender identity (mis)assigned to them at birth, and experience discussion of their past selves in those terms as an incredible source of anxiety, disrespectful, hurtful, wrong. I understand this. But when I think about what my relationship with past-Jack meant to me, when I consider how defining that relationship was for me precisely because it was gendered in a particular way, I know things are not so simple.

If I'm honest, I started to come to terms with Jack's transition properly only when I found a way in which to speak about the past. This came from Jack himself. In the early days at least, he referred to Jill directly, to *her*, in the past tense, as if she were another, separate, person. It was a linguistic device as much as anything, but what it enabled for me was something quite important: it lent legitimacy to my experience of the relationship with the person Jack had been, and allowed me to process the change – to speak about it as a temporal (as distinct from *temporary*) thing in the timeline of our friendship, even as I simultaneously knew that Jack had felt his body was somehow wrong for a long time, and experienced femaleness as an obstruction.

So when I say that I had a relationship with a woman, when I talk about that person and call her Jill, I am not trying to deny Jack his transition, or suggesting that his true gender identity is anything but the one he articulates now. But neither can I retrospectively apply to our past relationship the knowledge I have about Jack's identity now. What would that even mean? That he was lying to me by presenting as a woman throughout our relationship? That he should have known better? Identity doesn't work like that, and society is hard enough on those who express gender diversity without adding that kind of personal blame to the mix. So when I talk about my relationship with Jill, more than anything it is a way of speaking that allows me to be honest with myself: to respect my own experience of our relationship and how significant it was for me, which hinged on who Jack was at the time – living as and presenting as female, while nevertheless in conflict with it.

*

A little while later, Jack and I met for coffee in the city. He had a new girlfriend, and he'd started lifting weights. We had only seen each other a couple of times since he began testosterone treatment, and I was still getting used to the changes in his appearance, and his voice. Jill's speaking voice had had a melodic tone, although flattened and drawn by the shape of her accent. Jack's voice was raspy and deep, and it took me by surprise the first few times I heard it. I was embarrassingly curious, but he smiled and reassured me that he was okay with my stumbling. It was pretty common, he said.

I asked him how testosterone felt. He paused over his short black, squinted out the window across the street, as if fixated on the church opposite.

'It's like squares,' he said finally. 'It's hard to explain. Like, for example, the other day my girlfriend sent me this text saying I should come over to her place. It was really kind of flowy and getting in the mood, you know? Like, *Drop everything and come over right now because I want you* kind of thing. I was really excited, so I wrote back, *Okay, I just have to go home first and have a salad.* And she was all like, *Well, I've never been stood up for salad before!* It was only then that I realised I'd totally missed the point. It seemed perfectly logical to me – I'm on this proper lifting diet, you see, and my brain was like, *I have to do this work-out and then I have to have a salad and then I can go see my girlfriend.* Squares.' He made shapes with his hands, indicating the thought structure. 'But I never used to think like that.'

'Is it true that men have these conversations when women aren't around that ...'

I didn't even need to finish the sentence because Jack was shooting me a grave look and nodding firmly.

'Dudes communicate differently, and I can *see* it now. I'm kind of part of that – I understand it in a way I never used to. But I'm not totally part of it either. Like, when they're saying all that sexist stuff, I can't just dive in and say, *Hey, that's not right.* It's not my place, you know? When there's a group of women together it's different too. The way conversations grow between women – it's so familiar, and some part of me still wants to get up and go over and be a part of that conversation. But I can't enter that space anymore – I can't catch on to the rhythms and the flow in the way I used to.'

I didn't know what to say. Here was my friend, my ex-girlfriend no less, telling me that not only did testosterone change his body, it changed his *mind*: the very mechanisms by which he interpreted the world and constructed thoughts.

'Being a man suits you,' I said, suddenly. 'I was going to say that you're still the same person but you're not. And yet ...'

I was lost for words. Jack believed in spirits and human essences, a separate soul that inhabited the body. In that respect, the body was a house for the person Jack was, and therefore the person I called 'Jack' was a constant, albeit changing, presence within that material form.

But I didn't believe in spirits. And it wasn't until later that it struck me how much of a dilemma that was. If the body was all there was, and that body could change quite dramatically – hormone levels could be recalibrated, breasts removed, organs replaced with artificial parts – what did that mean for our understanding of what constituted a person? What, exactly, was it that I named when I spoke of myself? Or Jack, or my mother, or anyone? If I was no more or less than my body, did that make me more or less of a person depending on the kind of body I had, if parts of it were missing or fundamentally altered, whether by accident or through my own choices? And what about my thoughts and feelings? Brain chemistry changes all the time, with or without the intervention of drugs, so what is the identifiable constant in any one person?

I remembered a philosopher once saying that the universe was a negotiable alliance of things. I couldn't remember who the philosopher was, or where I heard them say it, but the proposition rang true: I am the aggregate of thousands of molecules, electrons that fire and fade, impulses and substances that process nutrients and expel waste, atoms that are absorbed and shed and replaced. Each one of us is the locus of a mass of material movement, a cluster of intricate physical relationships. This mass we identify as the body, the movement as thought and action: a collection of experiences that leaves marks and scars, interpreted and understood as narratives, as history; as a past, present and future. In Marxist theory, the word for it is *dialectic*: constant flow, constant change, development through movement and essential contradiction. I am simultaneously an individual and a system of processes: an identifiable thing, material in the world; and a cluster of perpetually moving, changing and developing entities.

'You are a unique collection of experiences,' I said finally to Jack that day. 'You are memories and events and changes and processes, all bundled together. We used to call that Jill, but now we call it Jack.'

To My Man of Seventeen Years

Henry von Doussa

Doctor Duncan in the river was before my time. The homosexual university lecturer tossed into the Torrens at a spot under a bridge where, allegedly, the Adelaide newspapers said, men met for sex. 'Number One Beat' I would later learn it was called. 'Grab 'em, give those poofters a swim. Give 'em a dunking. Go ...' But me, in 1972, I knew nothing of such things. The attack was talked about by Mum and Dad while I skidded about the kitchen floor, learning to crawl; a toddler in a blue flannel growsuit, sopping up the mirthful language of small-town gossip and innuendo.

Sopped up other conversations too as Leonard Cohen and Bob Dylan played on the record-player in the kitchen, and later *The Naked Vicar Show* and Betty Blokk-buster playing on cassettes in the Datsun as Mum drove us to swimming lessons in the Adelaide Hills. Conversations my parents didn't shy away from: 1973, homosexuality declared not a mental illness; 1975, South Australia, the first Australian state to decriminalise gay sex. Me, I was turning four in 1975.

The lecturer drowned. His companion made it to the riverbank and survived. Dad was a lawyer in a town constrained by churches while at the same time lurching forward under the direction of a state premier in pink shorts. Dad's talk about the attack – alleged police involvement and the circus that followed – hung in the air around me. Did I hear him mock the premier? Was it the colour of his shorts or the colour of his labour politics? Did I hear that the lecturer was a bad influence on young students and not that much of a loss? 'He had it coming. Those men, what a life.' Did I hear Mum defend the dead man and admonish Dad for his views? Did I?

Never early to bed, what did I hear as they smoked cigarettes and she poured him another drink while I kicked about on a rug by the fire? 'Give the nipple another squeeze,' he would say, referring to the plastic nozzle on the wine cask.

How to illustrate the time that's passed? In order or just the important bits? Is it chronology or relevance that should govern a story, govern a life? I may have to jump about as I illuminate what I need to show you: all that must be cordoned off in the pursuit of belonging, the discounted residue that must be pushed away to become as clear and seamless and functional as a sheet of glass, to become a normal person. 'Fuck that shit,' my friend tells me. 'I've never been able to sustain a relationship, and I've given up trying. I don't think I'll ever feel love, you know, deep down, long-term, forever.'

At four I was a pretty boy, with a penchant for piggy tails in my hair and the tartan kilt my parents bought me on a trip to Scotland. Mum reassured my siblings that such a 'skirt' was appropriate attire for men in a faraway land. For me it felt so much better than pants and flew up when I spun. But I was a farm kid. Dad worked in town, but we lived on a farm in a rundown house with a big old English garden of camellias and rhododendrons. My older brothers rode their motorbikes around the paddocks while I picked flowers to decorate my cubby house. While they hosed mud off motorbike wheels, I tied back the curtains, put violets in a vase on the windowsill and straightened the old doormat Mum had given me.

*

Everywhere, nothing. All about me nothing but the long, flat day ahead. Summer holidays: cattle to be mustered from one paddock to another; sheep who'd missed crutching to have their arses doused with kerosene to kill the maggots; a long climb uphill from the pump house by the dam where I had to turn on the pump to fill the tanks, top of the list on a hot north-wind day; jobs to be done before I was left to the drawn-out day with my brothers. The long, hot day of bored adolescent boys, harassing, tormenting, prodding and poking.

Any reaction we could get from animals on the farm was a good one. Masking tape wrapped around a pony's nose so he bucked and thrashed up the paddock, chased by shotgun fire to really get him going. Constable the prize bull corralled into a small yard, menaced for hours with a red raincoat off the laundry floor until he crossed over from reliable old mate to something quite unrecognisable; later sold and then destroyed after 'inexplicably' chasing Dad across a paddock with murderous intent. Pet rabbits riddled with myxomatosis set free to blindly hop about the duck-house paddock with their eyes pustulent, their hair in clumps, easily picked off with the slug gun. 'Spaz, get out the way,' my brother shouting as a bloody carcass sails passed my head. One from another direction slaps me in the back. The neighbour's sheep shot in the fleece with the same gun, the butt steadied on the stone parapet of the verandah that stretched around the house and to the west overlooked the neighbouring paddocks. A feeble, slack old gun that fired pellets in such lacklustre fashion the sheep jumped but did not fall. Fifteen chickens squashed into the pellet feeder in the chook house. A record. When we took off the lid the first one jumped out flapping its wings in distress, the one on the bottom not so much. Four boys and a stretched-out summer's day. The small fox terrier tied to the large German short-haired pointer, collar to collar with a length of bailing twine, then a stick thrown into the dam to see what would happen as the little one trailed through the brown water on its back struggling for air. Hilarity, success, the helpless yelping of the poor little fella. Guinea pigs, mice, rats, cats, all with a role to play. The fecundity of farm life: pulling lambs, watching cows mate, the foreplay of a bull's muzzle under a stream of warm piss and then his pizzle extended. The mad gyrations of a bullish buck rabbit, the corkscrew penis of the house boar. The unrestrained language of the farmhands who narrated the scene – 'the bitch is hot for it', 'stick it to her old fella' – as they guided the ravenous veined penis of a stallion into a nose-twitched and hobbled mare: 'she's buckled down for ya old mate, what ya waiting for?' Too many kittens smacked dead with the head of a shovel.

Before they were used for crutching at the start of winter and then shearing in the summer, the rusty-but-just-functional clippers in the dilapidated shearing shed needed lubrication. So did my dick. The pot of dirty Vaseline that sat behind the shearing stand was put to good use. Me, I used that lotion in a rushed, shameful moment, probably repeated countless times in hot sheds and private crevices on farms across the country – boys making do in the experimentation of desire. A watermelon with a hole in it or the sheath of a used toilet role – boys making do.

There were few hard and fast rules in the liberal household I grew up in, but Mum once quoted statistics from some American study about the number of boys on farms who have sex with animals. This, she said, as well as the backward fifteen-year-old doing laps of the neighbouring front garden on her three-wheeled bike, was off limits. It seemed there were few limits in our house back then: sex, sexuality, coarse language, challenged bloodlines, infidelity, women leaving their husbands, husbands pursuing other men's wives, parents experimenting with marijuana. Meat and three veg confronted by avocado pears, halva and feta cheese; experimentation and new offerings were embraced by my parents in ways I didn't often see in my friends' houses. Mum baking a cake for the opening of a feminist bookshop in Stirling. Dad having the money and the inclination to buy a piece of farm equipment one day and then a Pro Hart painting of a dead grasshopper covered in ants on another. The possibilities and limitations of the time were being tested as my parents pushed against the restrictions of previous generations into an uncharted world, governed, among other things, by the pill and the sexual freedoms it bought.

Me, the hot shed and, when I found a moment to steel away, a dirty old jar of Vaseline. My brothers? I could guess. Their relief and release, I don't know.

My older brother had stolen the centrefolds from a stack of *Playboy* and *Penthouse* magazines we found at the rubbish dump near our holiday house on Kangaroo Island. After a surprisingly easy consultation with Dad, we were allowed to take them home from the dump but instructed to leave them in the nightstand on his side of the bed. Over the years, the magazines moved from the nightstand as lines of desire radiated around the house; then across the water to the mainland. Some of the foldouts my brother kept and others, much to my father's fury when it was discovered, he sold at school, a sign of the entrepreneurial spirit that would see him one day become very rich. Privately I used the magazines as best I could, but other than the playful meta-frisson of desire they lent to our household, there was not a lot in them for me. As a group though, my brothers and I used them loudly and they shaped our thoughts about sex as we forged our way through adolescence. 'The holiday treat', those magazines were called, and along with one tube each of sweetened condensed milk from the corner store to suck on as we made beds and swept dead spiders and scorpions out of the house at the start of the summer, they were part of the holiday we looked forward to. As with the dictum, *I only read* Playboy *for the articles*, it was not so much the photos that were circulated among us but most often the 'letters', or silly cartoons, representations that allowed for a kind of distance from the bodies on display. A way of sharing our needs and desires together through dappled light rather than the harshness and humiliation of looking straight at them.

My sister, the oldest and the most confident reader among us kids, enthralled us after dinner (and sometimes before breakfast) by reading aloud the letters to 'Harvey', a type of Agony Aunt who dispensed advice about sex from one of the magazines. Harvey's pronouncements would then be regurgitated after dinner when Mum had gone to bed and Dad was drunk and leaning well back on a straining kitchen chair, or, and usually with more fun, on fishing trips in the boat when not much was biting. 'Harvey says take it slow and use lots of lube' my brother said as Dad fought to bring a fish into the boat. 'Keep your tip up, Dad, and take it slow, use lots of lube or you'll lose her, that's what Harvey would say.' Dad would laugh and shake his head, feigning a type of limit to our vulgarity, but really he enjoyed the banter of the irreverent children he was raising, children with so much more sexual information than he at that age, the only child of a shamed divorcee.

'The poor little bugger was so horny he wore a condom on his date ...', one of us said; 'Meat, we call the man Meat ... Oh my god, look at the size of that thing, the boy's deformed ...' I said in an American accent, and my brothers laughed. We egged each other on. 'Pee-wee is so small, we'll have to tie a board across his arse, he's liable to fall in,' another brother said. These were the lines we would recite as the boat bobbed about and we tossed stinking ground bait into the sea. Lines from horny American teenagers in the '80s film *Porky's*. Us boys watched that film over and over, borrowing the tape from the local petrol-come-convenience store in town repeatedly, when VHS home video was all the rage.

'Cherry Forever' was the busty hooker. She was the sexual tutor of the film, guiding young men to adulthood when they visited Porky's, the riverside brothel across state lines. She was talked about endlessly on the boat too. 'You'd get your brothel slippers off for Cherry, Dad, wouldnya?' we'd laugh. Dad had recently started wearing slip-on shoes, which had never been done before by the men or boys in our family, and for which we quickly coined the term 'brothel slippers' because, we reasoned, they were quick to get off and quick to get back on when you only had a lunch hour to spare. 'Wouldnya Dad, off and on at top speed for Cherry Forever?' Again, he would smile and sip his can and smoke and then, 'Stop your carryon damn you, I've missed a bite,' as he jerked the tip of his fishing rod into the air. Within the rarefied legal circles in which he spent much of his life, his potty-mouthed children, 'wise' beyond their years, I think he saw as a strange badge of honour. I think we were a way to feel he resisted the stifling expectations of being a big fish in a small pond.

As you can see, sex was never a taboo topic in our household, but it was framed by the language of the day, the limits of representation.

At about the same time Harvey and Cherry Forever were working on the shape of our desires, a series of abductions and murders of young men were detailed in the Adelaide papers, in what became known as The Family murders. Grim but salacious daily reports of a sinister group of suspected homosexuals and the places in Adelaide never to be walked alone at night – moral lesson, cautionary tale, spicy titillation, all with a role to play in the fashioning of a small-town identity and its curtailing of new identities and their struggle for acceptance.

I was never a strong reader. On a farm with a pack of siblings it was always outside play, and there were endless jobs to be done after school or on weekends, like chopping wood in winter and slashing grass in summer. But I read those sinister articles as best I could. I was drawn to the scandal and the pictures of boys around my age who, the paper explained, had been found (and for the fortunate ones, woken) with lubricant on their anus. They said that in the papers! The young men who looked out from the pages, where had they been going? Why them?

The boys, the paper said, are walking along the roadside when a car approaches, slows and stops, words are exchanged; a local mowing his front lawn looks on without registering the significance of the moment; the boy, for whatever reason, gets into the car, is offered a drink doctored with tranquilisers, and is taken to an isolated cabin in the Kuitpo forest or some such place on the outskirts of Adelaide and held for days. Sexually used, touched, lubricated, forced, hurt, killed. *Lubricant on his anus.* I quietly folded in on myself and in a faraway place in front of the fire with the hurly burly of *It's A Knock Out* or the frenzied titillation of *Benny Hill* on the TV, I read and reread that line. *Lubricant on his anus.* 'We don't often see you reading the paper,' Mum commented. I think she was curious, but did not inquire further. The first time I came across the word 'discrete' was in one of these articles. Without caution I asked Mum what it meant and she explained but asked for no explanation in return.

Four boys to sleep in the same room, with less than an arm's length between beds. Breathing, farting, coughing, torches on, torches off. What are they thinking as the lights are switched off? Them, I don't know: pocket money; school; Cherry Forever; Dad cutting the nuts off a calf with a rusty razorblade (the calf screams and thrashes, Dad shouts, 'sit on its bloody head, keep it still', the dog waits and licks its lips); the long walk home from the school bus when the holidays are over; the women from the magazines (one dressed in an airhostess' cap and neck scarf with her pubic hairs shaved into the shape of a pilot's wings, another riding a bicycle with a dildo where the seat should be); Harvey telling a woman the calorie count of semen and explaining that swallowing it won't spoil her diet. What are they thinking as I hear them breathe? Them. Who knows? Me. Where do I walk to meet these men? You won't need to drug me or pressure me. I will do it because I want to. Pick me. I will be the one walking with the blue schoolbag and uniform. I will be by myself if you tell me when to walk there. You will not need to hurt me. I won't run. Put on the lubricant and I will stay by your side. I will give you my all.

The newspaper reported that a beer bottle was inserted into one of the boys. What are the limits and possibilities of the body? Of a boy's body? Of a body like mine? Tell me where to walk and I will be there. I can take the bus. Tell me where to get off and I will wait.

*

And then, before you know it, the holidays are over. School. At fifteen the expectation was that kissing a girl was appropriate, titting one was game, and fingering one was a scandal or legendary depending on who found out. I moved among the lockers in a liminal zone, the onslaught of images from the past summer swilling about in me. I moved through the change rooms and the sports lockers in 1986. In the classroom I made myself belong wherever I sensed safety. Ebbed and flowed. I was a malleable chameleon-like creature who learnt to read clues and anticipate actions minute to minute, hour to hour, sometimes in, sometimes out. Sex Ed, History, Ag Science, Maths, Religious Studies, Art, parties, repeatedly watching Brooke Shields in *Endless Love* instead of doing my homework, smoking down the back of the oval, stealing clothes and sunglasses from shops in Rundle Mall on a Friday night, tucking them under my school blazer, the emblem on the pocket suggesting a crime not based in economics. A crime of need nevertheless. At home after school I was rough with my brothers, cruel to animals some days and dependent on them for love on others. Same with Mum. The first time I called her a cunt she was at the stove frying eggs. She swung around and whacked me open-handed in the face.

*

In another room on the TV leather queens in New York are dying. The news reports flick between good-looking men celebrating in the street, hospitals and funerals, the clash between church, science and politics. 'Twenty sexual encounters a night each man might have in a sex club,' the reporter says. On another channel, Lady Di touches a young man's hand; more than anything he looks frightened. With great compassion, touches a skeletal man's hand and makes it to the front page of the world's papers. The Patron

244

Saint of Sodomy, she was cruelly labelled. Again, clumsily, sitting in front of the TV on Sunday night with toast and tomato soup, 'What is sodomy?' I ask Mum. 'Men can love women; men can love men,' she said without derision or distain. Like avocados and feta cheese, she did not look away from what many around her kept at a distance.

She never fitted in well with the other school mums. She didn't really like talking about other people's lives. I think I was lucky. That year she bought a box of condoms and left them in the pantry near the muesli bars and other stuff for school lunches. She didn't mince words: 'There is a thing out there called AIDS. I don't care if you are having sex or who with. If you are doing it, put one of these on.' It was not the fear of her sons getting girls pregnant but the fears of AIDS that brought condoms into our house for the first time, without Pee-wee or Cherry Forever around to soften the blow. After the first time I had sex with a man, I washed my mouth out with straight gin and gave myself a solid talking to that it would not happen again.

*

Is it respectable chronology or relevance that illustrates a good life, a worthy life, one that is valued, nourished, treasured? Desire, hope, possibility, need, love, isolation, fear, all that has gone before, the grime and the crime woven into a matrix with few outsides. The tiny spaces between the fibres of this web, I wriggled through and found you. I wish I wasn't embarrassed by the sight of two men in white suits, embracing after they exchange rings. I wish my elbow did not lock when you take my hand as we walk down the street. I wish I did not feel caught out when my neighbour sees me arranging flowers on the front verandah. Flowers to make our home even more beautiful. I wish I did not try to catch the eye of good-looking men who walk past – even with you at my side – in the hope one might drain from me what I can't show you, can't afford to show you. What I look away from too. Where will that stuff sit? Harvey and Cherry Forever and Reg Livermore and Leonard Cohen and *Endless Love* and dead young men and vicious older ones and a hard-working dad and a socially progressive mum and a little brown dog yelping for its life as it gets dragged through dark water on its back – where do we put all that? My question to you, dear man: where? But I suppose in each celebration, each milestone, each argument or embrace, each pause or stumble, each sexual moment with you that gets there and the ones that miss or do not happen, you see a little more of me growing up gay in Adelaide and hopefully that moves us closer.

Angry Cleaning

Nathan Mills

Every so often, my dad would wander into the kitchen, open the refrigerator and begin to clear it out. To the unassuming, this probably sounds like a solid end-of-the-week activity – evidence of discipline and good housekeeping. But it was his catharsis, a release, after a week of demanding, twelve-hour work days. Come Sunday, if he was unlucky enough to find a tidy fridge, his back-up was yelling at a telemarketer who called while he was reading the paper. But, if all went to plan, Dad would look inside that fridge, at its long-expired leftovers, and loudly, proudly, expel the frustration that had been building inside him – one spoiled spaghetti dinner at a time.

Sundays were particularly useful for this. For one thing, Dad usually had Sundays off and, for another, we were all around on Sundays. Mum would be folding washing or falling asleep to day-time TV, my sisters and I would be in our bedrooms or on the couch. So when Dad complained about the state of the fridge, there was always someone within earshot to listen. His favourite way to do this was to sigh emphatically at something he'd discovered and then ask (to no one in particular), 'Does anybody still want this?!' As if we all knew intuitively what he was referring to and, in that moment, were only too grateful to be part of this crude substitute for self-care. At the end of it all, the fridge would be clean, and Dad would return to his paper. But everything about this was performative: not once have I known the man to clean quietly. If he's going to do it, he'd better have a fucking audience. Maybe this is a skill passed down to all once-closeted queer children – we can smell an act a mile off.

You see, Dad rarely had an audience when he was younger. Like most big families, they were too busy – getting everyone to school on time or making sure the one footy uniform, shared between four brothers, was washed and dried each night – to pay much attention to any single family member.

I never had a brother and, to be honest, when Dad told me about the number of times his older brother, stumbling in drunk at night, had climbed onto the top bunk above him and peed onto Dad through the mattress, I was pretty happy to stick with sisters. Being loaded into the car each night while Mum drove my sisters to and from their dance classes was pretty much as bad as it got.

Still, there's a nagging feeling you develop as a kid when you're the short, skinny, closeted son of a sparky from a very big and very male Catholic family. You notice your differences first, and everything else second. Dad would take me to the football, and I would whinge. Two guys on TV would kiss, and Dad would whinge. Our relationship was defined by opposing politics and interests. Nothing about my worldview and my dad's worldview lined up.

It's not as if he didn't try to meet me halfway. There were several father–son bonding days: trips to the movies (we will always have the time we saw *Cars* together), to the footy, or to a job site he was working on. And I, in turn, put myself out there and took up sport. The year my family moved from Brisbane to Hobart to be closer to our relatives, I signed up for football, started karate and played tennis. This was a big deal for me: getting up early on the weekend, the temperature just over two degrees, pulling on footy shorts or a karate uniform, and trudging out the back door to mum's Toyota Spacia. This was never my idea of a weekend well spent, no matter how happy it made my dad.

In retrospect, there is something comical about me at age eight, standing on a footy field early in the morning, while frost melts on the grass, surrounded by boys twice my height, wearing a jersey that didn't fit me ('This is the smallest one they sell,' Mum would always say), trying just hard enough so that we could all count this as me giving it a go. But for the rest of my life I would remain as effeminate and uncomfortable on a footy field as I would remain short.

For what it's worth, I was an altar boy the same year. But I navigated Sunday Mass with ease. Like sport, there were uniforms and spectatorship but, unlike it, I left Mass clean and in under an hour – our priest kept things to the point.

While I was there, I never forgot the grim relationship between religion and my sexuality, but God and Hell were removed, abstract concepts to me, and being an altar boy was just a decent way to pass the time. What mattered was that I got to wear an outfit, hold everyone's attention and keep my dad happy.

*

The family moved back to Brisbane a year later, into our old house, and picked up life where we'd left off. There, my attempts to fake an interest in sport began to wane; I never played football or tennis again, and I eventually quit karate.

'Nan cried when Mum told her you'd stopped going to karate,' my sister told me a few months later. 'Nan said: "But Nathan can't give up on his karate!"'

'No, she didn't!' I insisted, but unsure. I was thirteen years old at the time.

It was like they could all see it: the steady decline of my mission towards adult masculinity. Surely, they all thought, if I just kept at it, maybe found a sport I was good at, toughened up a little, I'd be right. I'd grown out of that knitting phase when I was seven; my barbie of Dorothy from *The Wizard of Oz* sat disregarded and unloved in a cupboard somewhere. I would grow out of this.

If I'm honest, I thought I might too. Puberty, surely, would be my saving grace. When my body changed, so would I. And everything certainly did change: my voice deepened, a trail of brown hair grew from my balls to my arsehole, a tiny but reassuring patch of hair appeared on my chest, and my interest in guys moved from an innocent curiosity to full-on obsession. I think it was the same year that Daniel Radcliffe starred in *Equus* and, not by coincidence, the first time I ever Google-searched images of a naked man. The last glimmer of my heterosexuality was fading in front of my eyes.

It's easy to look back on this time with a sort of knowing warmth for my innocence. Poor little gay Nathan, trying so hard to convince himself that he's straight. But if I were to sum up queer childhood in one word, a catch-all descriptor for kids attempting to come to terms with themselves, I'd say that it's lonely – remarkably so.

Loneliness seems to be the most consistent marker of queer adolescence, shared among all queer kids and shared yet among none.

All minorities struggle in their own particular ways – feeling pain, disadvantage, isolation – but there is something about being young and scared and gay that draws you out of the world around you. You don't have a family of queer people who understand that; you are a minority of one in your own life. Trying, in my case, to reconcile the facts that I was a boy, and from the moment I was conscious of this I was also certain I should tell no one that I liked boys the way that other boys liked girls. I'm not sure how I knew that so early on, but, however I did, I knew it as clearly as I knew my eyes were blue, my name was Nathan, that I had sisters, a mum and a dad, and I couldn't tell any of them that I was gay.

At some point, much later, I think I realised that dad and I had been stuck on the same conveyor belt, slouching towards the masculine promised land. We had learnt the same rules, willingly or not, and had both done our best to follow them. But something happened to me that probably happens to most out queer people – when queer kids become queer adults, when they stop praying to God at night to make them normal (*Nope, still a homo*, I'd think the next morning, before turning over to cry into my pillow), where everything sort of clicks, somewhere around eighteen, maybe; you step off the conveyor belt, abandon any idea that you will ever be the cool, apathetic straight boy you always wanted to be, and start to get on with living. In fact, something about the whole thing becomes so unappealing. You start to wonder, *Why do these straight guys keep punching each other? Where does all that anger come from? Do none of them just sit down and talk to each other? No, I guess they probably don't.*

Earlier this year, Dad came home one day and told me he had cancer. He said it quickly, as if by accident, and I remember being grateful that I hadn't already gone out for the day. This wasn't the kind of news anyone should bring home to an empty house. When he told me, it was like something in him snapped, like the fibres that held him in place completely dissolved. He cried, and I hugged him, and all I could think was that this was the first time in my life we had done this. My dad didn't cry often; he still doesn't. But when he did, it was like everything in him, his years of stoicism and the most Australian kind of middle-aged masculinity, vanished in an instant. He was unburdened, for a moment, from what I had to let go of years ago.

*

I should qualify this by saying that, despite his diagnosis, Dad still likes to clean out the fridge while everyone's around. Perhaps, in a family with three women and a gay son, he's desperate to prove that he is the most dramatic member. Some guys like to punch other guys when they're angry; at least cleaning out the fridge is productive.

The cancer, as it turns out, was a false alarm, but Dad's doctor recommended that he start drinking green tea to help with his ridiculously enlarged prostate – the cause of this false alarm. And he drinks it, every day – with milk. To me, that was the shocking part: that my diabetic father, who refuses to even own a blood-sugar measure ('I can tell how I'm feeling just fine. I don't need that thing to tell me'), was actually taking a doctor's advice. But, you know, small steps. These things take time. It is only green tea.

Unlike Dad, my life hasn't been marked by life-altering news or some major crisis. Growing up queer was more of a slow burn, anyway. The big stuff was simply a lot of small stuff, from childhood until now, that helped shape who I am: all those times kids at school called me gay (shit, they weren't wrong); the time my sister told me that boys shouldn't try to knit; when I decided I no longer wanted to kill myself; the time I went travelling and saw gay men embracing in public as if there weren't whole swathes of the country where that just didn't happen; my first drunken kiss with a curious friend, who told me the next day that he regretted it; or the time I gave a guy a small amount of head on the side of the Brisbane River (I really wouldn't recommend this, although it did feel like a humble ode to the city that made me to get some next to the river that made it). Small steps and small moments, all leading to here. None of those moments, thankfully, involved me getting cancer or fearing for my life, but they stick out anyway, like waypoints on a map. And while I can now go on dates and watch porn (unashamed), like any other sexually frustrated gay man, it all mostly just means that, even though I wasn't then, I'm fine now.

The Exchange

Alice Boyle

When I was seventeen, Mum insisted we host a Belgian exchange student. The email had pinged into her inbox: a plea for a host family, any host family, who were prepared to take on a Belgian vegetarian with a fear of dogs. It was accompanied by a personal profile headed by a photo of a tall, pale girl with a mess of ginger curls. Mum called me into the study and asked me what I thought. According to her, the vegetarian thing was a non-issue – I still had a lingering reluctance to eat meat after my heart had been broken by a vegan a year earlier. Apparently the dog thing was fine too – our cocker spaniel, Max, was more like a very hairy black slipper than an actual dog.

Mum's face lit up as she read the profile. Words were jumping out at her: 'loves reading', 'theatre', 'learning languages'. Just like me, in other words. Words jumped out at me, too: 'Roman Catholic', 'youth group leader', 'small town'. I said that definitely, categorically, under no circumstances was I dragging a Catholic youth group leader around for six weeks. I'd only just extricated myself from the closet a couple of years prior, and felt lucky to have made it out alive the first time. I refused to fold myself back into a space that had been too small for me since my first homo make-out dream at the age of ten. No bloody way was it happening. Point blank no, Mum.

So that's how we ended up hosting a Belgian exchange student.

*

I was a shit to Annelien before she even arrived. Rather than go to the airport with my family like a dutiful host sister, I blew off her arrival for my friend TJ's black-and-white birthday party – my last moment of freedom before being saddled with a conservative religious nut, I figured.

TJ's doorbell rang at around ten, and I was summoned to meet the Belgian. I dragged my beribboned heels the length of the hall. It's no mean feat to be sullen in a French maid outfit, but I have to say I handled it with aplomb. Annelien stood on the doorstep, bursting with more energy than was properly decent immediately following a twenty-hour flight. My parents looked exhausted by comparison; maybe they were just reeling from the incessant stream of chatter.

'Hi, my name's Annelien, it's *so* nice to meet you, I've been looking forward to coming to Australia for the longest time, and now it's here, and the flight was so long but it's fine, I'm not tired at all, and your parents said you're attending a party – would you mind terribly if I stayed and joined you?'

Her accent was, disconcertingly, full British. She flung herself at me and gave me a hug. I was thrown off balance in more ways than one. I invited her in. She was decked out in a rainbow jacket and a purple scarf, a rosella in a flock of magpies. She didn't shut up the whole night. I already adored her.

*

I'm not sure how Annelien didn't clock my queerness for the six weeks she lived with us. Maybe she did but was too polite to say. Even though I thought she was amazing, and even though we could each talk the hind leg off a donkey – leaving the poor donkey almost legless – I didn't say anything. Even though I figured out pretty quickly that she wasn't Catholic and that her youth group was actually a theatre troupe full of queer kids and art freaks, I still kept my mouth shut. Call it internalised homophobia or self-preservation or whatever. When the topic of romance came up, I fudged; technically, I told myself, it wasn't a lie to say that I didn't have a boyfriend. Thankfully, Annelien had enough to say about her own boyfriend to compensate for my supposed chastity.

Once or twice a week, I'd send Annelien home on her own, ostensibly because I was 'hanging out with friends. You wouldn't like them.' My girlfriend and I would meet up in the city, she in jeans and a hoodie, her hair stiff with gel, me tugging self-consciously at my snooty private school uniform. We'd make out behind flower beds in the Alexandra Gardens, lying on the damp, cold ground and pushing frantically at each other. One time we went to the movies just to have somewhere warm and dark to go. A white baby boomer spun around in her seat and told us off for making spectacles of ourselves.

It was winter, and options were limited. At that point, my parents were still alternating between rage and denial over having a gay kid. My girlfriend was deeper in the closet than I'd ever been, trying to hide her queerness from the entire Vietnamese population of Melbourne. I followed her lead and kept our relationship hidden from all but my closest friends. Secrets were how we lived. What was one more?

*

I didn't tell Annelien the truth until a couple of years later. She went home without ever knowing, but we stayed in touch. I'd always sucked at long-distance friendships, and yet, somehow, this one seemed to stick. We both finished school, started uni, had literary aspirations. My long emails contained most of the truth, although a few important details were carefully omitted. For example, the fact that my girlfriend and I had gone our separate ways, me having been a dickhead and dumping her in the thoughtless way that comes so easily to teenagers. I was already dating a sweet painting student who loved David Bowie and wore fifties-style dresses when my dad, so fit and healthy, started having chest pain. Mum had him at a cardiologist that afternoon, her GP training making her swift and decisive. Yes, there was a blockage. Yes, he needed surgery. No, it couldn't wait.

I don't know why I sent Annelien that email. It's not like Dad wasn't totally fine. He came home from hospital, pale and slow, but otherwise his usual self. Still, I emailed her in a mess of tears. Something about mortality and not living a lie. Some carpe diem shit that I probably picked up at my fancy school. The message was something along the lines of: 'Dad's just had heart surgery and I thought he was going to die, oh, and also I'm gay, didn't want to lie to you anymore, sorry 'bout that.'

Mainly she was just pissed that I hadn't felt like I could trust her.

It felt like breathing out. And so our friendship went on.

It was also around that time that my cousin proposed to his French girlfriend. The wedding would be happening the following European summer, and would I like to come? As one of the few English- and French-speaking guests, I would be Very Valuable for cross-cultural translation. France is right next to Belgium. Of course I said yes.

*

Annelien and her mum picked me up from the station in Bruges, and we drove back to their family home. Rumbeke is little more than a blip on the map, a stretch of road with a bakery, a pharmacy and a few houses surrounded by cornfields. A funny place for an arty theatre-book nerd to grow up. I met Annelien's kind blonde sporty family. She and I were the off-kilter peas in the proverbial pod.

We stayed in Rumbeke for two days, crisscrossing the paths through the cornfields and filling each other up with our news. I told her about my latest girlfriend, a strong-willed theatre student who lived by the beach, made excellent poached eggs, and when pressed supposed her favourite musician would probably be Michael Bublé. Annelien told me about moving halfway across the country to study, about her boyfriend (yes, still the same boy) and her dream of becoming a writer.

Once my jetlag wore off, the two of us made the three-hour pilgrimage to Antwerp, where Annelien was studying. Our train pulled through stations with names I couldn't pronounce: Kortrijk, Waregem, Sint-Niklaas. The train had long benches arranged in open compartments, with luggage racks and hooks for passengers' coats. Nobody was wearing a coat. It was the hottest summer Belgium had had in years. The heat was different to that at home. Melbourne summers were a sharp, dry, burning heat; crispy grass; air-conditioned supermarkets and cinemas; and ghost-town streets as everyone flocked to the shore. In Belgium the heat was still and damp, and the countryside was so green, even at the height of summer. We cracked open the train windows and inhaled the smell of the foliage. There's no air conditioning in Belgium – there's usually no need – and our sweaty legs stuck to the vinyl banquettes. Belgians often joke that summer is the nicest day of the year, but that year, summer went for weeks.

Annelien's room was a blaze of sunlight in a shitty old building. The communal kitchen smelt like mildew, but at least it was cool. I slept on a mattress on her bedroom floor, flung out and exhausted after spending each day walking along broken-up cobbled streets in clogs, drinking beer on terraces, and talking with Annelien, always talking. We met her friends for pizza, we went to the chocolate museum, we shopped for vintage suitcases. She told me the legend of how Brabo had cut the hand off a giant and thrown it into the Scheldt, giving Antwerp its name. It was a fucked-up story. We also visited her uni to pick up her exam results. The place was straight out of *Harry Potter*. Tall girls in floral dresses pushed their bikes around campus, calling out to each other in Flemish. My life in Melbourne paled in comparison.

*

I was still half asleep the morning Lise showed up at Annelien's door. Lise spilled into the room, her clothes full of holes, talking a mile a minute about how she'd failed half her exams and her dad was going to kill her. She had masses of hair and a ready laugh. She was breathtaking. I yanked my nightie down, covering my nakedness. For once, I kept my mouth shut.

Later, as Annelien and I tucked my mattress out of sight for another day, I fished for information. I found out that Annelien had been friends with Lise since moving to Antwerp two years earlier. Annelien also told me that Lise had had a crush on a girl while on exchange, and that she, Annelien, had been sworn to secrecy; but she could tell me because what role was I going to play in Lise's life?

I knew I was in trouble the afternoon we walked around the dock. Antwerp is a port city, and a fleet of old sailing ships had berthed for the week. We met up with Lise to walk the water's edge, looking at the ships but not really looking. For the first time since I'd met her, Annelien couldn't get a word in edgeways. Lise and I bounced off each other with fizzing energy. I gathered more titbits of information: Jewish, single-parent household, fluent in five languages, always flunking exams. She made my stomach flip.

We were nearly home, the shadows of the brick terrace houses stretching long on the cobbles, when Lise asked what I only found out later was her benchmark question: who was my favourite musician? I answered without hesitation: Jens Lekman, Swedish pop-folk crooner, and top-ten reason not to kill myself when being a bespectacled gay scholarship kid had felt like a burden too big for my weedy shoulders.

Jens Lekman? Lise loved him. She was especially into his 2005 EP compilation. How did she feel about Michael Bublé? She would rather poke her eyes out with a fork.

So you see, I was in trouble.

*

Annelien left town with her sporty family for their summer holiday. Would I be alright alone in her room in Antwerp for three days? She promised to ask Lise to look after me while she was gone. We'd got on so well that time we walked around the port, that time we went to the movies, the trip out to Lise's family home in Essen, that time we drank beer until the early hours. We were already such good friends! Would it be okay?

I said it would be okay. I resolved to play it cool. I did not succeed.

Our first date was only one in hindsight. I invited Lise to visit the contemporary art museum with me. It would've been great if either of us gave a shit about contemporary art. I was sweating in my jeans that were way too hot but made my bum look reasonable. Lise bought some cake to share and it tasted like stale sawdust. It was hands down the best date of my life.

That evening, we cooked together, orbiting around each other while chopping vegetables in the kitchen of her tiny studio, unspoken things swirling between us. Lise's friend Sidney arrived with fresh berries from her mum's garden, and booze. We drank it all, then bought more. We stumbled to a gay bar where Sidney stole the candle holders and Lise and I pressed up against each other in a dark corner.

We didn't sleep together that summer. We didn't even kiss. I was twenty and had a girlfriend back home. A girlfriend who liked Michael Bublé, but a girlfriend nonetheless.

Our three days evaporated in a tangle of guilt-tinged arousal. Three days was at once both brutally short and long enough to realise that this thing right here was unlike anything else in the world. Once our days were up, Lise put me on my train to France. My cheeks became wetter as the landscape dried out. I met up with my parents in Paris, and we travelled to the middle of the country together. I used all my pre-paid credit calling Lise, clutching the phone like a portal back to where I'd left my insides.

The wedding was beautiful. The population of rural Anzy-le-Duc, the bride's home town, almost doubled for the weekend. Our sprawling family filled every *chambre d'hôtes* in Saône-et-Loire. Mangled French and broken English combined to broker an understanding between the two clans. The party went for two days and two nights. I switched from French to English and back again. I was neither here nor there.

I flew back to Melbourne after the wedding. I broke up with my girlfriend the night my flight landed. She picked me up from the airport and had made me the most beautiful homecoming gift. She had had her hair cut especially. I felt like a cruel piece of shit, but I also felt free.

*

It would take me a whole year to make it back to Belgium. I postponed uni, got a second job, turned down expensive nights out. I sent Lise lollies and books in the mail. I used my tax-return money to buy a laptop and fell asleep with it in my bed, Lise's voice easing me into slumber. I treated every shift pouring Belgian beers for handsy, red-faced old men as another step towards a beer with my own Belgian.

My parents were reluctant to see me go. It was ridiculous, far-fetched, a stupid waste of my time. Also, why was I still persisting with this gay business? My friends were also reluctant to see me go. What if I my heart got broken? What if she was an appallingly bad kisser?

My university was the most reluctant of all – not through any particular affection for me or concern for my wellbeing, but because they couldn't be arsed doing the legwork. But I was persistent to the point of obnoxiousness. I pestered the exchange office for months until they finally relented. Fine, they eventually said, I could go to Belgium. Fine, I could count it as an exchange. But no, they wouldn't help me with the paperwork. It didn't matter to me, though. I was going.

*

I landed in Belgium expecting another sweaty summer, but instead touched down into rain and chilly winds. This time it was Lise who picked me up from the station. She held my hand so gently and smiled so shyly. She was shorter than I remembered. She was perfect.

That year in Belgium was magnificent and terrifying and exhilarating. For the first time in my life, I had my own sun-drenched room, my own shitty kitchen. Annelien and Lise's friends lent me sheets, plates, pots and pans. Those friends slowly became my friends. I got chubby on fries and beer, and flunked French. I learnt some Flemish, and wandered through the Harry Potter halls in my own floral dresses. Mostly, though, there was Lise. Lise at dinnertime, Lise on Christmas morning, Lise getting up to pee in the middle of the night and then crawling back into bed, snuggling into my nook. That year made us real. It was a good year.

That year was followed by another good one, and then another after that. We were long distance, and then we weren't, and then we were again. Sometimes it was hard. Sometimes we pissed each other off, had no money, didn't understand each other's cultural point of view. Occasionally it felt like too bloody much.

But like Annelien all those years before, our love has stuck. When people ask how long we've been together, the number sounds strange to me. We have become one of Those Couples. We have friends who have met, married, had children and split up in less time. We've had shitty jobs, shitty haircuts, shitty housemates. Loved ones have passed, and babies have been born. Annelien has even had two. They have her hair and her husband's smile (yes, still the same boy).

We've bounced back and forth between our countries and visited a few new ones in between. We've seen each other through surgeries, homesickness and a gruelling bout with the Australian immigration department. One day soon Lise will be an Australian citizen. They're going to give her a tree to plant, but her roots have been growing in this soil since the night we lay on her futon, buzzing with vodka and wonder, and just looked and looked. When Australia voted for marriage equality, we danced to John Paul Young, both of us soggy and frizzy in the rain. I cried while drunk on cheap cider and she held me tight.

We live in the same place now. We even have a lease. We own a coffee table and a stick blender. Somewhere among the long distance, the books read and the meals cooked, we've become adults. Despite all of that, I still feel free.

*

My queerness was born in a hot dry land that was never ceded. It took its first steps in underground parties in disused warehouses, eyeing cute girls on the cross-river bus and getting frisky in the back rows of Cinema Nova. It was born Australian, but along the way it veered off course. It's grown strong on a jumbled diet of pavlova and pralines. Its 'heaps good' is sprinkled with some '*ongelooflijk*' and more '*ik hou van jou*' than you'd think. It's drinking beer brewed by monks on a forty-degree day. It stands steady on cobblestones in the rain, and bobs in the waves off the coast of Victoria. Its roots stretch far and deep and are inextricably buried in the soils of two continents. It's carried within the person by my side, who still holds my hand gently, but no longer shyly. I'm thankful every day that she stuck.

Faggot

Beau Kondos

I wasn't always a self-proclaimed faggot. With all the homophobic connotations tied to the f-word, I understand why it's so cringe-inducing, I really do. I'm a strong believer in the potency of words, particularly the idea that the intention behind them cradles their power. My dynamic relationship with the word evolved over time.

In high school I was a typical closeted Aussie-Greek with the unusual habit of never speaking the f-word. Paranoia had dug its claws into me, convincing me that a simple utterance would be too close an association, and would tip-off the homo-police – the bullies who took it upon themselves to make a spectacle out of every limp-wristed, gay-slurring stereotype they could find in the school halls. I gifted the other f-word more liberally to said homo-police (behind their backs, of course, for the sake of self-preservation).

Horror stories of gay wog boys getting booted out of home were constantly doing the rounds. Greek news travelled fast thanks to the insatiable thirst that drove yiayias to watch soapies all day: for gossip, and their obsession with bad boys. These old ladies might have *looked* innocent, but they had a very *real* addiction. Imagine if a crack addict was forced to sit through thirty episodes of *Days of Our Lives* to get their hit? The yiayias don't have the patience either. That's why they are stocked up with endless trays of shortbreads and baklava – it's a culinary ploy to loosen their victims' tongues and allow the gossip to flow freely. They'll later use whatever they've scavenged and spill the juice to the who's who of gossip traders at the local Greek Club, who shoot it up at their weekly meet-up.

In Years 7 and 8, these conditions created a conundrum: I yearned to learn more about my emerging same-sex cravings while steering clear of anything that could give the Greek yiayias a quick fix. My parents were the people I trusted and respected the most, so naturally I had the most to lose if they found out and lost their shit.

Yiayias have their sweets and it's no secret that Greeks in general are feeders. When your stomach is on the brink of exploding from a single serving of *yemista* or *pastitsio* that could've easily satiated a family of three, the Greeks have done their job. They greet you with a bear hug, and farewell you with that same tight squeeze on your gut: the hug that lasts. That's how they show their affection, by making sure you feel embraced both inside and out. The burden of Greek shame of gargantuan proportions I could handle, but the prospect of being disowned and losing that double-squeeze shattered me.

So, naturally I turned to television to find the answers. We only had the single monolith boxy TV in the family room. Never mind what the Greeks tell you about Orthodox religion, they pay respects to the holy trinity of kitchen bench, dining table and couch by cooking, eating and vegging out respectively.

Unfortunately, the TV was carefully and centrally placed as a sacred item to be accessed while worshipping the holy trinity, making it near-impossible to sneak a peek at an episode of *Queer as Folk*. And struggling through prime-time Aussie shows like *Neighbours* just to get a glimpse of a G-rated gay kiss between men wasn't an option – that wouldn't happen for over another decade. Although *Will & Grace* gave me gays in their thirties to laugh with, none of these shows helped me believe that my cravings were normal – not just my cravings for the big juicy biceps of AFL players, but also the yearning to be held by a dude in a loving embrace. A movie like *Love, Simon* would have been a godsend, regardless of its unrealistic pitch: *Catfish* with a Disney filter.

The omission of man-on-man tenderness from mainstream TV when I was young indicated to me that it was something unspeakable and unacceptable. And, because TV was the gospel, I was filled with self-loathing for seeking such tenderness. And that's why the f-word was so dangerous: it was an admission of abnormality, of being 'the other'.

While everyone else seemed to be online, it took forever for the tinny crackle and ping of dial-up internet to pervade the Kondos casa: I was missing out on my self-taught beginner's course of 'Growing Up Homo at Home 101: Illness or Totes Norm Bro?' While I was far from the turmoil faced by Sandra Bullock in *The Net*, online privacy conspiracies engulfed my headspace, which prevented me from searching for gay stuff on the net at the public library or at school. If going incognito on my browser had been an option back then, after furtively searching for two men sucking face I would have braced myself for a fatal diagnosis and dropped in to WebMD to ask: 'Do my nuts slip back into my body because I'm gay?' (I mean, why else would my balls go back in after they had dropped, unless I wasn't man enough? I was too embarrassed to ask my dad in case it set off a glitter canon on his gaydar.) When I was older I discovered that it happens to every guy when their littles mates get cold while they're hanging out together. Mind. Blown.

The distinct lack of positive representations of men loving one another, combined with the self-censorship of my online searches, left me feeling alone and vulnerable while all these hormones raged for control of and action through my adolescent body. And guess what breed of bloodhound has the uncanny ability to sniff out insecurity in a heartbeat? Spoiler: it's the homo-police.

In the grand scheme of things, I survived a public high school in the naughties relatively unscathed. The thing about bullied victims is that their trauma is relative – everyone's pain is the only pain they know and it therefore packs the biggest punch. My bullies' homophobic taunts mostly occurred when I was alone, sewing seeds of abjection with a facial expression to match. 'I know you're *gay*' was delivered with that grimace that appears on your face when you realise someone has chucked up in the only cubicle in the nightclub, and you're desperate to take a dump. 'Do your friends know you want to root them?' An accusation delivered with furrowed brows, by the righteous straight hero seeking to protect his vulnerable heterosexual kind (no prizes for guessing that this particular bully now enjoys sex with men, which speaks volumes about projecting internal insecurities onto others). And the impatient 'Just admit you're a *faggot*!' – which is paired with that look you'd find on the face of a middle-aged shopper just before they ask a casually employed teenager to speak to their manager.

Everyone recalls moments of primal humiliation from childhood. Often it is the witnesses to our mortification that cement the moment and make it real. Some people, sometimes, are easily able to sweep these memories under their medial temporal lobe (I have access to the net now – watch out). But shame is given a boost from the knowledge that witnesses will carry the memory of your disgrace. If a tree in a forest is humiliated and no one is around to hear it, did it really happen? Or is it just bark off a giant sequoia's back?

After the private exchange of verbal abuse, physical confrontations would follow when the homo-police could corral an audience. I'm not sure if the homo-police were bright enough to realise what they were doing, but it worked. Two indelible moments I experienced of physical bullying were crushing, literally. One of the homo-police ground my hand into the asphalt with the heel of his shoe; another attempted to use the back of my neck as a lemon squeezer, kneading shattered glass into my nape. Oddly, I didn't nurse traumatic echoes from the physical wounds. These were defining moments not because of what was done to me, but because of how I reacted.

There was no fight. There was no flight. Only pure submission.

These bloodhounds targeted me because I was different, because I was a *fag*. In their private verbal confrontations, they made sure I knew that they knew my secret. Then, before an audience, a chorus of shame-witnesses, when the physical attacks happened, I couldn't fight back because if I did, it would be the catalyst for a further scene: a grand stage for the bullies to broadcast to everyone the faggoty reason I had been targeted, why I had been *chosen*. What if I risked swinging a punch only to lose the fight? I would've been *such* a fag. No thank you. Take it like a man whose balls can't even commit to staying dropped. Suffer in silence.

In retrospect, both bullies were a little unhinged – perhaps something intense playing out at home, or something more confronting unfolding in their heads. I heard a rumour that one of them had a brief visit to the psych ward a few years back. Sadly for me, hindsight wasn't handy at the time the bullies cornered me.

264

Not physically cornered, but detained in a self-loathing-riddled corner of my mind.

Feelings of worthlessness and humiliation reigned supreme. The tone the bullies used when they inflicted that word on me made my heart tighten. My blood felt like it had thickened into a tar-like substance, turning me into the thing they saw me as: dirty scum. I figured that if I felt like scum whenever they used that word on me, I must be scum. It was a simple recipe to cook up a hearty meal of low self-esteem with a side of future intimacy issues. If I had copped a larger helping, it could've potentially led to suicide. I was weak and I couldn't stand up for myself because the bullies were right.

I *am* a fag.

*

Thankfully, television and movies were my saving grace. Their heartfelt stories drew on the power of metaphor and subtext to make me feel like I wasn't suffering alone. *Buffy the Vampire Slayer* was my safe place. I was obsessed. I identified with the protagonist, who had been cursed to be different, 'chosen' for something she had no control over. I idolised the strength she cultivated to grow and fight the good fight regardless. Spider-Man was my favourite superhero because he understood the struggle of keeping his double life a secret from those he loved. Both of these hero mythologies gave me scenarios to identify with vicariously, and gracious moments of cathartic release when the hero overcame their obstacles. But though they offered models of coping that helped me accept my fate, they didn't show me – and hence I still didn't believe – that being gay was *normal*.

I was raised surrounded by jokes about how the Ancient Greeks started the 'gay thing'. It now seems obvious that if homos were banging in their togas as far back as BC, then being gay is a natural phenomenon. But when everyone around you is telling you something different, their opinions tend to become contagious and to override pragmatic thought. When I visited the pantheistic Greek island of Delos, I was surprised to find more dicks than I'd ever seen crudely drawn on a high-school desk. Not nude depictions on a statue or painting, I'm talking oversized sculptures of an erect penis on a pedestal. I kid you not. They literally put the D on a pedestal. The Ancient Greeks didn't just love dick, they worshipped it.

It was after this trip to Greece when my *Buffy* obsession transitioned into an obsession with Greek philosophers. I read Plato's parable about the origins of humans from the *Symposium*. Each had four arms, four legs and a head with two faces. They came in three genders: man, woman and androgyne (which had both male and female genitalia). Each of these three was split in half after inciting the gods, and the halves were then destined to spend their lives searching for the other: their soulmate. Men searched for men; women for women; and the male and female half from the androgyne for each other. After reading that story I was forever changed. Where *Buffy* had helped me *accept* that being gay didn't mean being alone in high school, Plato helped me *believe* that homosexuality was normal. Faggots had love stories too – two male halves searching for their lost lover. There's something powerful and truly life-altering about hearing an ancient story that allows you to feel valued for being just as you are.

Faggot is more than a word for me; it represents a journey of self-love. Now when I speak the word, I have no fear of conjuring any bigots, nor am I bound by the tar-like feeling pulsing through my veins when it was used against me. In hindsight, the word was a gift when inflicted upon me, because now I can use it to heal.

The word 'wog' was once an open invitation for my dad to smash his fist into someone's face in the schoolyard, but now being labelled a wog is celebrated. Why can't the word 'faggot' evolve as well? It's already undergone a journey from originally describing a bunch of sticks, to being fashioned into an insult in North America for a fella with a penchant for dicks, before that new insult-meaning spread throughout the Western world. I couldn't tell you how much it would've changed things for me when I was younger if one of my idols who didn't fit with the clichéd gay stereotype had stood up and proclaimed themselves a faggot, without malice, with only pride and joy in their heart. It would've been so refreshing to see the intention of the word reversed and reclaimed.

I've been known to upset people with soft skin in some circles. A friendship with me is initiated by a verbal baptism by fire.

266

People often misunderstand when I steal words that others have used against them in the past, words with a burden of trauma and insecurity, and attempt to recycle them in an endearing or playful context. I hope I can convince those gentle souls that I am one of them too, that I'm on their team, that I'm trying to strip the malice from the word, to take it back. Like Plato did for me, I'm trying to show them that I *see* their difference; I've embraced it and I want to celebrate it with them. I want to transform the intention behind the word and use its power to heal.

I recall the moment I felt truly celebrated in Australia for my difference. In 2017, on the evening the 'Yes' result in the Australian plebiscite for same-sex marriage was announced, I found myself at the official street party in Melbourne. It was held on Lygon Street – which has belonged to the wogs for so many years. I danced with a group of mates, ignoring the rain and soaking up the joy radiating from the sea of strangers smiling, laughing and screeching around me. We were the happiest faggots in the world. And in that moment I was proud to actually *feel* that there was absolutely nothing wrong with that.

So You Wanted Honesty ...

Sue-Ann Post

This is a photo of me and my best friend from church. I like to call it 'Tomboy and Not-a-Tomboy'. Don't be fooled by my dress: it was Sunday, so I had to wear it. No points for guessing which one is me. It would only be better if my fists were clenched and one of my socks were halfway down.

They say that the past is another country, but I've still got my passport. I grew up in rural Australia in the 1960s. The only phones were big black Bakelite rotary-dial landlines. Television was still in black and white and we only had two channels. There were no drink-driving laws, seatbelts weren't compulsory, you could still smoke in hospitals and it would be another twenty years before homosexuality was decriminalised. Throw in a fundamentalist Christian upbringing and I had not a single clue that gays and lesbians even existed. I'm part of (hopefully) the last generation of kids to grow up thinking they were the first, or indeed the only ones to be attracted to the same gender. It was a profoundly lonely experience.

I didn't find out that homosexuality existed until I went to college at eighteen. And it wasn't the best introduction, as it came courtesy of my *Abnormal Psychology* textbook. There in Chapter 11, 'Psychosexual Disorders: Gender Identity Disorders and the Paraphilias', after incest, paedophilia, voyeurism, sado-masochism and rape came homosexuality. I cannot begin to describe the shockwave that hit me when I read the definition. My first thoughts were, *You mean it's real?! It's an actual thing? There are others like me? Where are they? Can I join the club?* Sadly, that was followed by an intense, internal fundy-Christian backlash that had me wrestling my demons and desperately praying not to be gay for the next two years.

After that, I gave up. I accepted that I was a homosexual and came out to pretty much everyone I knew. Despite the fact that I had never even kissed a woman or met an actual lesbian. I just knew it was true. With apologies to '80s band Hot Chocolate, it doesn't start with a kiss. It starts with a look and your stomach doing backflips. You don't need to kiss someone to know that you are attracted to them. When I came out, my friends were surprised, my family was shocked! Horribly, horribly shocked!

I would have sworn on a stack of Bibles that I had never heard of homosexuality until I read that textbook. Except, it wasn't really like that. My friends were surprised it had taken me so damn long to figure out what I was. They'd guessed years ago. My family, especially my brothers, were shocked, but as for my mother claiming to have had no idea, well, I'll get back to her later. The truth is, all sorts of homosexual references had been floating around me the whole time, but they were in code and you had to read between the lines. Although the words 'gay' and 'lesbian' were never spoken, there was a constant sneering cultural disdain for sissies, nancy boys and old ugly spinsters who couldn't catch themselves a man. A fake lisp and a limp-wristed wave conveyed all the contempt needed, without using actual words. And that contempt ran through pretty much all of society. Gay and lesbian themes appeared only rarely in films and on television, usually in subtext, and they always ended badly. The Hays Code for film censorship in America may have officially ended, but the hangover carried on for decades. Among other things, the Hays Code had decreed that homosexual relationships could not be depicted as happy, healthy or successful, so for decades there were only four ways for a gay relationship to end: murder, madness, (straight) marriage or suicide. I think of them as the Four Horsemen of the Gay Apocalypse. It took until the 1980s for a film about lesbians to have a happy ending. (It was *Desert Hearts*, if you're interested.)

I may have completely missed all the subtle references and subtext, but evidently people around me were more aware. Even in high school, girls walking past me in the hallways would hiss words at me. From the tone of delivery, I knew they were intended to be insulting but I had no idea what 'lemon' or 'lezzie' meant. One time they hissed the word 'lesbian' at me and I foolishly asked my mother what it meant because I couldn't find it in a dictionary. She slapped me and told me to never use that word again. And here comes the truly odd thing. When I said earlier that I had no idea homosexuality even existed, it's a tad more complicated than that. It seems my subconscious was trying to protect me from cognitive dissonance by grabbing uncomfortable memories almost as soon as they were formed and stashing them away in a locked file that I wasn't able to access till years later. That memory of my mother slapping me when I said the word 'lesbian' was one that quickly disappeared. Another one was even more astonishing. At a high-school party I attended, two couples were sitting cross-legged on the floor opposite each other, making out. One of them said, 'Hey, let's swap,' and suddenly the girls were kissing each other and the boys were kissing too. Not that I really noticed the boys; I was absolutely fixated on the girls. It was completely mind-blowing, but that memory was captured and locked away before I even walked out the door to go home that night. It only returned when I came out four years later.

It is one of the great oddities of life that as you get older, you realise the past is not fixed, that ripples of various historic events are still moving through our culture. Looking back with new eyes can completely change the way you perceive the past. One small example: all my female teachers in primary school were called 'Miss'. None were married. Then one of my teachers got engaged to one of the other teachers at the school and I was shocked at how angry the other female teachers became. She was virtually ostracised. It was only years later that I realised it was because she was one of the first female teachers to be allowed to marry. Until 1966, by law, married women weren't allowed to work in government jobs, so if you wanted to be a teacher or a nurse you had to stay single. My teacher was one of the first to take advantage of the change in the law, and the resentment of the other, older teachers was palpable.

A more personal revelation came when my gaydar was officially installed, shortly after I came out. I looked back over my life and one incident in particular completely shocked me. When I was sixteen, another member of my church suddenly started attending our branch despite the fact that it was a long drive from where she lived. She always brought her teenage son along, and she and my mother constantly threw the two of us together. We ran Junior Sunday School together. We went to church socials together. We were cast in a play together. It didn't last long – they eventually went back to their local church branch – but later in life my gaydar kicked out a reading and I realised, 'Oh my god. He was gay! And not just a little bit. He was as camp as a row of tents! He was Thorpe-ingly gay!' Despite my mother's protestations that she had no idea I was a lesbian, she quite obviously had suspected something and had conspired with this other woman to throw their two ugly-duckling queer kids together in the hope of creating the beautiful swan of heterosexual marriage. It failed.

Despite all the confusion, doubt and fundy-Christian pushback in my brain, I came out as a lesbian in 1984. A few years later, I moved to Sydney, where I was enthusiastically embraced by the gay community and felt at home for the first time in my life.

Except, it wasn't really like that. My first trip to a lesbian bar was a thoroughly disheartening and depressing experience. I rocked up wearing a jacket and tie because I thought that was what all lesbians wore. I stood at the bar, ordered a drink, glanced around the room and … nothing. No one looked at me. No one spoke to me. I was too shy to approach anyone so I just sat there and was completely ignored. Half an hour later, a huge fight broke out and just like back in the schoolyard, everyone gathered around and shouted encouragement. 'Kick her, Deidre! Harder!' I fled the bar and got a taxi home, thinking, *What the hell? Is that what I'm meant to be like? Are these my people?* I didn't understand the night at all. I didn't think I'd done anything wrong. But then, I didn't really know anything about the community. It's not like they held orientation days for new lesbians or handed you a manual. I thought it was me. I thought I was just as unattractive to lesbians as I had been to boys. After all the drama and trauma of coming out, I felt as lonely as ever. It kind of broke my heart a little bit.

It took me a few years to figure out what had happened. It turned out my outfit had a lot to do with it. The Sydney bar scene in the mid-'80s was still very much about the butch/femme dynamic. By wearing a jacket and tie I had signalled that I was a butch. The unwritten rules for butch/femme interactions were that butches did not approach other butches ('Are you crazy? That would be like two men going out!') and femmes also did not approach butches. Butches had to put in all the effort. I had no idea about any of this and if anyone had asked me, I would have said, 'But I'm not butch. I'm a big old tomboy and I want to romp with other big old tomboys.' Being attracted to butches rather than femmes didn't fit within that dynamic, so sadly I have never picked up at a lesbian bar. Such a shame, really, because as my partner of twenty-three years always says, 'I like my men to be men and my women to be somewhere in between.'

To be fair, it wasn't all the bar culture's fault. When it comes to flirting with women, I can be as dense as a Queensland Liberal politician. I had already started doing comedy and was garnering notoriety as one of the first 'out' comedians in Australia. Early in my career I often referred to the 'short hair and comfortable shoes' lesbian stereotype, and after one gig I was approached by a rather stunning woman with long red hair who smiled at me and said, 'You know, not all lesbians have short hair.' My response? 'Well, of course you're right and I probably shouldn't perpetuate the stereotype.' I blathered on for a bit, and then she walked away. Sometimes I am such a fricking doofus, even I can't believe it.

As I soon discovered, being the only out lesbian on stage was a double-edged sword. My first paid, professional gig was an all-women cabaret at the Trade Union Club and the response was overwhelmingly positive. My second was a week later at main-stream comedy venue the Harold Park Hotel, where after the gig an extremely angry lesbian stalked past me and hissed, 'You sell-out!' Seriously? My second bloody gig and I was already a sellout? And from there, things just got weirder over the years.

Some women thought I wasn't lesbian enough and should stop talking about it on stage. Some thought I was too lesbian and would just confirm the stereotype and scare the straights. It was even suggested that I wait till a 'shorter, prettier' lesbian comedian came along first. Some angrily questioned whether I had the right to speak on behalf of all lesbians, a right I had never, ever presumed. Hardcore lesbian separatists were outraged that I said anything at all about lesbians in front of male audiences. New Age lesbians disapproved of me because I 'used too much masculine energy' on stage. I may have been picking up awards and playing sold-out houses in mainstream clubs, but lesbian nightclub gigs turned out to be nightmares. Once I followed two straight female comedians, who the crowd loved, but when I came on they started yelling 'Get off! Put k.d. lang back on!' I did a gig in the back room of a suburban pub for a crowd of closeted suburban lesbians who flinched every time I said the word 'lesbian'; within five minutes they'd turned their backs on me and started playing pool again. The last time I was interviewed on a gay radio station, I was kind of stunned when one of the hosts said to my face, ''Cause really, you're not the best comedian in the world. But you're a good role model.' Even sadder, I no longer accept lesbian-only gigs unless I know the group or at least the organiser, because the last time I did one, they tried to sue me for breach of contract. They said my performance was 'offensive to lesbians'. Now that was a real kick in the guts. In my darker moments, I fear that the legalisation of homosexuality has led to the boganisation of homosexuality.

But you know what? I don't care and it doesn't bother me. Well, maybe it does a bit, but I knew that most women are batshit crazy long before I became a lesbian. I embrace the crazy and run with it. I started doing comedy in mainstream venues because there was no real gay circuit. I didn't set out to be a role model or lead a revolution. I was just a big doofus tomboy lesbian who liked to make people laugh. People said I couldn't be 'out' and have a career in comedy, and that was a challenge I was more than willing to accept. I'm not everyone's cup of tea and that's fine by me. My fans are as weird and wonderful as I could possibly want. For every awkward or horrible gig, there has been an equally awesome and amazing gig. I've performed at the Opera House! Twice! (Three times if you count the time I performed there in a Mormon children's choir, but that's a whole other story.) In the thirty-four years since I came out, I have seen the queer community go from the butch/femme nightclub scene run by the mafia (they were the only ones willing to take our money), to mainstream acceptance and, bugger me, gay marriage. Who would have thought! And what a wild ride it has been.

As nice as it is to live in an era of acceptance and (notional) equality, there are some relics of the previous era that I would be sad to see disappear. I am (still) a tomboy, and I know some people now disapprove of that term and wouldn't mind if it disappeared, but please don't be too quick to ditch it. The idea of 'tomboy' runs through most cultures and has been around for at least six centuries, but probably longer. My favourite definition comes from the *Wordsworth Concise English Dictionary*: 'a high-spirited romping girl'. That was me. I romped and wrestled and played most of the sports that girls were allowed to play. I hated wearing dresses, climbed every tree in our garden, and occasionally beat up boys who hassled my friends. In primary school, when a teacher came to fetch the boys to move chairs in the assembly room, I was usually invited along as well. When we practised dancing for an upcoming school social, there were always more girls than boys and I always danced as a boy to make up the numbers. Always. To this day, I still don't know how to dance backwards like a lady.

Everyone knew I was a tomboy. I even got called a tomboy in two different languages. When I was being particularly noisy or rude, my mother would call me a *hoyden*, which is the Dutch term for tomboy. (For extra points, the German version is *Wildfang*. How cool is that?) I embraced the concept of tomboy with pleasure, and found relief and comfort in a cultural niche that fit me perfectly. I had no idea that I was growing up queer, but I did know I was growing up a tomboy. There were no lesbians in the books I read as a child, but there were heaps of tomboys. Jo from *Little Women*, and George from the *Famous Five* series by Enid Blyton.

Scout from *To Kill a Mockingbird* and Pippi Longstocking. The truly great thing about growing up a tomboy was that it didn't place a question mark over your gender or assume a sexuality. There were just as many straight tomboys as there were lesbian ones. More importantly, it was a term that everyone 'got'. From teachers and preachers, to shop assistants, cops and crusty old farmers, the phrase, 'Don't mind her, she's a tomboy,' was more likely to prompt an indulgent grin, not a frown of disgust.

I hope there is still room in this modern era for such an old-fashioned but incredibly useful term.

Sometimes I Call You Even Though I Know You Can't Answer. It's a Symbol, I Think …

Anthony Nocera

When I was younger I had problems with phonetics. When I first wrote that, I typed it all in capitals. Like I was yelling or REALLY EXCITED about my illiteracy. Trouble with forming words and correlating them to meaning, with reading and comprehension. I couldn't follow stories. It stemmed from an inner-ear problem that affected my ability to hear.

My mother took me to a doctor and said, 'Is this why he's slow to pick up reading?'

'Yes,' the doctor said. I, of course, couldn't hear him. But he nodded, so I put two and two together.

'What are you talking about?' I asked.

'WE'RE TALKING ABOUT YOUR READING!' Mum shouted so I could hear.

'YES!' the doctor shouted, 'YOU'RE SLOW!'

*

'Have you seen *Call Me by Your Name*?' he asked.

I was sitting with a friend in a loud bar. He got the drinks. Beer. I hate beer, but I drank it anyway, making 'ah' noises after every sip to hide the fact that it tasted like a foot to me. It felt intimate, though, despite all of the noise. We made conversation in the pockets of quiet when we could.

I said, 'Yeah.'

'My first time was exactly like *Call Me by Your Name*.'

'How so?'

'I was sixteen, and we were camping down by the beach and me and my friend were in a tent and I remember we'd been swimming all day, yeah …' He trailed off, and his eyes lingered on the distance like he was back on that beach looking at the way the water ran down his friend's body like tears, or like sweat, or ropes of cum, and how the muscles moved underneath his skin like they were moving just for him. 'Yeah, and we had this moment in the water when we swam together, swam into each other and we both felt something. And later that night, when we were in the tent, we just started to touch each other and kiss, and then I was balls deep for days.'

'That sounds … romantic.'

'It really was,' he said. 'I'm glad you think so. When did you see the film?'

'With my boyfriend a few weeks ago.'

'That's right, you have a boyfriend.'

'Yeah.'

'How's it going? Are you two in love?'

'I think so … I guess.'

'Don't you know?'

'I don't know how you could ever definitively know.'

He nodded. 'That movie, it just …' He took a sip of beer and I did too, to make it seem like I was keeping up. 'Good, isn't it?'

'Love it,' I said. 'And I love beer. Ah!'

'But that movie, it's just like my life … you know? It's so beautiful. It explained so much to me.'

'How do you mean?'

'I saw myself in it,' he said. 'What I wanted and all that.'

'Like your life corresponds to it?'

'No, but it … talks to it,' he said, and I thought how nice it would be to talk to something, to be in conversation but not have someone talk back.

He told me that his first experience set the tone for his entire sexual existence. He said, 'Sex for me is, like, sunny, you know? Total euphoria, man. I just bliss out.'

*

A film studies lecturer once told me that quite often films tell us how to watch them in their opening moments. They show us how to read the film, how to understand it, the lens through which we should examine what's being considered by the work. For example, at the beginning of Christopher Nolan's *Memento*, a polaroid photo un-develops – it's shaken into blankness – signalling to the viewer that this is a film in which parts will be told backwards. In the opening sequence of Catherine Hardwicke's *Twilight*, a predator chases a deer through the woods and the perspective shifts back and forth between the predator (a vampire, Edward Cullen we assume) and his prey. It's an opening that says: 'This is a film that is going to play with the notion of the gaze; it's going to tinker with ideas about watching and being watched.'

I thought about my first sexual experience, my sex, my gaze, and how it was much more like William Friedkin's movie *Cruising*, an '80s slasher movie set in New York's gay leather scene. It begins with a severed arm floating in a river. This opening said, 'Being homosexual is dangerous' or 'To be gay is to get hurt'. After we made out for about an hour, he, my first lover, just turned his back on me. I asked him, 'Where did you go?' and he said, 'Somewhere else'; I took it as a challenge to get his attention again. I kissed his spine, each and every vertebra until I got low enough to make him stir and turn back around.

'How was that?'

'It was good,' he said, 'I suppose.'

We had sex and it was okay, I guess. He inserted the tip of his penis into me and came immediately, groaning, 'Oh my god, yes, yes.' Then he collapsed on top of me and asked, 'Was it good for you, Anthony?' I should have rolled over and turned my back on him, and gone somewhere else during my deflowering, but I just silently nodded, and he asked me to leave as he tossed a condom on the floor, and I watched his cum ooze out of it as I packed up my things.

For the next few weeks I kept thinking about the cum oozing out of the condom and how it felt loose when he was using it and I called my mum in a panic and screamed, 'What if I have AIDS?'

'Did you use protection?' she said, coolly.

'Yeah, I did, but what if it happened anyway?'

'Well,' she said, 'did he seem AIDSy?'

'What is AIDSy?'

'I don't know … Was he wearing a lot of leather? Did he look menacing and have a handlebar moustache?'

'No. What the fuck?'

'I'm just asking the questions that need to be asked.'

'I don't think that needed to be asked!' I said.

'Anyway, you don't have AIDS.'

'How do you know?' I said.

'Because, Anthony, if you had HIV you'd be thin.'

*

The film begins with a title card that reads, 'Somewhere in Northern Italy'. It's an opening that says, 'This is a fantasy. This is a romance.' I wondered what my opening said about me, what the opening of my sex life was trying to tell me. Probably: 'This is not going to go well' or 'It's only going to get worse' or 'This will make you anxious, you will be unnecessarily stricken with panic'. Or maybe, 'You didn't think it was possible to sprain your arsehole, but it is, and you will'.

*

'You should know,' my friend said as the bar quietened down again. He took a sip of his beer and so did I.

'Delicious,' I said.

'The beer?' he asked, and I nodded.

'Know what? What should you know?'

'Whether you're in love or not,' he said. 'You should know where you stand. It should be definitive. You should be sure.'

*

Call Me by Your Name is interesting in that it takes male queer desire and wanting, traditionally associated with violence, corruption, infection and monstrousness (if it was depicted at all) and places it within the language of mainstream feminine desire.

One of the first texts I studied at uni was 'Ripe Figs' by Kate Chopin: a short story about a girl, Babette, and her godmother waiting for figs to ripen from hard little green marbles into soft, supple fruit before they go and visit their family. The ripening of the figs and the waiting symbolises adulthood, sexual maturity and how everyone needs time and patience to ripen.

I remember a girl in my tutorial hated the text. 'Women aren't fruit,' she said.

'It's a symbol,' said the tutor.

'I'm no palm reader. I don't need to understand symbols,' she said.

*

In *Call Me by Your Name*, Elio and his sexuality – and his coming to terms with it – is the ripening fruit, the fig that Chopin was writing about; he is the apricots that Oliver, the older, handsome lover, gobbles down by the basketful, he's the nectar that Oliver drinks and is re-energised by every morning. I think it's very romantic to be eaten. Especially when you start to soften towards someone. Like Elio does with Oliver.

Well, Elio, you're not the only one who is a piece of fruit, I thought. When I was eighteen I used to go on camming sites and jerk off with people halfway across the world. When one of them saw my naked body and I told him I didn't have a dildo, he said, 'Get a banana from the kitchen and fuck yourself'. And I did as he said: I waddled to the kitchen with my hard-on painfully bouncing around and grabbed the smallest banana from the fruit bowl and then sat in front of my computer screen with my legs in the air and tried to fuck myself with it. I didn't really know what I was doing so I just kind of lifted the banana like a dagger and rammed it into myself. And it just hit the wall of my arsehole so hard that the skin of the banana loosened, and the fruit shot out the other end onto my bed and I just lay there, yeah, I just lay there looking at the ceiling and used my leg to subtly close my laptop.

*

It wasn't the first time fruit had entered my bedroom. When I was fourteen, or thirteen, young and ripening like an apricot or a fig, I decided that I wanted to stick something in my arse. After watching a lot of porn, I wanted to see what it was like. I googled 'what to put in your arse that isn't a penis' and came upon a Yahoo! Answers page that said to use a vegetable that is penis-shaped and to microwave it until it feels human. I determinedly grabbed the most manageable, slimline carrot I could find out of the vegetable crisper and put it in the microwave for two minutes. When I took it out, I felt it sear into my skin and I threw it down and looked at the long cylindrical burn across my palm.

I wonder what a palm reader would have seen. I googled it and apparently a long cylindrical burn across your palm from a make-shift dildo is a symbol for being a fuckwit. And for dying alone, probably.

I looked at Elio and his apricots and his fruit and thought, *Hey, you're not so fucking special.*

*

'But he spends so much time reading,' Mum said to the doctor. She wasn't yelling, but they were both talking just loud enough for me to hear, as if they'd been yelling for so long that they'd reached a new normal base volume for polite conversation.

'Yeah, look, he's probably not doing much of that.'

'What's he doing?'

'This happens to a lot of kids. He's likely looking at the pictures and making up a new story for himself to inhabit.'

'Is that bad?'

'It's not bad or good. He'll have a hell of an imagination.'

'What?' I asked again. And they both jumped back into shouting mode.

'WE'RE TALKING ABOUT YOUR IMAGINATION, ANTHONY,' Mum said.

'YES,' the doctor said, 'ABOUT HOW IT'S A BAD THING.'

*

'How do you know you love me?' I asked as we were finishing breakfast at his dining room table. It has recently become our din-ing room table. We were becoming an 'us', an 'our', a 'we'.

My boyfriend looked up at me. 'Hmm?'

'You just said, "I love you."'

'Yeah?'

'How do you know?'

'I don't, I just do,' he said.

'And you're okay with that? That not knowing?'

'Sure,' he said.

281

*

I saw *Call Me by Your Name* with my boyfriend on a stinking hot day in November. Or December. Or maybe January, I don't know – hot days like that have a way of melting into each other, joining up into one giant, sweaty block of time that you wish would end. We'd been feeling rather disconnected lately, like we were in two different places. We had been together for nearly three years and we were talking less. Fucking less. We were still having sex, but it was less urgent, more routine. I worried we were getting bored.

The thing about fruit – peaches for Elio, bananas for me – is that it rots. It ripens into its prime, and then it overripens. Elio ripens like an apricot and his love is all firm and juicy and ripe for the picking, and it is consumed, partially, but is then left half-eaten to rot. It goes bad. I wondered if my boyfriend and I were going bad.

The French philosopher Michel Foucault once said, 'For a homosexual, the best moment of love is likely to be when the lover leaves in the taxi. It is when the act is over and the boy is gone that one begins to dream about the warmth of his body, the quality of his smile, the tone of his voice. It is the recollection rather than the anticipation of the act that assumes a primary importance.' I thought about my boyfriend and me: how could we sustain something if neither of us ever left? How could I love him if he was always there?

I decided to spice things up. To keep things interesting. But I didn't want to be associated with anything that could go off, could go bad. I needed something unperishable.

We were lying in bed eating Oreos and I placed one between his teeth so half the Oreo was hanging out of his mouth, and I crawled up to him on all fours. I pulled the covers off him, making sure my body, my cock, gently grazed his as I prowled towards his lips.

'What are you doing?' he asked.

'Nothing,' I giggled coquettishly, and bit the other half of the Oreo.

'AH!' he shouted.

'Did you like that?'

'No, fuck!' he said, bolting out of the bed. It turned out that I had overshot. I didn't just bite into the Oreo, but through his bottom lip. I followed him to the bathroom to see myself in the mirror with his blood on my chin, while he washed his face in the sink.

'Why did you bite me?' he asked.

'I'm trying to keep our love alive!' I shouted. 'I'm trying to make this relationship work. I don't know what the fuck *you're* doing.'

We went back and lay in bed for a little while. I silently finished the entire box of Oreos while he just sat staring at the space in front of him, occasionally saying, 'what the fuck' over and over again. 'What the fuck, Anthony, what the fuck?'

Later, when I was driving home to my own bed, I wondered if he desired me more now that I had left. I wondered whether the bleeding had stopped and what what I had done had meant to him.

*

Recently I've been tracking through all my sexual partners, trying to find images and symbols to work out what it all means. To be in love. To know that you're in love. *Call Me by Your Name* is very clear with its symbols and their meanings. Love is messy and unrequited, yes, but in the film it's easy for the viewer to understand, to see the markers of it. I guess I wanted to see the markers of love in my own life. Have something I could talk to.

One of the first guys I hooked up with changed his display name on Grindr a lot, but never his picture. When I first messaged him, he had it set to 'Mates' but changed it to 'Gaggin 4 It' halfway through chatting. We decided I would go over to his place. Since he was gaggin 4 it and everything.

*

'I love getting out on the water. It's freeing. I love the salty air and the warm breeze. Salty like a good dick,' he said, as I walked into his house. I noticed his boat. I said, 'You have a boat.' And he said, 'Yeah, I love boating. I love getting out on the water. It's freeing. I love the salty air and the warm breeze. Salty like a good dick.' I wrote that twice because I think it's the type of thing that bears repeating.

*

Bodies of water, the ocean, rivers, creeks, lakes are almost always symbolic. I remember my Year 12 English teacher, Ms Back, talking about symbolism and metaphors and other literary devices, and she said, 'Over the course of your studies in English and Literature this year, you will cease being students and start to be active scholars. You'll stop having to look for meaning in the world around you. It will just jump out.' In *Call Me by Your Name* the bodies and busts of sculptures, muscled men, are pulled out of water. Desire lurks beneath the surface, but it is always dredged up.

Ms Back went on to talk about the simile and she said the key to effective simile usage was, obviously, not to overuse the device, but to create something tangible for the reader to sink their teeth into. Something tangible. Like a good dick.

*

'It's cloudy out … looks like rain,' I said.

'Did you really come here to talk about the weather?'

'I guess not,' I said, undressing.

'Did you see what the boat was called?'

'No.'

'It's called *Bent*. Like you. Like me. Bent.'

'Nice. It's a great boat.'

'I'm a true boater. Been boating forever. Do you boat often? Been on the water much?'

'No,' I said. 'My dad gets seasick so it's not something we ever did when I was younger and now I just … never think of it, I guess.'

'You should come up to Maslin Beach sometime. I try to go up as much as I can. The other boaters at Maslin love it. They love *Bent*, they think it's real clever, man,' he laughed. And then he grabbed me and kissed me aggressively. His kiss was hard. He slammed his face into mine like I slammed that banana into my arse all those years ago, but I didn't jump out of my skin as much as I wanted to. And his tongue was rough, yeah, rough, and he was really forceful with it, like he was trying to snake his way down into my stomach so he could exfoliate me from the inside out, and then he threw me on the bed and as I hit the mattress I felt it collapse in on itself, but it didn't bounce or spring back up, no, it just sort of rippled out underneath me and he must have caught my

284

look of surprise because he laughed and said, 'It's a waterbed. I told you I love boating. I'm always the captain of the ship.'

'I've never been on a waterbed before.'

'You're so fucken sexy,' he said, 'you really raise my mast.' Which I found confusing, because *Bent* wasn't a sailboat. It had a motor that could make it go real fast. Surely a true boater would know the difference. As he kissed me again and set about pumicing the back of my throat with his tongue, and then bent me over to fuck me, I thought about all the people down at Maslin, most likely all true boaters, and wondered whether this guy was a laughing-stock to them. And as he started thrusting in and out, in and out, in and out, in and out, I started to rock back and forth, and the bed started to rock with me, ripple and wobble and turn in on itself and my stomach turned and I started to get seasick like my dad.

'Oh mate, I'm gonna cum soon,' he said. 'Get me the lube.'

'Where is it?' I asked, trying not to vomit.

'On the starboard bedside table.'

'Starboard?'

'Yeah, it's the opposite of port-side.'

'I don't know what that mea—'

'Starboard. When facing the front of the boat, the helm, star-board means right-hand side, sailor. You should know that. Everyone should know the fundamentals of sailing and boat maintenance before getting on a ship!'

'Okay,' I said, and I crawled to the bedside table and got the lube and crawled back and lay down while he jacked himself off. After he was finished and he'd shot his load, he laughed and said, 'Job well done, boys,' as he looked down at the small sticky puddle of cum on his stomach. I realised that I wasn't one of the boys at all and that he was talking to his sperm. I wondered if he knew that they couldn't hear him. I wondered if he knew that we weren't on a boat.

I didn't cum and he didn't seem to mind. I got dressed and when he opened the door to let me out, or 'disembark' as he called it, it was raining and I remembered that Ms Back said that rain usually symbolised crying, at least when there were men involved.

'Wow, it's raining,' he said. 'Would you look at that.'

'I didn't really come here to talk about the weather,' I said. And I sat in my car and didn't cry as the rain fell around me.

'Are we catching up this week?' I texted my boyfriend, a few days after the Oreo incident.

'Yeah,' he replied. 'I thought we could watch a movie.'

'Which one?'

He sent me a link to *Interview with the Vampire* and I laughed until I cried.

*

'How do you know that you love me?' my boyfriend asked.

'Hmm?'

'You asked me how I know that I love you. How do you know that you love me?'

'Sometimes I call you when I know you can't answer,' I said, 'just so I can listen to your voicemail.'

'Why?'

'I don't know. It's a symbol, I think. Like in a movie or a book.'

'For what?'

'Loving you. Needing you.'

'Oh.'

'What?' I said.

'I always think that's really fucking annoying when you do it. I'm usually in a meeting and I find it very distracting.'

'Oh,' I said. 'Do you want me to stop doing it?'

'Stop doing what? Calling me, or loving me?'

'Either. Both. I don't know,' I said.

'Stop calling me. Keep loving me.'

'How?' I asked.

He shrugged. 'I don't think it matters how. Just that it happens.'

*

'Is this going to be an issue?' my mother asked the doctor.

'No,' he said, 'shouldn't be. So long as he doesn't watch anything he gets too involved in.'

'What happens then?'

'His mind will probably wander and he'll stress himself out,' he said. And then he said, 'YOU'LL BE FINE!' to me, making sure I could hear.

*

'You know it ends in tragedy, right?' I asked my friend, shouting over the noise of the bar.

'What does?'

'*Call Me by Your Name*. It ends badly.'

'Yeah,' he said, 'I know. I just stop watching before it all goes bad.'

'What if you get too caught up and forget to stop watching?'

'Deal with it … It's still worth it in the end. You want another beer?'

'No,' I said. 'I'm alright.' And I took another sip.

Ah!

How Not to Quench Your Thirst

Jean Velasco

2004 – Dry Vermouth

The only drink available at the fundraising event is dry ginger ale with vermouth, served in large plastic cups that need to be held with both hands. It's sickly and warm, but we order another round anyway. My friends and I shuffle to the edge of the party, far from the overbearing jazz band, and stand awkwardly with our heels sinking into the grass. As a shortcut to the formal dress code, I'm wearing all black, but still feel conspicuous. I down the vermouth in long gulps, in preparation for my imminent departure from college anonymity.

While I wait in the bar queue for a refill, an older student shouts at me, 'Before this night is over, your hair is on the ground.'

I flinch, but secretly hope he's right. My hair is long, mousy brown, untameable. I have no desire to keep it. The bartender tells me I've sold myself cheap, compared to other girls in previous years.

Around nightfall, fundraising efforts plateau a few hundred dollars short of the target, and I worry I'm not high-profile enough to raise the necessary money. But it turns out I was wrong to underestimate the spending capacity of drunk, privileged youth. Donations and drink sales spike as people get thirsty for the main event. Someone colours in the fundraising thermometer poster until the red hits my name, and suddenly I'm being led to the centre of the pavilion.

They sit me on a plastic chair at the same level as the crowd, and a horde of black-tie zombies leans in, fighting to get closer to the spectacle.

Someone puts my hair in a rough braid, and they take turns at sawing with ineffective scissors. Bristly bits stick to my sweat, in my ears and down my cleavage. My cheeks burn, and I imagine a rash creeping up from my chest, curling around my neck and spreading like red mould across my face. Lost for words and appropriate facial expressions, I keep drinking. When I finally hear the buzz of the razor, it has a calming effect.

Afterwards, I have trouble breaking free. Everybody wants to touch me, to rub my scalp. It takes effort to push past the blur of grasping people and escape to the sanctuary of my dorm.

There, I spend a long time in the shower, shaken by the intensity of the crowd. My head is hyper-sensitive, and I sway under the water, feeling every tiny drop as it splashes against skin that has not been this bare since I was born.

Next, I study myself in the mirror. Without make-up, I look pale, puffy, blotchy – the usual string of ugly adjectives that accompany close inspection.

But stepping back?

I love it. I look like a boy. If only my face was thinner, but this is better than expected.

With a little foundation, I'm ready to go back out there.

When I re-join the party, people comment on the nice shape of my skull. It's a strange compliment, that I accept with a self-conscious smile. Someone I don't know tells me encouragingly, 'You should have done that years ago.'

I'm only nineteen and not sure about 'years ago'. But in a way, they're right. Thank god I have done this, I feel so much closer now. To what, I have no idea.

1992 – *Sprite lemonade*

We're at the Vickick Pie Night, and I'm wearing my Essendon jumper with an incongruent white ribbon in my ponytail. The jumper is woollen, and I don't like how the sewn-on sash makes my torso feel asymmetrical and heavy in comparison to my bare arms.

Our club is aligned with St Kilda, which means the hall is decorated with red, white and black balloons. The floor is littered with food wrappers and semicircles of dried grass that have fallen from studded football boots. I can't see anyone from my team, so I run around with my little brother, popping all the white balloons to leave the red and black ones, until some grown-ups tell us off.

The best thing about pie night is the free pies, and soft drink, which we're not allowed at home. After stuffing ourselves silly, we loiter by the trophy table, unsure what to do. Some big kids are playing kick-to-kick outside, but we're supposed to stay in the hall.

When the speeches start, we go back to our parents. Regardless of whether I sit or stand, I can't see what's happening. So I crouch down, gazing abstractly at the crowd, half-listening to the MC's football jargon and clapping when everybody else does.

As he announces the Grade 2 prizes, Mum gives me an excited prod, but I'm confused. He's talking about a boy called Tom, and as far as I can remember there's no Tom in my team.

Then I hear my name being called, and people usher me towards the stage. When I climb onto the platform, the looming MC shakes my hand and presents me with the Coach's Award. It's a gold replica of a footballer taking a specky, mounted on a faux-granite block that's surprisingly light. I stand where they tell me to, clutching my trophy and trying to keep down the pie-and-lemonade reflux. Next to me appears Scotty, the co-winner, who gives me a massive smile. He's the nicest boy in Grade 2 and I have a slight crush on his freckles, even though he's Carlton.

In the car on the way home, I inspect the generic engraving carefully. Scotty is the coach's son, so it occurs to me the competition might have been rigged. If that was the case, maybe I won the prize because I'm the only girl, and not in spite of it.

My parents don't agree. They rave proudly, saying how sweet I looked in football gear with a ribbon in my hair. They quote the MC, repeating that thing about me not being a Tom-boy.

I don't know what a Tom-boy is, but one thing is clear: it is a good thing that I'm not one.

1999 – *Diet Coke*

In Materials Technology, we're supposed to be learning how to sew. Nobody ever makes anything more complicated than a calico bag, so the class is treated as a bludge period. The workbenches are covered in fashion magazines and Diet Coke cans from the vending machine, a visual analogy of our collective fifteen-year-old preoccupations.

The girls I 'sit with' are scheming about dumping Lorena from our 'group'. She's a 'fat bitch' for reasons that I'm yet to grasp, but I don't say anything to defend her.

I'm more interested in what's happening at the opposite table. The popular girls are talking about boys, out of the teacher's earshot but loud enough for the rest of us to hear. To me, the conversation seems incredibly explicit, and I'm once again conscious of being sheltered, raised in a bubble, the only student without the internet, or even a computer at home. The girls are describing things I've never heard of, but I get the idea and find myself blushing. One of them catches me watching her and calls me on it. I mumble a complaint about the heat in the art department, which makes no sense as I'm wearing the winter school jumper. It's an oversized, prickly thing, the same crimson as my face.

2004 – Sweat
It's a Saturday evening and we're flat out as usual. I work at one of the dodgiest Italian restaurants on Lygon Street, where they add flour thickener to the pesto, among other unforgiveable kitchen shortcuts. The staff are more authentic – a fleet of greying Italian waiters, and then me. We all wear white shirts, black vests and long aprons. My hair is an overgrown buzzcut that I try to offset with dangly earrings.

Tonight, there's a middle-aged gay couple in my section and they're being very friendly, despite the mediocre entrée. When their medium steaks turns out to be rare, I take them back to the kitchen. Chef Tony stops what he's doing to glare across the counter at the offending customers, and mutters something inaudible. He commands me to wait at the pass, sweating under the heat lamps, while he shoves the steaks in the microwave for a full two minutes. When I take the shrivelled things back out to the table, the couple are gracious. Later, one of them gives me a fifty-dollar tip, folding it into my palm with a kind smile.

On the other side of the restaurant, there's a group of women who keep trying to catch my eye. Ponytail Tony is supposed to be looking after them, but I end up taking over their table.

Even though the night is winding down, I don't have time for chitchat, and I try not to get too caught up with them. Young Tony, the owner's son, is always watching, and these women don't exactly scream VIP.

After their bill has been settled with a modest tip, one of them asks if I could recommend somewhere to kick on, as they're from out of town.

I have no idea what to answer – my social life is limited to grimy pubs within a small radius of campus. These women are at least ten years older: that's to say, real adults. I load a tray with glasses while racking my brains for a bar that doesn't serve beer in plastic jugs. Impatient, the same woman asks where I'll be going out later, which leaves me even more stumped. Why would she want to know where I party?

Then the knowing smiles and snickering click. With a shaved head, I no longer draw the attention of conventional sleazebags. But I figure these women are either flirting or making fun of me. I mumble something about asking my colleagues, but they tell me to forget it.

After they've left, I polish glasses as efficiently as possible, wondering if anyone noticed the exchange. Young Tony hands over my cash envelope with what I perceive as a smirk. Chef Tony yells at me to pick up my staff meal. I'm not hungry but I take it anyway so as not to offend him.

During the walk back to campus, the foil takeaway container of soft, disposable food weighs heavily in my backpack and on my mind.

In the small hours of Sunday morning, the college flats are dead quiet. The other students are out, or at home in the country. After throwing up all the pasta, I lie in bed thinking about the lesbians – I'm pretty sure that's what they were – and wonder if I blew an opportunity. I've no idea what I was supposed to do differently.

2014 – *Ginebra con tónica*
It's a weeknight in Chueca, Madrid's infamous gay neighbourhood.

I'm drinking free-poured gin and tonics with an old friend from college, who happens to be passing through Spain. About a decade ago he drunkenly came out to me when we were walking home one night, before doing the same, far more eloquently, to a standing ovation in front of the entire student body. He's a successful lawyer now, and while he has barely aged and his humour is just as sharp and irreverent, there is a heaviness to him that wasn't there before. *Life out of the closet isn't necessarily any easier*, I think, as we order yet another round. I know that I'm projecting, but he does the same to me.

My friend is describing Madrid Pride, which I missed because I live in another Spanish city. He raves about the drag queens, the beautiful, near-naked men and the emotion of the parade. But then his smile disappears, and he makes an observation which apparently implicates me.

'Who is waving the bi flag, Jean?' His tone is almost accusing, as if bisexual visibility is somehow my responsibility.

It's a valid point, further exemplified by the fact that I've never come out to him, or, as far as I remember, given him any reason to suspect. I wonder why gay men are so quick to point out my sexuality, while gay women are so quick to doubt it.

'How did you know?' I ask, before divulging my current conundrum. I'm smitten with my Spanish teacher, a heterosexual woman who is eager to be friends, and has offered for me to live with her during the summer.

My friend gets distracted by Grindr and struggles to balance on his chair as he hears me out. But when I finish my preformulated confession, he looks up from his phone, and asks with an offhand smile, 'What took you so long?'

2009 – Salt water

I'm in bed again, though it's barely lunchtime. The curtains are drawn, the waste-paper basket is overflowing with tissues, and I've covered the mirror with a towel. Next to me, my phone is charging on the table. Every now and then the screen lights up, a fluorescent square of jellyfish blue. I let the calls ring out on 'silent' and messages go unopened.

About an hour ago I called in sick. The conversation was easier than expected, my supervisor sounded genuinely concerned. Feeling guilty, I remind myself the symptoms are legitimate. Sore throat, blocked sinuses and lethargic, aching bones. It's amazing how the head and heart and body are all connected. I turn the phone upside down and set the alarm for late this afternoon.

When I wake up, it's not to the alarm but to the sound of my housemate's key in the front door. She wasn't supposed to be home today, but then again neither was I.

Hopefully she's just quickly dropping in and doesn't notice my presence or the food I stole from her shelf. Frozen stiff, I follow her footsteps as they circle the kitchen, then go to and from the bathroom and her bedroom. I hear running water, a flushing toilet, and the sound of high heels on floorboards. Maybe she has a date. I pray it goes well, for my sake. The front door clicks and I let out the breath I was holding.

After she's gone I have a shower, make tea and put on calming music. This is my usual healing ritual. Once it's dark, I'll go down the street to replace her bread and cereal.

While I'm waiting, I write in my diary. There's a lot to get down, and for the next hour I type manically, spewing it all onto the page.

I write a lot about work, and the knock-off drinks which start when my shifts do. I write about what drugs I've taken and who I've kissed. Who I've slept with and where, in which stranger's apartment, backyard, abandoned car park. I confess my guilt about one Sunday with the family, when I forced down lasagne despite having taken amphetamines.

I write about how I'm scared to cross the city to get to uni, because I can't handle the gauntlet of fast-food temptation, or the prospect of running into anyone I know on campus. In daylight, you can see the popped veins in my neck, and the weeping scabs beneath concealer that is now too dark for my washed-out complexion.

I calculate the exact amount of money I'm flushing down the toilet and the extra shifts I'll do to compensate. I decide there's no point in going to uni, as I just end up sleeping in the lectures. I'm getting sloppy, and almost killed a rabbit in pharmacology when I miscalculated a dose by tenfold. I showed up late, in pyjamas, to my Spanish exam. I'm behind on everything. Unreliable. A joke.

I write pitiful declarations of unrequited like, for the guy who rejected me on the grounds of my evident 'problems'. He thinks I might be gay, which seems totally unfair, given the context. Yet even though I want him to be wrong, I suspect there might be truth in what he says.

I tell myself I have 'too much on my plate' to worry about something as flippant as sexual identity. What does it matter who I'm attracted to, if I'm not deserving or capable of a loving relationship?

In a final fit of melodrama, I write about how I want to cut myself, but can't, because I'm too much of a slut for the marks to go unnoticed. So instead I dig and scratch at acne until it bleeds, then tell everyone it's a rash from food intolerance. Another excuse to limit my diet further.

Once I've brought the entry up to date, I drink another bottle of water and keep writing. After heavy binges, I don't need to pee for hours.

On a new page, I draw up a detox, exercise and study plan, which details everything from the long list of prohibited trigger foods, to the exact time I'll exfoliate, floss and do sudokus to repair my broken brain. It's a blueprint for impeccable vegan teetotalling. Perfectionism at its zenith.

Looking back at previous entries would've revealed a pattern in the rambling contradictions. Madness masquerades as honesty, no longer constructive, but telling in its omissions.

The truth I cannot see or bear to write is that I don't want to get better; I want to be 'properly anorexic'. Bulimia is a weak and wasteful habit that puts me in regular contact with toilet bowls. Simply not eating would be cheaper, cleaner and save me hours each day. It would also make me *thin enough*. To be taken seriously. To be cute and androgynous and erase any question of being with women 'by default' simply because I couldn't get a man. To draw people's attention and, at the same time, disappear.

The second thing I struggle to acknowledge is wanting to be a 'real lesbian'.

Of course, it would be easier to be straight, and I'm trying. Probably too hard. But it doesn't matter how many men I sleep with; the other unsettling feeling keeps creeping back. If I have to be gay, why can't it be unequivocally so? I'm sick to death of this limbo ambiguity.

To me, 'bisexual' is synonymous with exhibitionism. I hate the leering comments about threesomes and being roped into making out with women for a male audience. I'm tired of trying the same in private and finding they're suddenly out of their comfort zone. Tired of the contradictions, and how in my own, short-lived heterosexual relationships, my attraction to women is not a turn-on, but a destabiliser.

Given I'm so adept at lying to myself, self-doubt pervades my every thought. I wonder if it is about exhibitionism after all, the fetishisation of bisexuals and wanting to be attractive. I have an eating disorder, so I must be susceptible. If the media can brainwash me into a level of superficiality about my appearance that overrides my values and better judgement, then couldn't my sexual desire be equally impressionable?

Then there's the question of how much. What percentage do you have to be, to be bi? If it's not fifty-fifty, is it even worth worrying about?

I make up all kinds of excuses. 'Men when drunk, women when high', and repeat this like a mantra. Women are just fantasy, at most a one-nighter, a furtive pash in a nightclub cubicle. Straight women, that is. Without knowing any 'real lesbians', I assume they'd consider me fraudulent. I'm scared of their judgement and their feminism.

There are other factors. My skin, for example, wouldn't bear female scrutiny. Women see more, question more and have better sensitivity in their fingertips. Men, in my experience, are rough and undiscerning. Only they can satisfy my unrelenting masochism.

These are my unarticulated thoughts, as I get dressed, cover my face and neck with concealer and go down the street to the 7-Eleven.

There, I spend ages inspecting nutrition labels, filling my basket, then putting things back on the shelves.

In the end, I capitulate. How else am I to fill the manic wakefulness, when I cannot be seen, do not dare to even pick up the phone? I have $30 until my next paycheque, which is enough to replace the stolen food and get a four-pack of doughnuts, two

Maxibons, a hotdog and a giant tub of yoghurt. I eat the hotdog on the way home, so it doesn't stink out the flat.

Because I'm not sure when my housemate's due back, I binge at my desk and vomit into double, triple plastic bags, which I drop out of the window to where the wheelie bins are kept.

2001 – *Liquid nitrogen*
In Chemistry, I spend most of the 55-minute period decorating my school diary with razor-backed dragons. This isn't because I'm bored – the teacher has my complete attention. Ms W, soon to become Mrs M, is eloquent, funny and unconventional. I adore her classes, and the fact she's been criticised by parents for not being sufficiently 'exam-focused' appeals to my repressed sense of anarchy.

Under the enchantment of her voice, chemical concepts emerge with ease from previously abstract ignorance. Her analogies are so visual that I don't need to look up at the board to understand them. But if I do, our eyes invariably meet, and I feel like the whole time she has been speaking only to me.

During experiments, I follow her presence out of the corner of my eye as she flits from group to group checking Bunsen burners.

After school, I work at a popular fast-food chain, and have a similar fascination with one of the managers. I track his blue shirt around the restaurant and tense up whenever he comes close to me at the cash register.

One of these infatuations is obvious, easy to recognise as a crush. The other, I choose not to question, so I simply pass it off as admiration.

2018 – *Café con leche*
The lights in the cabin have been dimmed, and the flight attendant is doing a final round before we slip into artificial night. My girlfriend hasn't bothered with an eye mask or ear plugs, and is dozing next to me while a movie plays out on her screen. After a full month of speaking English and meeting every sphere of my Australian life, she is *hecha polvo*, made dust.

Unlike her, I'm wired, and keen to stay awake for as much of the flight back to Madrid as possible. I order a coffee and open my laptop to a fresh document.

Where my old, handwritten diary used to end up tear-splattered in melodrama, today's entry is so upbeat it's cringeworthy. The dominant theme is gratitude. Not just for the person sleeping beside me, nor for the warm reception we received in Melbourne. But for coming through, and the relative ease of coming out. My family and friends were enthusiastic and natural about my unprecedented presentation of a female partner, indeed any partner, something I'd never had the conviction to do before.

After following the same-sex marriage plebiscite from a distance during the lead-up to our trip, we were relieved not to encounter personally any of the homophobia or frightening ignorance we'd witnessed in the media. I was wrong to have ever doubted my people. Then I remember: it was never them I doubted.

It's almost seven years since I left Australia, and the time abroad has mostly been an exercise in unlearning. Language immersion is an effective tool for breaking destructive inner monologues. Cultural differences forced me to let go of control and opened my eyes to social conditioning. Having the luxury of time, to read and take an interest in the world, helped me break free of the toxic, cyclical introspection that dominated most of my twenties.

My girlfriend is a 'real lesbian', who's okay with the fact that I'm not. As a 'professional feminist', she has been instrumental in dismantling many of my long-held misconceptions.

I'm not sure if this relationship has succeeded because she's a woman, because she's uniquely her or because I was 'in a good place' when we met. Although having a partner shouldn't be necessary to validate oneself or one's identity, I can't deny it's helped.

It's a long way to Madrid, and even there I won't be home. There's still so much more unpacking to do. But despite the uncertainties, we're optimistic about our future. In either world, or in both.

Silence and Words

Aron Koh Paul

When I realised I was in love for the first time, I marked the day in my adolescent diary with a single blank page. In those volumes I never shied away from recording my thoughts about everything, from world affairs to the state of breakfast. The year was 1995 and I was seventeen. At the bottom of the page, where I liked to note the music I was listening to that day, I wrote the song 'Have I the Right' (to love you) – my musical tastes in those days didn't move much beyond the 1960s. The empty lines above were the only answer I knew then how to give.

On every other subject I was precocious. My VCE English teacher accused me of being florid. 'You write as if you're Francis Bacon,' she said, dragging on a cigarette in her smoke-filled car on the way to see a David Williamson.

In this florid tongue, I wrote long letters to my best friend, Matt. I kept a draft of one. In it, I wrote about Plato, about literature and philosophy, about the weather, politics, our plans for saving the world. I said nothing about love. He never wrote back. He wasn't the literary type, he said. 'I keep all your letters to me,' he told me on the phone, 'because one day they will be worth something.' I don't know if he realised how much his words could sting me.

*

When we say goodbye for the last time, we are each at different universities, in different cities. In the final two long years of school together, we took to calling ourselves 'the survivors'. In his parting speech, our headmaster told us that our school years would be the happiest of our lives. For some, it became truth. What a lie and a curse, it seems to me now.

We spend hours on that last night revisiting our teenage conversations as we sit in my room at college under the giant poster of the Lady of Shalott that I've pinned to the wall above my bed. 'What the hell is with that?' he asks. 'I'm into Pre-Raphaelites,' I say. Like Anne Shirley, I can recite the Tennyson poem by heart, without thinking too hard about why it means so much to me, as if I'm living the curse of unrequited love without realising that my life is just a nineteenth-century literary rehash.

We shake hands when I see him to the tram. I really want to hug him, but I resist the things I really want, afraid of the response. Love is easier as a dream. I watch the tram disappear, his profile in the window looking straight ahead, having said nothing I really wanted to say. 'You were always so good with words,' his father tells me only a year later, when he asks me to speak a eulogy at his son's funeral.

*

As a child I had always wanted a friend. My first year of school – I have a photo of me grinning broadly in my blue Sandringham Primary School pullover, carrying my red plastic lunchbox – I had two good friends, Adam and Nicole (Nicole had a trampoline). In one photo, I stand between them wearing paper hats at my sixth birthday party at McDonald's. I got a brand-new Malvern Star with training wheels – I remember hurtling downhill on the footpath with my mother running beside me. We went kite-flying on the Sandringham foreshore around the white rotunda.

I had enemies too. Two boys who ran around me in the playground calling me 'Japanese–Chinese'. I told them they were stupid for not knowing that China and Japan were two different countries. Mum told me they were only teasing me out of jealousy. Also, I was Aussie–Iban, a completely different mixture.

In another photograph, which my mother took when I was around four, she has dressed me in a 'Sarawak: Land of Headhunters' t-shirt that falls to my feet, and posed me standing on the bed with a raised wooden shield and spear. I look uncertainly at the lens. There were no digital retakes back then.

In 1983 we went to Sarawak chasing my father and mother's dreams, to live with my father's family, a five-hour boat ride up the Rajang River in a house surrounded by jungle and plantations. My mother told me it would be like *The African Queen*. I imagined her as Katharine Hepburn among the natives, and me as Humphrey Bogart. Instead of the puffing steamboat, there was a motorboat with overpowered air conditioning and hyper-loud kung-fu movies. My mother dyed her hair blonde so she would stand out more – there's a photo of her golden halo in the midst of the congregation in the little blue timber Methodist church. My younger sister and I are seated on either side of her. I look as unhappy as I do in almost every photograph from these childhood years. I don't belong here, the photos scream. I refused to go to Iban class because, I said, 'I'm Australian.' The vision I held of Australia was one of belonging, but that life had been put on pause – the bicycle rusting away, the kite grounded, the model boat I started building with my father on one of his visits sitting unfinished in a box on top of the cupboard.

When the other boys at the local high school wanted me to show them mine if they showed me theirs, I walked away. They wanted to know if it was true that 'white men' are uncircumcised, and wasn't I curious to see theirs too? Boys walked about the school innocently holding each other's hands, and I stayed among the clever girls. One of the girls wrote me letters that I never answered. I only wanted a friend like me – though I didn't really know what I was like. I liked opera, musicals, political discussions, Narnia and *The Lord of the Rings*. My mother read romance and crime novels for hours while I lay on the floor, drawing maps of my own fantasy worlds, which gradually took over the whole lounge room. My mother read to escape, and I scribbled to do the same. On other days I read my mother's anthropology and history books, pausing to trace the images of naked Greek statues with pencil and paper. When the *New Idea* magazines arrived from 'home', I secretly cut out the male underwear models and kept them in a locked box under my bed.

When we came home, I was not yet fifteen. I went to a country school where everyone asked me where I was from and mixed me up with the Thai exchange student. A quiet sandy-haired boy used to talk to me about growing tomatoes and write me letters about Jesus. My best friends were the two old librarians. I would sit at the piano in the hall outside the library and play them 'The Blue Danube'. I always got along with old ladies, like Great-Aunty Irene, who travelled the world in a steamship, collecting teaspoons from every port. We got along so well that the night she died her ghost appeared at the end of my bed. She probably knew more about me then than I did. She gave me a glass turtle and a musical box that played 'The Music Man'. We watched the Charles and Diana wedding together on her bed, and I used to race home after school to watch *Monkey Magic* there too and pretend the puffy pink satin doona was a cloud I was flying on. The Australia I came home to was different, of course. *Monkey Magic* had been cancelled. Paul Keating was the prime minister everyone hated because he was privatising everything. The morning after he lost the 1996 election, the Labor-supporting Lebanese milk-bar owner told me that Keating lost because of people like me. He meant Asians. Pauline Hanson had just been elected to parliament on a mission to stop us swamping the country.

Maybe difference had become a habit after so many years not fitting in. But even the principal failed to tell me apart from the exchange student sometimes. The country teachers didn't know what to do with me, so they sent me to the library to study on my own while the other students were acting up. One day, we had to give talks about a historical figure. Everyone else wanted to fit in, to not stick out, to be cool, and they wrote short paragraphs that made it clear they didn't care. I gave a long speech about Otto von Bismarck and the Concert of Europe. To calm my nerves I stared the whole time at the most beautiful blonde girl in the class, as if I was talking directly to her. She smiled back, encouraging me. Now I think about it, maybe she was embarrassed, but at the time I couldn't tell. Later that day her boyfriend wrapped me up in sticky tape in metal-working class. When I told Matt this story a year and a bit later, he said, 'What was his name? Me and my mates will go and mess him up for you!'

When I first saw Matthew, he was arriving at the boarding house with his parents. He wasn't anything like me. I was on a scholarship, and he was the son of an Old Boy. He was always grinning as if he'd just broken something. There was a rumour of some trouble in Canberra, for which he had been sent down to Melbourne to escape. White skin, red lips, roses in his cheeks, black hair that fell over his forehead when he hadn't brushed it back under his New Yorkers cap. I have two drawings I made of him in profile as he posed. I drew the dissected mice for his biology homework too. He wanted to be a marine biologist, or a mafia boss. He said his favourite film was *Pulp Fiction*. I didn't watch those kinds of films. His father was a lawyer and his uncle was a priest, so he said he'd probably have to study Law. His mother part-owned a racehorse. When my mother came down from the country for the parents' night, she wore her most elegant scarf and parked our old bomb around the corner so nobody would know we were 'poor'.

Matt said his favourite quote from the Bible was 'Rejoice in thy youth'. He liked to skateboard and play rugby and have shiny cadet boots. He liked the idea of being popular, one of the boys. They would go off together on 'missions from God'. Later, he told me they hid the marijuana under my wardrobe because nobody would suspect me. I was the straight and narrow one – it was an appearance I wore like armour, with intellectual walls and drawbridges.

The housemaster told us one day when we were arguing with each other that we were like a married couple. We fought about God (he was an atheist) and politics (he was a republican). On the last day of school, Matt played Pink Floyd's *The Wall* and I blasted Handel's 'Zadok the Priest' across the school oval. On breaks for exam study, we chased each other around the house, emptied the fire extinguisher at each other, broke furniture, threw (surprisingly painful) apricots at each other, and wrestled in the corridor. We watched *Gallipoli* over and over because we had to for English, and afterwards we listened to Albinoni's 'Adagio in G Minor' together in the dark of his room.

People like Matt make friends easily, as if everyone falls in love with them for possessing something they themselves lack. He told me once that he had had a girlfriend in Canberra, that she had thrown herself out of a moving car. I decided, without thinking about the implications, that I would do anything for him. I still thought vaguely that there was a girl out there for me, someone like Helena Bonham Carter in *A Room with a View* – an aloof mystery – but at the school disco I didn't want to dance near anyone except my best friend to 'I Wanna Be Your Lover' and 'Total Eclipse of the Heart'. I was Lucy Honeychurch, and Matt was the screaming boy in the tree who was questioning everything I thought I was.

But instead of talking about love, we studied *The Outsider* and *Richard III*, their questions ones of philosophy or politics. I didn't mind being nerdy – I thought that ideas really mattered, that there was nothing higher. I avoided sports and the gym, because I told myself I could never be or have anything like that – glimpses of bodies and snippets of locker-room banter posed a threat I couldn't yet name. I looked down on the Greek–Australian boys who painted cocks in Wite-Out on the lockers. 'Faggot' was their ultimate term of abuse, but I didn't attach such a crude word to myself. I was too busy standing out for different reasons – each difference a disguise. I argued in school essays that there is no such thing as race, but I couldn't get away from being in between, and yet defined by, those alien moulds. I chose all my battles out of defiance and called it loyalty – to the old Queen, to Reason, to ideals of God and of platonic romance too pure to be attained.

*

When Matt's father calls to tell me his son has died of a heroin overdose, I'm back at home in the country for the holidays, a long way from anywhere. I cry and my mum cries too. She tells me a story about a girlfriend she had at school with whom she felt really close. She's dropping hints or invitations to talk, but I don't want to talk about myself. When someone dies like that, everyone's grief is deepened by some form of guilt.

Matt's father pays for my flight to attend the funeral and, for reasons I don't fully understand, I have a place among the family. They say they know how much he meant to me, but I can't imagine that they do. Someone tells me Matt had a boyfriend, but I never see him. There's a girl in black carrying red roses at the casket. I don't see his body, but I imagine it lying there, drained of colour and hope. His uncle delivers a sermon about the evils of drugs and the waste of a young life. Matt wasn't yet twenty-one.

I'm angry. It feels like a lecture that says nothing about my friend, or of the things I remember about him.

I get up to speak, but all the words I want to say disappear. Am I really allowed to say how much I loved him?

Twenty years later, although I have loved, lost and gained so much more in that time than my old headmaster could've imagined, I still feel the burden of that silence.

homosexual

Mike Mullins

I don't relate to the word 'queer'. 'Gay' has never sat comfortably with me either. Perhaps I'm just old-fashioned, but I've always been most relaxed with the word 'homosexual'.

Growing up in a small town in Australia is challenging for anyone who is different. Especially when you are born in 1951 and your world is the monoculture that was Australia in the post-war years. It is doubly challenging when you are a male child who hates playing sport and displays a creative flair for doing things in his own unique way.

The Rock in New South Wales was established as a railway town in the later part of the nineteenth century, when the first steps were being taken to bring together the separate colonies into one nation. Down the road in the Victorian town of Glenrowan, the Kelly gang was blazing a trail of mythological proportions, the iconic *Bulletin* magazine was in its embryonic years, and many of the artists and writers and performers who thrived at the time – Mary Gilmore, Henry Lawson, Nellie Melba, and the painters Arthur Streeton, Tom Roberts and Fred McCubbin – captured a very romantic view of Australia. In 1883, the Sydney-to-Melbourne railway line officially opened – for the first time you could travel between the two cities by train. A railway engineer who took the route observed, 'There were no townships touched between Wagga and Albury, and the country is but thinly populated.' It wasn't until March 1885 that The Rock was proclaimed. The name was controversial as the township's station was originally called 'Hanging Rock', but the rock in question had actually fallen ten years earlier. So it became, simply, 'The Rock'. I was staggered to discover that the town had only been established sixty-six years before I was born.

My school years at The Rock were challenging, and few memories from that time can be recalled with fondness or nostalgia. According to a former teacher I was an effeminate child, which made me an easy target for bullying.

The playground was a place of torture. I dreaded recess and the seemingly endless lunch period in particular. The negative attention from the boys was relentless: regular rituals of ganging up on me, calling me nasty names and much worse. I have no idea whether my teachers were aware of this or felt any responsibility to deal with it. This was the 1950s, when a man had to be a man and if things were tough, you had to learn to toughen up.

These attacks also went beyond the boundaries of the school. On the way home, I was often stoned and bashed and my bike was frequently thrown into the creek. I remember on one occasion being held down by one of the boys while the others pissed on me. The culture that many now call 'toxic masculinity' reigned supreme at The Rock during my childhood.

One day the headmaster caught me walking hand in hand with a fellow student who I'll call Johnny. It was not sexual. Johnny was the only male student who I became friends with during the late primary-school years. He was the son of a farmer, but I don't remember why we connected. The next day, at the school assembly, the headmaster called us both up in front of the entire school and forced us to walk hand in hand. The kids screamed with laughter and the humiliation was intense. Johnny never associated with me again and I think that this was the day we both lost our innocence. Our childhood concluded. The message was clear: men don't touch each other except in formal handshakes and in contact sports.

More and more, I retreated to the company of girls. I felt safe in their presence – a refuge from the toxicity of the schoolyard. All of this changed, of course, when puberty arrived and the boys started sniffing around the girls. My presence was suddenly unwelcome to both genders.

Away from school, in the safety of our backyard and in the company of the neighbourhood kids, were more positive experiences. The creek that runs through the town was frequently dry and an exotic place to play: curved sheets of tin became slides down the grassy slopes; curves in the dry creek bed became battlegrounds for games of Cowboys and Indians; scaling fallen trees made for epic adventures; and the native birds provided a rich soundtrack to it all. Life at The Rock was not all negative.

My first sexual experience arrived with an unexpected visit from an older boy in the neighbourhood. He wanted to know if I had done 'it'. The enquiry was about masturbation (commonly referred to as 'wanking' or 'jerking'), and he was eager to show me the way when my answer was 'No, what is *it*?' This was not a homosexual act; there is no doubt in my mind that all he was doing was exploring and sharing the newly discovered capacities of his cock.

The games at the creek changed when testosterone became the driver. A couple of generous girls were happy to share their bodies with a group of us fellas on the banks of the creek, but it soon became apparent to me that I was more interested in watching the blokes in action.

My sexual life became very secretive. Suddenly, there was a compelling reason to be among the boys and some, who had so ruthlessly harassed me when I was younger, now found my company convenient. That convenience had its rules and restrictions and under no circumstances could it be discussed with anyone – including the boys themselves, until there was a need to catch up again. I enjoyed these clumsy sexual encounters and, in some ways, I think now I yearn a little for the purity of those first experiences. These days, sex has long lost its innocence.

Beyond the physical pleasures of these encounters was another, more complex dimension, which was a desire to be accepted. It would take a further five decades to fully understand the intricacies of that particular ache, its connection to my deeply entrenched anxiety and its associated fear of rejection. But in some small way in those early encounters, my tormentors accepted me and with that came a hint of empowerment and the beginnings of my life as a homosexual man.

In late 2014, I suffered a nervous breakdown. Triggered by a series of workplace bullying incidents, which had nothing to do with my sexuality, one day I started to shake uncontrollably. It wouldn't stop. These circumstances led to my resignation from the job and a period of intense therapy. It turned out to be the best thing that could have happened to me. I had long avoided dealing with the many issues that had influenced and informed who I was. In the therapeutic process I discovered that I was born an anxious person, due to the circumstances of my birth-mother. It's now been clinically proven that if a woman is stressed and anxious during pregnancy, it has an effect on the unborn child, predisposing them to anxiety. Being a young Catholic girl in 1951, pregnant out of wedlock, must have been extremely stressful. The stigma of unwanted pregnancies in those days was brutal, so she had no option but to give her child up for adoption.

I spent eighteen months with my psychiatrist, deconstructing my life. The circumstances of my birth, a childhood with a violent, alcoholic father and the toxicity of my school years were just the beginning. Having been a homosexual in Australia during the '60s and '70s brought a whole set of issues as well. Homosexuality was not only illegal in those days, but also seen as a human deficiency, in terms of both masculinity and mental health. I confronted all of this (and more) as we unpacked the jigsaw of my life, piece by piece.

When the therapy was finished, I was a new person. For the first time in my life I became very confident about my sexuality. At sixty-five years of age I suddenly became a highly active sexual being. I acquired a contemporary haircut, started to go to the gym six days a week, lost 20 kilograms, pierced my ears and had a tattoo inked on my left arm. My friends would ask, 'Is this the new Mike?' My answer was succinct: 'No, this is the Mike that always was but until now has never been allowed to be.'

In 2018, I watched the live broadcast of the Australian parliament passing the same-sex marriage legislation. When the strong contingent of advocates in the visitors' gallery broke into song with a rendition of 'I Am Australian', I started to cry.

I sobbed uncontrollably for forty minutes. I couldn't stop. The tears came from deep inside and they were cathartic.

Afterwards, I wondered: *why did I cry like that?* The answer was simple: as an adult, for nearly fifty years, I had felt a lesser person, a sub-citizen, an inferior man.

Suddenly – finally – that was all gone.

A Robust Game of Manball

Patrick Lenton

At the University of Wollongong, in the school of creative writing, as I learnt about particularly sick short stories, about the wildest of rhymed stanzas, about the loosest literary philosophers, I also learnt about other, just as important, things: friendship, the dangers of trying too hard, and the inherent stupidity of masculinity and men.

Creative Writing was a weird degree in both purpose and setup: a tight-knit collection of around twenty to thirty students who were just keen as shit about sentences. You know the old army maxim of 'put 'em through hell together?' Well, Creative Writing kind of worked on the opposite notion – put them through something truly absurd and useless and fun like studying creative writing, and they'll bond through the shared realisation that they'll never get a job or earn any money.

One weekend, it was announced that a bunch of the girls in our friendship circle would forgo the usual pleasure of smashing cheap jugs at the North Gong or drinking boxes of goon in someone's sharehouse, or crashing one of the actors' interminable house parties, to have a 'no men' night. I supported the notion in theory – men are pretty terrible, and it's nice for everyone who doesn't identify as a man to have some peace. However, this left *me* alone with the dudes. A lone wilting queer flower in a garden of boys who wouldn't feel comfortable comparing themselves to flora. Admittedly, nobody in a creative writing degree was overtly masculine – more poetry-reading effetes than football-throwing bros – but it was still upsetting. I assumed I'd have to listen to jazz.

I used to see my inability to relate to men and their communities as a fault on my part, a deficit. I saw their scorn of me and my obvious queerness and nerdery and fluttery weirdness as something wrong with me. I used to attempt to think of ways to fit in, like the time I pretended to have a favourite type of truck.

So, on the 'no men' night, rather than simply enduring a nightmarish evening of high testosterone, of shouted arguments about the relative merits of lit bros like Hemingway or Bukowski, of cheap beer and posturing, I thought I'd try to lean in and experience a true boys' night. I didn't know exactly what a boys' night was precisely, but I had grand dreams of using my organisational skills to foster a deep rapport, a raw emotional masculine truth, like when men go out into the woods and shoot things or rip copper out of the earth or round up cattle on a lonely mountain – I realised I was thinking of *Brokeback Mountain*. You never know: perhaps I was actually a man's man, but I'd just never had any male friends to test the theory out on.

Consequently, with great excitement, I put together a party-planning team to organise the first ever Creative Writing boys' night out. We called it 'Mandate'. My friend Anna actually came up with most of the good ideas. Why was Anna there? Who knows. Why was Anna anywhere?

Mandate had everything – the slogan was 'mandate, get it in ya', which Anna printed on super cute buttons to give to all the participants. We created a signature cocktail for the event. We made canapés, we decorated the random sharehouse we were in with streamers and lights, we even made a playlist ('It's Raining Men', sung by Geri Halliwell, twenty-three times in a row).

Strangely, despite getting a great turnout, the party first stuttered and then failed to launch. Our guests milled awkwardly in the immaculately decorated living room, seemingly too on-edge from my highly curated fun to sit down and relax. The more alcohol that got pumped into the room, the more somnolent and slow the conversation became. A cute boy I was trying to flirt with kept calling up girls at the other party and pleading to join them.

I was pissed off. Somehow, as the night progressed, my failing mandate morphed into a competition. I could only imagine what the non-men event was up to, but I was convinced that it was fun and frivolous and everything my shitty party was not. I gathered the party-planning committee, and tried to brainstorm ideas.

'Drugs,' said Lachie. 'Pranks,' said Anna. But then, in a flash of genius, I realised that what they needed was the *opposite* of what I wanted. All I had to do was think of my worst party scenario: men would be sure to love it.

'Mandate,' I announced loudly, interrupting literally no conversation. 'It's time to play sport. It's time for ... Manball.'

We traipsed to a local sports field (well, everyone except Anna, who decided to stay behind and organise an undetermined prank).

There was a *Friday Night Lights* aura to the evening now, the big lights filling us with vigour and patriotism, the hot night making us boisterous and rough. There was jostling and hooting and the loud hyena cackles of the young at night, and while normally I'd hate every part of that nonsense, now I was just thrilled, grinning in the darkness. *Yes, my simple boys*, I thought, *we're all in cahoots now, my stupid man-babies.*

Having never played or watched a sport in my life, it took some time to develop the rules of Manball. As far as anyone can remember, there were two opposing sides, a sack of goon and a lot of running and pushing. If you'd told me before that night that a bunch of pretentious philosophy students and book nerds and power-Goths would spend their evening running and strategising and pouring goon over themselves while taking a victory lap, I would have spat in your face. But, against all odds, Manball worked. Even I was running, all hysterical and red-faced and boisterous, like a sugared-up toddler at the beach.

Maybe I had been missing out, I thought. Maybe my dislike and fear of men and their activities was something limiting, a fragment from another time. If we kept Mandate inclusive and open to everyone – not just men – maybe I'd grow to love things like physical activity and being interrupted when I talk. As I was thinking this, I watched a boy named Dane bounding along with the goon sack – like a newborn gazelle, all flying tongue and big hooves until he slipped and smacked his beautiful noggin against a tap, knocking himself out instantly.

Halfway to the hospital, with the poor concussed lad hoisted on our shoulders like a fallen king, Dane recovered enough to argue that he didn't actually need to go. He was trembling and slurring, but at that point of the night, with the amount of fruity lexia coursing through our veins, who wasn't? Instead, we went back to the house, babbling with excitement, sporting Dane and his smashed head like an emblem, a trophy.

*

I wish that this night was as ridiculous as my memory paints it – but the fact is that at the time I was lonely and closeted and scared. I was seriously attempting to discover who a secret queer boy could be friends with, testing whether there could be a treatise between me and straight men. I held my queerness inside tightly, like a gallstone, like a rapidly developing pearl in a disgusting oyster. In high school, straight males had beaten me up, locked me in a bathroom for eight hours, forced me to move from school to school. I was afraid of men. I didn't just want their approval and friendship because I was a dumb closeted self-conscious weirdo; I wanted to find the trick to getting them to stop beating me up. This party was a test, which I was pretty sure I was doomed to fail.

Finally coming out years later was, for me, not so much about gaining the freedom to date men (I was in love with a woman at the time) but about tearing off the final remnants of the ragged cloak of masculinity I'd been wearing as an attempt to blend in. I don't think it was a massively successful disguise, but it was heavy and burdensome. It felt so good to kick it off.

*

When we got back to the sharehouse, we had to kick down the front door. Anna had constructed an elaborate fortress by piling every piece of furniture in the middle of the room, for reasons that we never deciphered. In the kitchen sink, a fire raged. Every door to the house was barricaded against entry. Anna herself was passed out in the corner, wrapped in a curtain. Somehow, in its absurdity, in its elaborate frailness and lack of any utilitarian benefit, the entire night – and Anna's prank in particular – seemed a fitting metaphor for masculinity, for manliness, for mandate.

The Equality of Love

Yamiko Marama

After the results of the same-sex marriage postal survey, Gina started holding my hand in public. Not just the grab, squeeze and release type of hand-holding either.

The first time, it took me by surprise. We were crossing the road in Melbourne's CBD on our way to a movie. The white lines on the bitumen guided our passage, holding off the grumbling traffic waiting as we crossed into the throng of oncoming pedestrians. Gina's hand curled spontaneously into mine, enveloping my brown hand in its whiteness in the familiar way that it does, as if it's been moulded for that purpose, protecting me from the chilly Melbourne breeze. Just another day, but not really.

We'd handled those months in the lead-up to and during the survey differently. I cried. She got angry. I tried to ignore it until I couldn't and would then find myself crying in the car on my way to work, as I cooked dinner, in the shower. The tears were usually sparked by a reminder of something from earlier in the day: a conversation I'd overheard, a news report that interrupted my morning drive, one of the many articles that flooded my newsfeed. I'd get through my day because I had to, but underneath I felt brittle, a fragile rawness easily opened up by words.

While I tried to look away, Gina, always curious and probing, would read the comments. The hateful and gratuitous ones people left under articles and opinion pieces posted on Facebook – comments floating in little beige bubbles, unsolicited opinions adjudicating our humanity. Gina would rant and rage to our friends, to her colleagues, to me when we spent time together doing innocuous everyday things like walking to the supermarket.

I imagined her alone, still ranting to an audience of herself, unable to turn off the stream in the same way that I couldn't turn off the tears.

It's hard to know what is being in love with a woman and what is being in love with Gina. Before her I'd only had flings or relationships with men. I'd believed myself to be happy – and I still think I was – although perhaps with a little question mark on the end.

Our romance started abruptly. The first time Gina kissed me we had been walking back to her place along the sand of St Kilda beach, shoes in hand, toes squelching. We were intoxicated and giddy; we had the beach to ourselves, with the stars and sea our only witnesses.

Things quickly escalated from that first kiss and Gina soon became the fabric of my every day. I made myself comfortable in her home, and it became my home a mere six months later, her routine playing out alongside mine like two arms on the same body. I'm attuned to her habits now: watching breakfast news with a steaming cup of coffee in the morning, the plunger and milk carton sitting like well-behaved children on our carpeted floor. She's always up before me: I reach out to find she's left the bed during my attempts to savour the final drops of sleep, but I'm reassured she will be there, on that couch, coffee in hand, as I kiss her and tumble out the door on my way to another day.

And she's usually home when I return, although sometimes I'll beat her and get to watch her sloping through our apartment car park, admiring her confident gait through the kitchen window as I do the dishes, and then greeting her as she comes through the front door, stories bubbling out of her. Later, we relay the events of the day as we walk along the foreshore or juggle dinner plates on our laps, the darkness from outside announcing itself as winter always does.

My side of the couch in our small apartment is where I perch to put on my boots (my armour) in the mornings before work, and where I lounge in the evenings, the crook of the couch a resting place for my head. It's the very same spot that I sat when I first entered Gina's home on the night I told her I'd never kissed a girl before, tentative but emboldened by drink. This would be one of those turning points, a moment with a pre and a post.

My pre had been comfortable, but like all comfortable things also somewhat small and stiff. I'd been ready to outgrow it, but I hadn't been sure why or how, and it no longer felt sustainable for me to pack my bags and travel the globe every time dissatisfaction burbled within me. It turns out coming-of-age stories are not only for the teens. I'm a late(ish) bloomer – my queer coming of age happened in my late twenties, at a time when many of my friends were creating whole new, separate life forms whose welfare they are completely responsible for. I still congratulate myself for finding matching socks in my cupboard. I'm still busy exploring my own life, digging around and feeling amused by what I find.

And so, I fell down the rabbit hole, like Alice, like all people falling in love. And I arrived in an upside-down world where I was required to integrate this new identity – one that felt revolutionary in its authenticity. It was Gina who became my personal handbook to queerdom.

Gina, on the other hand, had experienced a lifetime of queer adventures: world travels with various ex-girlfriends; booze-soaked nights with lezzo cliques that would rival *The L Word* for drama; the transformational world of women's Aussie Rules football, the sport that had been dominated by men but saw the emergence of a whole club, and league, that didn't really require any.

'You wouldn't have liked me then,' she'd say dramatically, as she likes to do, proceeding to relate some kind of debaucherous event she'd been a part of. She's a storyteller, Gina – not like me, who hides away in our apartment to type words into a laptop screen that looks blankly back. She likes the theatre of it, an audience that she can amuse.

You could see snippets from these tales on her Facebook timeline: Gina dressed as a pot-bellied Santa at the football club Christmas do, Gina on the piss, making silly faces with her best friend Dawson, Gina at a friend's hens' party riding a giant pink inflatable penis. It's one of the things I like about her the most – her willingness to be playful and juvenile, perhaps because she spent so much of her teenage life missing out on that. There's a freedom in being able to enjoy yourself, unapologetically, regardless of your age. I too find myself becoming more playful the older

I grow. Worrying about meeting others' expectations means less when you've already announced who you authentically are.

Being queer, if you're lucky, means you can dodge certain expectations: getting married, having kids, finding some lukewarm but stable job that will pay for your house deposit in the suburbs. Nothing wrong with all that, should you want it – but maybe you don't? Instead, you can go to lesbian events on a Sunday night, or a rainbow festival where you dance on a mountain with other queers, the twisted, cindered trees echoing your own movements. And it's not either/or: you can slip between these queer worlds and the worlds of your non-queer friends, and decide where you fit.

The ferocious passion of early-days romance can create something like a cocoon: coffee in bed; talking for hours; lounging in sheets that become a kind of personal fort, eyes itchy from lack of sleep, and yet minds wired, invigorated by the compulsion that is early love. It's a gift when you feel so known so early on by someone, and I was surprised by the detail to which Gina understood me. She could see how being a little different had made me vulnerable to prioritising other people's needs before my own; she saw a playful side that was often hidden within the responsible person I had always been.

Living with Gina has given me the confidence to put myself out there, to be outraged, to write, to say no. Below its glittering facades, queer culture is about being who you are, unashamedly. The clichéd gay anthems that we all love to sing at the top of our voices, blissfully ignorant of how bad we sound until we listen to our Snapchat stories in horror later – Cher, Lady Gaga, Beyoncé, Whitney Houston, Frank Ocean, Queen, George Michael, Prince – often speak to the celebration of us as a community. They're one of the ways we learn to celebrate ourselves as individuals, which is not something that has been handed to us, but for which we have had to work.

Looking back, I realise that Gina had initially been cautious, treating me delicately despite her confident and at times brash demeanour. It had been harder for her than it had been for me. She had spoken of getting into relationships with 'straight women' who had wanted to dip their toe in but had little interest in weathering the complexity of actually being a queer woman. I realise now that she had actually been giving me an out, early on, perhaps knowing what might be in store for me at a time when I was intoxicated and blissfully ignorant of what that might mean. It was easier for me to see her caution as a relic of old times, given her twelve years' seniority to me – there wasn't, I was certain, going to be any alarmist meltdown from me, no massive freakout.

But once I was faced with my own experiences of homophobia – from the world at large but sometimes even from people who loved me, and in subtler ways than I'd anticipated – I understood Gina's trepidation. On reflection, it had started right from the beginning, from work colleagues who declared that 'Yamiko's not gay!' when my new relationship was mentioned, as if they'd been privy to some earlier office memo confirming my alleged heterosexuality based on how I dressed or acted. I soon realised that being queer was something of a full-time job: having to correct people's assumption that you had a boyfriend; being presumed to be straight; overhearing flip and degrading comments about you; having to censor affectionate behaviour with your partner to avoid the leering of certain men; pulling up friends when they were thoughtlessly negative or dismissive. Even, during the period of the postal survey, debating friends who would seek to justify a 'no' vote, because they had family members who were voting this way and they thought I should understand why, even as the whole country was allowed an opinion on whether we deserved the same rights as others.

I found that on occasion Gina wasn't invited to events, and I had to wonder if particular family and friends were reluctant to explain me and her to everyone else. Gina wore my sadness on the first Christmas I spent without my family, when she had not been invited to Christmas lunch because I refused to label her as a 'friend'; she forgave me when it took me longer than it should have to stand up to what this injustice signified. It was melancholic, but we still made it special: she cooked a ham, the fat cut up in decorative squares with cloves poking out, and we spent the day drinking Moët on the beach and doting on a little Christmas tree that barely reached our hips. That Christmas, Gina became my family, as we spent that day together, alone.

I guess she had been through enough of it herself to know. The part of Gina who can change a car tyre, has a truck licence and can fix most things in our house – abilities that to me seem like signs of tough autonomy – created the same Gina who has a long list of stories: events to which she had routinely not been invited as a partner; intrusive questions about her sex life; open discrimination at work; even being threatened by a pack of men on one occasion. All the stories she had accrued in her life as a queer woman, and all the stories she had of friends who had been disowned or kept their lives hidden – these were all real stories with real pain, not over-acted television entertainment.

I couldn't help but feel guilty about the ease into which I navigated my queerness by comparison, having grown up in a relatively progressive bubble in which it was assumed that you would uncon-ditionally accept people. The shock, of course, is that liberal, middle-class progressives can be every bit as discriminatory as any-one else – they often just have the language to hide it. Obviously, it's easy to see my naivety in hindsight: perhaps all of us imagine that things will be different for us – that life is not waiting to serve up the big old dose of pain that is the requirement of being human. However, Gina remained patient throughout it all, a steady hand as I dealt with the adjustments; she was likely more irritated at my less-than-adorable habit of leaving wet towels on the ground and my general day-dreaming disorganisation that leaves cyclones of mess behind.

And if I'm honest, I did have access to many accepting people – close friends, family and confidants who have revelled in the life that I have created with Gina and in our happiness. They have included and accepted her, us, sometimes to a surprisingly – or sur-prisingly uneventful – extent. Despite the initial difficulties, Gina has been so strongly and proudly adopted and loved by my family, that I sometimes wonder if she's been hiding within us, all along. Maybe this has, in time, made her less cautious, while I am some-times more so, as if we have met somewhere in the middle between her initial tentativeness and my cringe-worthy ignorance.

I wish I could feel as free as I did when Gina and I first started dating, the way that I would snog her on the dancefloor at a straight club, or reach for her hand without thinking – and then feel per-plexed when she let go of my hand like it was on fire. But I'm no longer sure that the Yamiko I was back then is realistic in the world that we live in. It amuses me to think that at times I am probably more cautious now than Gina. I feel a slap of anxiety when she does something intimate like squeezing my hand or kissing me while we're both sitting in a cab. I check to see if the driver is observing us in his mirror. I'm used to being observed now, in this world, and I'm aware of how it exposes you.

I was surprised when she had reached for my hand, that day in the city, in such a public way and with such a firm, confident grip. She'd shrugged her shoulders in response, as if to say, 'Well, the majority of these fuckers voted on our lives, and voted in favour of supporting us, so fuck it.'

My friends talk of 'home' as the set of walls they grew up in, whereas mine is with Gina. Even as we sit in our shitty one-bedroom apartment that neither of us own and which we decorate temporarily. It's amazing to think that I have attached myself to this other person so fiercely in four years, that there is no longer any other home outside of her intimate grasp.

A City Set Upon a Hill

Dang Nguyen

There is a city on the horizon. That's what I've always been told: that far off, in the west, if you look out across Melbourne from the top of a very high hill, or from out of a tenth-floor window, or while you're climbing a fig tree with your hands all sticky with sap and bugs, you can see a city in the direction of the sunset shining as bright as winter, as white as light. If you stare unblinkingly, and train your eyes not to water, and focus with your soul, you can make out ivory towers, and a wall like nacre, and pale cathedral spires rising spans and cubits over the buildings below.

When I was a kid, people held me up to windows and pointed and said, *Look, see? Can you see the harbour and the ships like swans, and the starlight on the battlements and waters? Can you see the snowy banners shining in the sunset, and the lamps of crystal?* And I would strain and squint and beg them to stop playing tricks on me.

It got stranger as I got older. People expect toddlers to be stupid and not to get things or see what's right in front of their faces. It's a little less tolerable when you're five, or seven, or nine, and every person you meet can see something white and shining floating in the far-off ether but you can't. It was like there was a spell that had somehow passed over me, some god or goddess who hadn't set their sign on my hand or a memorial on my brow.

We visited Vietnam when I was six. Đại Nam, the Great South, which loomed huge and mysterious in my child-mind, at once the realm of bedtime stories and ancient kings and a place my parents told me we were lucky to have escaped. It was the first time I'd met my cousins, my aunts and uncles and my grandmothers. It was the first time since fleeing the communists that my parents had

321

seen their families and friends and all the loved ones who had peo-
pled their lives before I knew them. I think I was kissed more in
that first half-hour at the airport than I'd been in my entire life
leading up to that point. Outside, it smelt like Footscray, but a
thousand times bigger, weirder, damper. It was my first real experience of humidity, and the tropical air was so wet I could taste it
when I breathed.

And there, in the far south, shining yellow as butter and golden
as sunshine, floating over the horizon, was a pagoda.

I screamed with excitement when I saw it, pointing and bouncing in the back seat of my uncle's car. Sài Gòn is a very French city,
with huge broad avenues and boulevards connecting roundabouts
and civic buildings and monuments, all webbed with wild tangled
thickets of side streets, so I enjoyed a clear view on the drive to my
aunt and uncle's villa. My bedroom was on the fourth floor and
I spent the whole time at the dusty window, squinting through the
smog and smoke at the gleaming temple-tower in the distance,
thrilled to my heart and blood and soul with the joy of knowing
that I was capable of seeing visions too, that there was a magic circle that included me after all.

I told everyone I met, from my cousins who got tired of hearing me talk about it to the policeman we met when my grandmother
took us to the zoo, that I could see a pagoda on the horizon. They
smiled and nodded indulgently, and gave my parents faintly incred-
ulous looks when they thought I wasn't looking, the same sort of
looks they gave when I opened my mouth and Australian-accented
Vietnamese came out – glances and furrowed brows that suggested
there was something wrong.

'Why can't he see the rest of the palace?' my grandmother
asked my mother, in a tone that implied the deficit was my parents'
fault. She didn't think I could hear her, or maybe that I didn't
understand. There's always been an assumption in my family
that I'm a little slower than everyone else, so it's okay to talk over
my head.

'It's just the way he is,' my mother replied good-naturedly.
'He's just strange, that's all. In Australia we have a white city, and
he can't see that properly either.'

'He's a little slow,' my father said to my uncles in the awkward, grinning way that he reserved for when he was making excuses for something. 'He probably doesn't know what to look for.'

Well, that showed how much they knew. I wasn't slow, or strange, or ignorant. I just couldn't see what they could. But here, in Vietnam, the land of my people, where the food smelt of coriander and tamarind, I could see a golden pagoda. Maybe it wasn't the palace that everyone else in Vietnam could see, but it was something. It was a balm to know that I wasn't defective after all: I wasn't stupid or blind or not trying hard enough – I was just different, just not like the rest of them. And I knew as well as anyone that being different was good. Being different meant I was the main character: *Look, there she goes; the girl is strange but special – a most peculiar mademoiselle* ...

I couldn't see it when we flew back to Australia. I fought my sister for the window seat on the plane, and watched as the shining pagoda dissolved into clouds and sunlight and blurred into the horizon and away.

Strangely enough, once we got back to Melbourne, I sometimes thought I could see something on the northern horizon. Not a golden temple, nor a white city, but something like a dome of sapphire, the exact shade of the sky at noon of high summer, visible only by the sunlight gleaming on its polished edges and vertices. It floated over what I would one day learn was the direction of magical kingdoms with names like Brunswick, Collingwood, Fitzroy and Northcote, remote and lovely as a mountain peak. I wondered if it had always been there, just waiting for me to realise that I could see cities on the horizon after all, and to stop straining to see something in the west and turn my eyes northward.

Nobody else seemed to notice that it was there, so I didn't bring it up. Even at six years old, I knew I didn't need the aggravation of trying to explain something that would sound like nonsense to the people who could see the white city. I turned my face east and west and south, to the city I knew and all its streets and gardens and spaces where I lived my life, but all the while I felt the heat of the north pushing on my mind, like I was living with my back to a bonfire.

My favourite show, I decided at eight years old, was the Japanese *shōjo* anime series *Sailor Moon*. I don't think my parents knew what I was drinking in every morning, this show about a silly blonde girl with a talking cat and magical powers. Sitting directly below the television, I learnt about friendships that would last to the ends of the solar system and back, about finding your family, about courage and the power of unconditional love. I learnt that when I grew up I wanted to be a princess in a long, rippling white gown, a moon on my forehead and a light in my hand that held back the darkness.

And then there was Tuxedo Mask, the dashing, immaculately tailored love interest with his top hat and white tie. I hadn't known that I liked tallness, dark hair and a mocking smile, but sitting at that television every weekday taught me all that and more. It took me a while to articulate it, but eventually I realised that when I grew up, I wanted to marry Tuxedo Mask. And, from that moment on, the shining blue dome that I saw floating in the north was joined by a slender cluster of minarets, the sun radiating through their translucent pink quartz walls like a rose-coloured fire.

Over the years, the strange thing in the north grew. When I kissed Rob, trembling, in Year 8, I saw a red-gated Japanese *honden* appear, brighter than passion, hot as my blood when his hands quivered on my waist. Its vermilion columns and carved screens enshrined that kiss, soft and shy and a little too wet, with a dozen candles flaming eternally before it in worship, a bell rope that would turn pale and threadbare with thousands of rung prayers, and stone steps that would one day become worn-smooth with the weight of ten thousand prostrations.

When I was banished to the margins of the schoolyard, a palace sprang up in my visions. Schools are savage ecosystems where the brightly coloured things get pecked and slashed and torn apart by their duller peers. Flinching from soccer balls and not knowing how to join hateful, envious conversations about women made me an obvious target for stones and arrows. Exiled from the adolescent war council in which teenage boys used profane slang to plot their strategies for conquering the strange and savage territory of girls' bodies, I gazed at the palace that rose over the north, half-listening in revulsion as I watched the sun blaze on the limestone facades, its domes and spires capped with brilliant brass.

When I got called a faggot for the first time, a city wall appeared in gleaming green jasper, its polished stone shimmering dark and flecked with red like blood. I would learn to hate that word, and ten thousand guard towers grew up in the green wall, one for each time it was used against me. I had no idea it was possible to hate something as much as I hated the sound of that word, all ugly guttural Anglo-Saxon noise and spittle, like the sound of someone coughing up phlegm, each utterance of it carving out crenels and arrow slits, raising the shining wall to sheer and dreadful heights.

When I discovered that the internet had uses other than homework research – when I found fanfiction and erotica, pornography and fitness models, the glossy, eternally gasping, always-thin and invariably white beauties of certain websites; when I felt the low, dark thrill of reading something I knew I shouldn't, poorly punctuated stories that initiated me into the arcane rites of lube and fingering, that answered questions about anal sex and hygiene that I would never have dared ask the science teacher who taught Sex Education at my Catholic boys' school – gardens appeared on the jasper wall's terraces, overflowing with flowers and fruit trees in pools of dazzling colour. I spent hours staring north from my upstairs bedroom window, breathless from the pleasure of looking at them. Daisies and violets and scarlet poppies nodded their heads by the thousand, and chrysanthemums shone pale and perfect as full moons, and marigolds bloomed so bright I could almost taste mango and lemon curd and orange blossom honey at the sight of them. Vines put forth grapes like clusters of amethysts, apples winked scarlet from under the dappled shade of their trees, and when the wind was in the north the perfume that floated across the world made me dizzy with delight.

As I learnt to fear walking too close to other boys, or getting caught staring, the gardens grew roses. When I realised that scorn and humiliation were the likely result of another boy sensing I wanted to kiss him, briars twined their way through the garden, unfurling flowers as full and red as hearts and thorns like curses, crowning the curtain wall with wreaths of wicked spikes. When I learnt how many people like me had been beaten dead, thrown from bridges and strangled under motel beds, the thorns quivered with rage and dripped something slow, black and poisonous.

One day at Flagstaff Station, I saw two teenage boys kiss. They were older than me, and scarcely seemed human in the ease with which they moved, the carefree grace of the way they slid together, mouth to mouth, breath to breath. I'd never seen two boys kiss like that before, not on television, not in real life. Porn didn't count in the same way – its kisses stirred my flesh and blood, but this kiss hit my heart and lodged there, glimmering like a jewelled dart. Those beautiful strangers on the train platform blazed like dreams, and I knew somewhere in my soul I would one day be kissed like that, the way people in movies kissed when the music swelled.

I never did see the white city in the west, but as I learnt to navigate the world – as I began to want and hate and kiss and fear and touch myself – I came to see a city in the north shining every colour under heaven like sunlight blazing through stained glass, with its sapphire pleasure dome alight with jade lanterns at night, and gardens that bloomed all through winter, and a lotus-choked river flowing through it as brown as skin, and diamond-coloured streamers, and a rainbow of banners that proclaimed the virtue and everlasting splendour of its inhabitants.

I didn't tell anyone about it, of course; I knew what would follow: *Oh, he's different, he's silly, he's always making mistakes, he's not like us, he can't even see the white city, look at him thinking he can see something in the north*. I didn't need the drama. The world didn't deserve the strength and courage it would take me to tell them about what I saw. I bared my teeth and drew myself up to my full, unimpressive height, and the jasper walls gleamed as hard and impenetrable as my resolve.

And that would have been the end of it, if not for something that happened in my twentieth year that overthrew and toppled me with the violence of a sea that hates the shore. I fell in love, not wisely, but deeply and well.

I looked into a pair of grey-blue eyes, shining in the light of the fireworks that exploded pink and purple and blue over us from the MCG as we sat on a hill in Birrarung Marr, hand in hand. My heart fluttered like a harp string as we kissed. The fires in the sky faded, leaving behind a faint illumination that gilded his pale features – a light, I suddenly realised, that shone from the north, from a sapphire dome and fiery beacons in tall watchtowers made of green jasper, reflecting off minarets and cupolas of polished brass.

'Kim,' I said a little unsteadily, my heart in my mouth. 'Can you ... see that? The city?' I pointed wildly to where it glimmered beyond Federation Square.

I would learn later that he could in fact see the white city in the west as well, that he had grown up with its light on his face and known from his earliest days that here was a place for him. But, at that moment, all I knew was that his answer delivered me from a shadow I hadn't even realised lay over my heart; it soothed fifteen years of fear and reassured me that I wasn't alone after all, that there was a tribe for me, a nation of people that could see the many-coloured beauty in the north.

Trust Me (Tips for My Teenage Self)

Thomas Wilson-White

- You are right about Anthony Callea.

- Christian school sex education will leave a lot to be desired. Save yourself the grief and google 'douching' immediately.

- Kissing guys is always going to be great, so keep doing it. Also, porn is fine in doses – more experimental searches won't trigger horrifying sleeper urges, as you fear they will. Except for that one that does.

- On that note, sex doesn't have to look like porn. You will feel pressure to have it all the time because you are a gay man and that's apparently what gay men do. This is a lie the creators of *Queer as Folk* invented because they couldn't think of better storylines.

- You're going to spend years writing from a heterosexual perspective, mostly because every aspect of life on Earth – and everyone – says you should. Your work will only start to get noticed when you stop doing that, so stop doing that. Trust me.

- Loving Tina Arena doesn't make you gay, it makes you a decent human being. (So stop turning down the music in your headphones in case people can hear it.)

- Some of your friendships – even your favourite ones – will fall apart. And because of your deep-rooted belief that you are inherently flawed, you will take 100 per cent of the blame. Don't.

- Your dad is going to break your heart into pieces and you'll quickly turn the pain into a joke to survive. He'll never reach the potential he had to be there for you, but you will have a good relationship with him, and in the end that will be enough. There will be times when you will hate the parts of yourself that are like him. But you wouldn't curse the moon for causing oceans to ebb and flow, so don't curse him either.

- Your mum would say comparing him to the moon is overly generous, but she is wrong because this makes her the sun.

- You will get really good at being broken up with, and you'll think it will always be this way. It won't; you're fine. Try to care less. It works.

- That full-time babe on the school bus, whose eyes are like dark pools of Coca-Cola, who you swear made you gay with private school voodoo or some shit – you know, the one you'll paint in the stars each night, who'll never know the beauty of the constellations you crafted for him or the time it took to find the gumption to speak a hello – well, I promise there is more to that story, and it's worth the wait. I can't say exactly what I mean by 'worth the wait', but I'm raising a *very* suggestive eyebrow, so you do the maths, kid.

- People will sometimes be dismissive of you or condescending, and you will spend years thinking it's because you're gay. This is entirely incorrect. It's because you are young with perfect skin and they are old and broken.

- Anything mustard-coloured makes you look pale and underfed, like a vegan art student. Do me a favour and just skip that whole mustard phase. Also vests. Take it off. Now.

- The only girl allowed to ask you for fashion advice is your big sister; the rest are stereotyping you and deserve nothing (unless they actually look amazing – then it's your duty to tell them so as loudly and extravagantly as possible).

- You won't have a single positive role model for a long time, and your path will often feel directionless and doomed. To make matters worse, the world will tell you what you are, and you will even play along with that for a while to please it, but that will get uncomfortable.

- You will never be good at vogueing, but your hips don't lie and lots of girls in clubs will want to be your friend. One day a girl will buy you a drink and say, 'I was so sad when I found out you were gay,' and because you are naturally accommodating you will apologise. Let's work on 'sorry' not being the first thing out of your mouth in these sorts of situations. Are you sorry for having brown hair? For having blue eyes? No, of course not, so don't be sorry for being gay. Ever.

- Your siblings will hurt you sometimes, but they will save you more often. Be really good to them, because they get rich before you do.

- You won't listen to me, but try not to get drunk so much. It will never suit you, and parties will always give you anxiety.

- On that note, when that awful thing happens to you in the bathroom stall of a gay bar when you are twenty-one, please believe me when I say it didn't happen because you were drunk. And you didn't ask for it. And it wasn't your fault. People do bad things to other people. You'll spend years bound by silence and regret and it will deform your early twenties. For what it's worth, if I could I would reach into your future and push you out of the way, back out onto the dancefloor, away from the darkness that found you that horrible night, so that you could keep dancing in that gormless and innocent way, unaware and careless and wonderful. But I can't, so your consolation prize is the strength you'll find in the aftermath. And I'll say it again: it wasn't your fault. And you didn't ask for it. And no one can take your good heart away from you; that's not how it works. Use it to forgive yourself.

- There will be a heartbreak, the biggest and hardest of your young life. Oh baby, it's a big one. You will have sworn he was going to be the one: a dark-haired dreamboat sailing the seven seas of life. But he won't have an anchor, and you'll be too sweet to taste the salt water filling your lungs. It will turn your heart into a foreign country, where they speak a different language, where the food has unpronounceable names and you can't afford the return airfare. You'll cry from night until day until night again, and as the sun rises on the second day you'll promise to never let another person hurt you this way. The country inside you will enter a long winter, and years will pass. Another man will come along and build a house in this wintry landscape, but like most settlers he will be opportunistic and blind, unable to recognise the history and lore etched into the land where he's found his city, and it will crumble. Yes, the winter will pass like winter does, but this new heart will remain. Eventually you'll download Duolingo and learn the language of this place. You'll learn the names of its foods and you'll even enjoy them. It will be hard to be as bright and open as you once were, but one day you will realise you are grateful for this more cultured heart. There may be no greater lesson.

- And often you will find yourself wondering where it's all going and what it all means. There won't be a stretch of ocean on the entire east coast that you don't search for answers, nor a pillowcase dry from the heavy tears you'll shed, and in those times I urge you to wrap your arms around yourself and breathe into the chaos of it all. Because time will pass no matter how much you wish for it to remain static, and the ones you love will grow old, and they will leave you on this wretched earth without their light and their loving pokes and prods; and when you're stuck to the ceiling, bone-chilled from the injustice of being human, wishing you could find a place to scream and scream until your throat resigns, just remember that the sun rises every morning, and it will warm your skin, and – I say this to make sure someone has said it to you – *it will always get better.* You will be okay. And when you finally see those you loved so deeply, whose best and worst you took to proudly build yourself, whose love defined this huge life of yours, in whatever way it happens, you'll have such an almighty story to tell them. Trust me.

About the editor

BENJAMIN LAW is the author of the memoir *The Family Law*, which he adapted for SBS TV, *Gaysia*, and a Quarterly Essay: *Moral Panic 101*. A columnist for Fairfax's *Good Weekend* magazine, Law has also written for over 50 publications internationally and is a co-host on ABC Radio National's *Stop Everything*.

About the contributors

ADOLFO ARANJUEZ is editor of film and media periodical *Metro* and formerly editor-in-chief of sexuality and gender magazine *Archer*. He is also a freelance writer, speaker and dancer. Adolfo's nonfiction and poetry have appeared in *Meanjin*, *Right Now*, *Screen Education*, *The Manila Review*, *The Lifted Brow*, *Cordite* and elsewhere.

ROZ BELLAMY is a writer, editor and researcher, whose writing appears in *The Big Issue*, *Huffington Post*, *Junkee*, *Meanjin*, *SBS* (online), *The Sydney Morning Herald* and *Ten Daily*. Roz is a contributor to *Living and Loving in Diversity* and *Going Postal: More Than 'Yes' or 'No'*.

ALICE BOYLE studied creative writing, French and Spanish at the University of Melbourne. She's a writer, ESOL teacher and some-times-photographer. She lives in Melbourne with her Belgian partner and is currently writing a queer young adult novel.

JAX JACKI BROWN is an LGBTIQA+ disability rights activist, writer and educator, whose work has been published widely. Jax has a passion for intersectional equality and is eternally hopeful that a fair and just world is possible.

JOO-INN CHEW is a writer, and a doctor working in general practice and refugee health. She lives in Canberra with her partner and two kids. She loves diving through green waves, zooming along on her bike, and finding words to decipher the world.

STEPHANIE CONVERY is the deputy culture editor of *Guardian Australia*. She was formerly deputy editor at *Overland* magazine and a freelance writer and arts worker in Melbourne. Her first book, *Who Killed Davey Browne?*, will be published in 2020.

HEATHER JOAN DAY is a mixed-race trans femme witch, writer, musician and multidisciplinary artist living in Melbourne on Wurundjeri land. She writes poetry and short memoir, as well as music that she describes as transsexual gothic grunge pop.

STEVE DOW is a Melbourne-born, Sydney-based journalist who writes for *The Saturday Paper*, *The Monthly*, *Guardian* Australia, *Spectrum*, *Vault* and *Art Guide*. His 2012 collection of essays, *Gay: The Tenth Anniversary Collection*, is available as an e-book.

MICHAEL FARRELL is a poet from Bombala, New South Wales, now living in Melbourne. He is the author of *I Love Poetry* and *Cocky's Joy*. He co-edited (with Jill Jones) *Out of the Box: Contemporary Australian Gay and Lesbian Poets*, and he published an alternative scholarly history of Australian poetics, *Writing Australian Unsettlement: Modes of Poetic Invention 1796–1945*.

NAYUKA GORRIE is a Kurnai/Gunai, Gunditjmara, Wiradjuri and Yorta Yorta freelance writer.

PHOEBE HART is a writer, director and producer of documentaries, factual content and children's television. She is also a lecturer in film, television and digital media at the Queensland University of Technology, and principal of Hartflicker, a video and film production company. She is known particularly for her autobiographical road trip movie, *Orchids: My Intersex Adventure*.

NIC HOLAS is campaigns director at Change.org and the co-founder of The Institute of Many (TIM). He has written for the *Guardian*, *Archer*, *Hello Mr*, *Star Observer*, *Junkee* and more.

JUSTINE HYDE is a writer, critic and library director who lives in Melbourne. Her work has been published in *The Age*, *The Saturday Paper*, *Lithub*, *The Australian*, *Meanjin*, *Seizure*, *The Lifted Brow*, *Kill Your Darlings* and various anthologies. She hopes to one day write a perfect essay.

ATUL JOSHI was born in Myanmar, to Indian parents. He migrated to Australia as a child in 1971. A former classical musician, he lives in the New South Wales Highlands and works in arts management. His short fiction has been published in *The Big Issue*, *Seizure* and *Ricepaper Magazine* Canada.

GEMMA KILLEN is a writer, editor and academic in gender studies. Her writing focuses on the everyday minutiae of queer life, community and friendship. Her work has appeared in *Australian Feminist Studies*, *Autostraddle*, *Feminartsy* and *The Big Issue*. When she's not writing, she's probably sewing or admiring some handsome cats.

JACK KIRNE is a writer based in Melbourne. His work has appeared in various publications, including *Meanjin*, *Exposition Review* and *Subbed In*. He has published *Discount Fabric: The Campaign*, a graphic narrative, with his partner, Aaron Billings. He is currently undertaking a PhD at Deakin University.

ARON KOH PAUL is a historian and heritage consultant based in Melbourne. He teaches urban planning, and writes history, historical fiction and occasional political commentary.

BEAU KONDOS is the author of the YA fantasy novel *The Path of the Lost*. He has also written for *The Monthly* and *The Saturday Paper*. When he's not working at a publishing house, you'll likely find him making big decisions at his local supermarket's ice-cream freezer.

SAMUEL LEIGHTON-DORE is a queer artist and writer living on the Gold Coast.

PATRICK LENTON is a writer from Sydney. He is the author of the short-story collection *A Man Made Entirely of Bats* and the entertainment editor for *Junkee*.

NATALIE MACKEN is a Sydney-based word tamer. She is the creative director of The Content Folk.

YAMIKO MARAMA is a writer, therapist and food-truck owner. She lives in Melbourne with her favourite person, Gina. Yamiko is a 2018–2019 inaugural Next Chapter Wheeler Centre recipient and is currently writing a memoir on otherness, based on her experiences as a queer woman of colour in Australia.

DAVID MARR has written for *The Sydney Morning Herald*, *The Age*, *The Saturday Paper*, *The Guardian* and *The Monthly*, and has served as editor of the *National Times*, reporter for *Four Corners* and presenter of ABC TV's *Media Watch*. His books include *Patrick White: A Life*, *The High Price of Heaven*, *Dark Victory* (with Marian Wilkinson), *Panic* and six bestselling Quarterly Essays.

TIM MCGUIRE has written for *The Lifted Brow*, *Kill Your Darlings*, *The Big Issue*, *Going Down Swinging* and others. He was longlisted for the Richell Prize in 2015 and was a Wheeler Centre Hot Desk Fellow in 2017. He's appeared at Men of Letters, the Emerging Writers Festival and more. From Brisbane, he lives in Melbourne.

M'CK MCKEAGUE is an ex-vegetarian from the Beef Capital of Australia (no Casino, not you). Currently surviving the whims of Melbourne weather, M'ck is a performance maker and set and costume designer working across theatre, installation and social practice.

SCOTT MCKINNON is a postdoctoral research fellow in the Australian Centre for Culture, Environment, Society and Space (ACCESS) at the University of Wollongong. He is the author of *Gay Men at the Movies: Cinema, memory and the history of a gay male community* (Intellect, 2016). Scott's research on LGBTIQ history has been published extensively in academic journals, as well as *The Conversation*, SBS Online, ABC News Online and *Star Observer*. Scott is vice president of Sydney's Pride History Group.

NATHAN MILLS is a Brisbane-based arts administrator at La Boite Theatre Company. He is in his final year of undergraduate study at the University of Queensland, majoring in Politics and English.

THOM MITCHELL is a non-binary slashie now living in Naarm.

MIKE MULLINS OAM is the founding director of Performance Space in Sydney. Between 1973 and 1986 he created a number of boundary-testing performances. He then became an executive producer of cultural and corporate events. He is currently writing his memoir, *Anxious: The Story of No-One*.

DANG NGUYEN was born in a refugee camp in Malaysia in 1992, and was raised almost entirely in Melbourne, Australia. Although he was brought up a child of Flemington, North Melbourne and St Albans, his heart has always belonged to the cafes and gay clubs of Brunswick and Collingwood.

GISELLE AU-NHIEN NGUYEN is a Melbourne-based Vietnamese–Australian writer and bookseller, the commissioning editor for the Feminist Writers Festival, and an inaugural recipient of The Wheeler Centre's Next Chapter fellowship for 2019. She has been published in *Meanjin*, *The Saturday Paper*, *Kill Your Darlings*, *Rookie* and *Frankie*, among others.

ANTHONY NOCERA is a freelance writer and full-time homosexual from Adelaide. His work has appeared in *CityMag*, *Krass Journal*, *Overland* and *Vice*, among others. His work has been rejected by numerous publications also.

KELLY PARRY loves her girlfriend, kids, mates and writing stories – ferociously. A self-confessed laugh slut, she enjoys nothing more than a good cup of tea, an episode of *RuPaul's Drag Race* and a quiet night at home, plotting to overthrow the patriarchy.

VIVIAN QUYNH PHAM is an engineering and human-geography scholar interested in making visible the invisible. Recently an Australian Endeavour Fellow at University College London, and the Liveability design expert for the award-winning Desert Rose, Vivian is currently completing her MPhil at the University of Wollongong on moisture in social housing and looking for her next contribution.

SUE-ANN POST was Australia's first 'out' lesbian comedian. She has won several awards for her comedy, published two books and wrote a column for *The Age* for three years. She is also a poet and playwright. Mostly, though, she is a big tomboy doofus.

OLIVER REESON is an essayist and screenwriter. They co-created and wrote *Homecoming Queens*, a web series on SBS about chronic illness in your twenties.

REBECCA SHAW was on the writing team at *Tonightly with Tom Ballard* and has written for *Hard Quiz* and *Get Krack!n*. She was deputy editor at SBS Comedy, and is contributing editor at *Kill Your Darlings*. She's written for most places you can think of, and in 2018 a song she co-wrote won the ARIA for best comedy release.

TIM SINCLAIR is a writer of young adult fiction and poetry. His latest novel, *Run* (a CBCA Notable Book), is a paranoid parkour thriller set in Sydney, which uses concrete poetry to capture the speed and energy of the discipline.

NADINE SMIT is a Registered Nurse and is transgender. She has successfully changed careers and transitioned from living as a man to being the woman she has always known hid within. She has had a fulfilling life, but nothing compares to being true to herself.

THINESH THILLAINADARAJAH is a Tamil Canadian lawyer whose views on queer identity and multiculturalism were shaped by his upbringing in Toronto, where he never felt like he had to pick between his Tamil and Canadian identities. He has found Australian culture more monolithic, and his work focuses on creating space where people can embrace and present all facets of their identity.

HOLLY THROSBY is a songwriter, musician and novelist. She released four critically acclaimed solo albums, a collection of children's songs, and an album as part of the band Seeker Keeper. She is the author of *Goodwood* and *Cedar Valley*.

JEAN VELASCO is an Australian writer, of mostly specul She is currently based in Madrid, where she works as translator.

HENRY VON DOUSSA is a writer and social scientist from Melbourne who grew up on a small farm outside Adelaide. He works for La Trobe University at The Bouverie Centre (Victoria's Family Institute) and The Australian Research Centre in Sex, Health and Society. The health and wellbeing of families, particularly those affected by parental mental illness, is the current focus of much of his work.

THOMAS WILSON-WHITE is a queer writer, director and screenwriter. His feature debut, *The Greenhouse*, is set for release in 2019.

FIONA WRIGHT is a writer, editor and critic. She is the author of two collections of essays, *Small Acts of Disappearance* and *The World Was Whole*, and a poetry collection, *Knuckled*. Her poems and essays have been published in *The Australian*, *Meanjin*, *Island*, *Overland*, *The Lifted Brow*, *Seizure* and *HEAT*.

CINDY ZHOU works as a high-school teacher in Melbourne's inner west. When not shaping young minds, you can find her gardening, sampling beers or cuddling her greyhound, Fran.